Just for...

Personal Investment Calculator

Edited by **Fred Dahl**

Contributing editors:

Michael T. Curley
Wall Street Training

John P. Geelan
Merrill Lynch, Pierce, Fenner & Smith, Inc.

William A. Rini
New York Institute of Finance

Elmer F. Synek
Ohio Real Estate Commission
E&R Advisory Committee

Joseph A. Walker
Consultant to the Financial Industry

Random House New York

Library of Congress Cataloging-in-Publication Data

The Random House personal investment calculator: how to calculate
    profit and loss on your personal investments / edited by Fred Dahl.
        p.   cm.
    ISBN 0-679-72800-7
    1. Investments—Mathematics.   I. Dahl, Fred.
HG4515.3.R36   1990
332.6′01′51—dc20   90-32223

Manufactured in the United States of America
1 2 3 4 5 6 7 8 9
First Edition

Contents

How This Book Can Help You

You can benefit most from this book by keeping it handy and turning to it again and again for reliable, quick answers to your investment math questions. *No advanced math background is necessary.*

Here's how to use this guide:

- Look up the page number for the information you need in the comprehensive index at the end of the book (starting on page 388).
- When you have found the page, go to the question in boldfaced type that you need answered.
- In response to the question, you will find the solution you are looking for in two parts: (1) A practical explanation, accompanied by a simple formula (as needed), and (2) a clear example to show you how to use the formula.
- At the end of each chapter, you will also find a glossary of terms used in the chapter.

Try a question right now!

Note: Decimals are automatically converted to percentages. For example, ".085" becomes "8.5%" by moving the decimal two places to the right.

I

ANALYZING FINANCIAL STATEMENTS

Analyzing the Balance Sheet

YOU WILL LEARN...

- What the "accounting equation" is.
- How a balance sheet is constructed.
- What to look for in the balance sheet.

INTRODUCTION

Corporations differ from other types of businesses, such as proprietorships and partnerships, in that they are legal entities of their own. In most cases the owners of a partnership or proprietorship are also the managers of the business. The owners of a corporation, however, may not be—and usually are not—the managers. Management reports to the owners largely through financial statements. If a corporation has total assets of $1 million or more and is owned by 500 shareholders or more, it is obliged to register with the Securities Exchange Commission (unless it is a bank, an insurance company, or nonprofit organization). Registration with the SEC means, among other things, submitting annual financial statements.

Because the information in financial statements is, for the most part, uninterpreted, investors should analyze and assess them before they buy the company's stock and thus become owners. Some of this analysis and interpretation is subjective and thus varies from one investor to the next. A great deal of it, however, can be accomplished systematically by means of simple arithmetic methods.

THE ACCOUNTING EQUATION

What is the accounting equation?

The accounting equation, which summarizes the total financial structure of a company, is:

Assets = Liabilities + Stockholders' equity

This equation includes anything that impacts a corporation's financial status:

- Property owned, bought, or sold.
- Loans made to or by the corporation, as well as interest owed to or by it.
- Taxes for which the company is liable.
- And so on.

Example: Growth Corp. has assets (cash in its accounts, securities under its control, inventory in the warehouse, property, etc.) of $2,500,000. It has liabilities (bills to pay, accrued expenses and taxes owed, interest on loans to pay, and so on) of $1,750,000. Its stockholders' equity can be computed as follows:

Assets   = Liabilities   + Stockholders' equity
$2,500,000 = $1,750,000 + Stockholders' equity

which is the same as:

Assets   − Liabilities   = Stockholders' equity
$2,500,000 − $1,750,000 = Stockholders' equity
                          $750,000 = Stockholders' equity

What is "stockholders' equity"?

Stockholders' (or *shareholders'* or *owners'*) equity, sometimes called *net worth,* is what is left over after a company matches its assets to its liabilities. For example, if a company were to liquidate (that is, sell off or otherwise convert all its assets to cash) and then pay off all its liabilities, the remaining cash would represent equity. That equity belongs to, and would go to, the owners of the corporation—the stockholders or shareholders.

Example: In the Growth case, $750,000 would be distributed among however many people hold shares in the company.

What if liabilities are greater than assets?

The accounting equation can never be "out of balance."
Whereas assets and liabilities are matters of documenta-
tion—the information is drawn from the company's records—the equity component is the result of a calculation. If
a company's assets are less than its liabilities, stockholders'
equity is a negative number, that is, the owners have no
equity.

Equity

*How is equity distributed among stockholders in a small
corporation?*

Some companies with limited assets choose to restrict
ownership to a small circle. Their stock, which represents
ownership of the business, is not traded openly on a stock
market, such as the over-the-counter market in the United
States. Such companies are referred to as being *closely* (or
privately) *held*; they typically have few owners—sometimes only one. They have not *gone public* (that is, they
have not offered their shares for sale on the open market).
So the value of their stock depends solely on the difference
between assets and liabilities, not on supply and demand
forces in the stock market.

In such cases, each owner's portion of the equity can be
calculated on the basis of the number of shares of stock
owned. Put another way, each owner's equity interest is
based on the percentage of the total number of shares
outstanding owned by the holder. The more shares someone owns, the greater the percentage of ownership.

Example: Growth Corp. is a relatively small company that
is owned by just a few people (that is, it is "closely held")
and whose stock does not trade on the open market (that is,
it has not "gone public"). In this simplified case, Growth
Corp. has ceased operation, converted assets into cash, and
paid off its debts. So there is a sum of money to be
distributed. If Growth Corp. has issued 100,000 shares of
stock to 5 stockholders, a stockholder who owns 5,000
shares has a 5% interest in the company's equity:

$$\frac{5,000}{100,000} = .05 \text{ or } 5\%$$

Let's assume the following:

Investor A owns	20,000 shares
Investor B	10,000
Investor C	5,000
Investor D	55,000
Investor E	10,000
Total	100,000 shares

Given $750,000 in stockholders' equity, 100,000 shares outstanding, and 5 owners, equity is distributed as follows:

	No. of Shares Held	Percentage of Ownership (no. of shares owned times total shares)	Equity Distribution (% of ownership times total equity)
Investor A	20,000	20%	$150,000
Investor B	10,000	10%	$ 75,000
Investor C	5,000	5%	$ 37,500
Investor D	55,000	55%	$412,500
Investor E	10,000	10%	$ 75,000
Totals	100,000	100%	$750,000

How is equity allocated in large corporations?

All corporations (except banks, insurance companies, and nonprofit organizations) with $1,000,000 or more in assets and at least 500 public shareholders must register with the Securities and Exchange Commission under the Securities and Exchange Act of 1934. Companies with these kinds of assets and this many shareholders very often offer their shares publicly (that is, "go public"), and the shares trade on the open market. As a result new buyers of the stock are less likely to be familiar with the company than "private holders." The SEC's role is to assure investors that the company's disclosures are in accordance with legal and regulatory requirements. This ensures neither the honesty of the company's management nor the profitability of the investment, but it does at least make the playing field a little more even for investors.

When stock trades among many owner/investors, its value depends less on the difference between assets and liabilities and more on the market value as perceived in the marketplace. If there are more investors who want to buy the stock than those who want to sell it, demand outweighs supply, and the price rises. If would-be sellers outnumber buyers, the price declines because supply is greater than demand. In some cases, the market value of a stock can rise despite "bad financials" (such as a large amount of debt or poor cash flow) simply because investors see the ultimate opportunity for great profits. Correspondingly, the shares of a financially sound business might trade at a market value below its real worth because the investing public does not perceive it as having great enough investment potential.

So, for publicly traded companies, the market value determines the value of the stock to the owner.

Example: According to the accounting equation, Big Business, Inc. has stockholders' equity of $50,000,000 and 1,000,000 shares issued and outstanding in the hands of holders. Theoretically:

$$\text{Value per share} = \frac{\text{Stockholders' equity}}{\text{Number of shares held}}$$

$$= \frac{\$50,000,000}{1,000,000}$$

$$= \$50/\text{share}$$

In actuality, Big Business may be trading on the New York Stock Exchange for $125 or $25, according to how investors perceive the value of the company. Let's assume that the stock is trading on the "Big Board" at $125 per share. If you own 100 shares, their worth to you is $12,500 ($125 times 100 shares), not $5,000 ($50 times 100 shares).

THE BALANCE SHEET

Managers of a corporation bear the responsibility of reporting the company's financial status to shareholders. One of the several basic documents used for this purpose is the *balance sheet,* which is a detailed representation of the accounting equation as applied to the company. The balance sheet contains all the itemized assets, liabilities, and equity.

What does a balance sheet look like?

The balance sheet is a three-part financial statement: one part lists the company's assets, the second the liabilities, and the third stockholders' (or shareholders') equity. A typical balance sheet is shown in Figure 1–1. Note that the Big Business balance sheet in that figure is dated December 31, 19XX, meaning that this is an annual statement. (It could also read, "For the year ending December 31, 19XX.") A balance sheet can be drawn at any point in time during a company's fiscal year.

Figure 1–1

Balance Sheet
Big Business Inc.
December 31, 19XX

Assets	
Current Assets:	
Cash	$ 650,000
Marketable securities	1,300,000
Accounts receivable	425,000
Inventory	550,000
Total current assets	$2,925,000
Fixed Assets: Property, plant, and equipment	$2,225,000
Sundry Assets: Prepayments	30,000
Intangibles	15,000
Total assets	$5,195,000

Liabilities	
Current Liabilities:	
Accounts payable	$ 680,000
Accrued expenses	945,000
Accrued taxes	325,000
Total current liabilities	$1,950,000
Fixed Liabilities:	
Bonds—7%, due 2006	$ 830,000
Total liabilities	$2,780,000

Stockholders' Equity	
Preferred stock—7% (Par: $100)	$ 750,000
Common stock (at par)	1,330,000
Capital surplus	100,000
Retained earnings	235,000
Total stockholders' equity	$2,415,000
Total liabilities and stockholders' equity	$5,195,000

Note how each of the three sections of the balance sheet compare with the three elements of the accounting equation.

Current Assets and Liabilities

How are "current" assets and liabilities distinguished from "fixed" ones?

The basic criterion is one year.

Current assets are any possessions of the company that are cash or that could be converted into cash within a year; they are also anything owed to the company that is collectible within the year. Within this category are included *quick assets,* which are those that can be converted into cash "quickly," that is, within days or weeks. In addition to cash, quick assets include marketable securities and accounts receivable. Inventory, which could take months to convert, is usually not considered a "quick asset."

Current liabilities are any debts that the company is expected to pay within 12 months.

What is "working capital"?

Also known as *net working capital* or *net current assets*, *working capital* is the excess of current assets over current liabilities. It represents the money left over if all current assets were liquidated and used to pay all current liabilities. If current liabilities are greater than current assets, the company is in trouble. Remember the accounting equation: Assets equal liabilities plus shareholders' equity. If current assets are not at least great enough to offset current liabilities, then those liabilities have to be paid for out of other assets. This puts the owners' equity at risk for as long as this condition exists.

How is working capital calculated?

The formula for working capital is:

$$\text{Working capital} = \text{Current assets} - \text{Current liabilities}$$

Example: The assets and liabilities sections of the Big Business balance sheet are as follows:

Assets	
Current Assets:	
Cash	$ 650,000
Marketable securities	1,300,000
Accounts receivable	425,000
Inventory	550,000
Total current assets	**$2,925,000**
Fixed Assets: Property, plant, and equipment	$2,225,000
Sundry Assets: Prepayments	30,000
Intangibles	15,000
Total assets	$5,195,000
Liabilities	
Current Liabilities:	
Accounts payable	$ 680,000
Accrued expenses	945,000
Accrued taxes	325,000
Total current liabilities	**$1,950,000**
Fixed Liabilities:	
Bonds—7%, due 2006	$ 830,000
Total liabilities	$2,780,000

Working capital (net working or net current assets) is computed as follows:

$$\begin{aligned}
\text{Working capital} &= \text{Current assets} - \text{Current liabilities} \\
&= \$2,925,000 - \$1,950,000 \\
&= \$975,000
\end{aligned}$$

Big Business has $975,000 in working capital.

What is the "current ratio"?

Current ratio is the proportion between a company's current assets and current liabilities. The dollar value of working capital does not really tell you much about a corporation's ability to meets its obligations. A small amount of working capital in one type of company may be perfectly adequate; the same amount in another company may signal oncoming disaster. Of greater value is the ratio of current assets to current liabilities. Once it is known, it can be compared to the ratios of other, similar companies or to industry standards.

Current ratio can be expressed in a number of ways— 1.5, 1.5×, 1.5 to 1, 1.5/1, 1½ times, and so on.

What is the formula for current ratio?

Divide current assets by current liabilities:

$$\text{Current ratio} = \frac{\text{Current assets}}{\text{Current liabilities}}$$

Example: In the preceding Big Business example, current assets were \$2,925,000 and current liabilities were \$1,950,000.

$$\begin{aligned} \text{Current ratio} &= \frac{\text{Current assets}}{\text{Current liabilities}} \\ &= \frac{\$2,925,000}{\$1,950,000} \\ &= 1.5 \end{aligned}$$

This current ratio means that Big Business can cover its current liabilities "one and one-half times." Is that good? In most industries, the norm falls somewhere between 1.60 and 1.90.

Types of Assets

How do you tell one type of asset from another?

The assets section of the balance sheet itemizes anything the company owns or has coming to it.

Current assets consist of:

- *Cash* includes bank deposits (the corporate "check-book") and any other currency, such as petty cash.
- *Marketable securities* is cash invested in securities. Usually the investments are short-term (U.S. Treasury bills are typical) because the cash may be needed for operation of the company and it should not be tied up in long-term instruments.
- The *accounts receivable* entry includes money owed to the company as a result of services rendered or goods sold. Some balance sheets will include an *allowance for bad debt,* which is a percentage of receivables that the company does not expect to collect for one reason or another.
- *Inventory* consists of anything the company needs to provide its service or to make its goods. It could be stockpiles of pig iron, bolts of cloth, silos of corn, and so on. Service companies are likely to have much lower inventories than goods companies.

Other assets, specifically *property, plant, and equipment,* are "fixed" because they are not expected to be converted quickly to cash. They consist of any real estate, machinery, computer systems, vehicles, or other high-value assets used in the operation of the company.

Sundry assets are a "miscellaneous" category, typically used to accommodate expenses that the company has prepaid. These *prepayments* consist of up-front payments on insurance premiums or a lease. When a prepayment is made, the amount involved is moved from the cash entry to the sundry, or prepayment, entry.

Intangible assets do not exist physically, as do warehouses, delivery trucks, or inventory stockpiles. Intangibles are the company's goodwill, patents, trademarks, copyrights, or franchises.

What are "quick assets"?

Quick assets are all of a company's current assets that can be quickly converted into cash, if necessary. Cash, of course, is immediately available, marketable securities can be sold in minutes, and accounts receivable can be either collected or factored for cash. The only type of asset on the balance sheet that is not considered quickly convertible is inventory, which might take weeks, months, or even years to turn into cash.

How is the value of quick assets calculated?

Quick assets are equal to the difference between total current assets and inventory.

Quick assets = Total current assets − Inventory

Example: The balance sheet for Piper Mfg. Co. contains a current assets section that looks like this:

Balance Sheet
Piper Mfg. Co.
December 31, 19XX

Assets	
Current Assets:	
Cash	$ 800,000
Marketable securities	750,000
Accounts receivable	125,000
Inventory	550,000
Total current assets	$2,225,000

To calculate its quick assets:

Quick assets = Total current assets − Inventory
= $2,225,000 − $550,000
= $1,675,000

You can also arrive at this value, without knowing a company's inventory, simply by adding up all other current assets.

Quick assets = Cash + Marketable securities
+ Accounts receivable
= $800,000 + $750,000 + $125,000
= $1,675,000

What is the "quick asset ratio" (liquidity ratio or acid test ratio)?

The proportion of quick assets to current liabilities is called the *quick asset ratio*. It is also called the *liquidity* or *acid test ratio,* because it tests the corporation's ability to meet its liabilities even more rapidly than the current ratio—if, for instance, all current liabilities became due immediately. The current ratio includes inventory as a candidate for liquidation. Inventory, however, can take quite a while to convert to cash. The acid test assumes that inventory cannot be considered an asset for ready liquidation. The effect is that the ratio determines how ably the company can meet its current liabilities out of a smaller portion of current assets.

How is the quick asset ratio computed?

This ratio is calculated the same as the current ratio but with inventory excluded:

$$\text{Quick asset ratio} = \frac{\text{Quick assets}}{\text{Current liabilities}}$$

Example: The Big Business assets and liabilities sections look like this:

Assets	
Current Assets:	
Cash	**$ 650,000**
Marketable securities	**1,300,000**
Accounts receivable	**425,000**
Inventory	550,000
Total current assets	$2,925,000
Fixed Assets: Property, plant, and equipment	$2,225,000
Sundry Assets: Prepayments	30,000
Intangibles	15,000
Total assets	$5,195,000

Liabilities	
Current Liabilities:	
Accounts payable	$ 680,000
Accrued expenses	945,000
Accrued taxes	325,000
Total current liabilities	**$1,950,000**
Fixed Liabilities:	
Bonds—7%, due 2006	$ 830,000
Total liabilities	$2,780,000

Quick assets are $2,375,000 (as calculated in a prior example), and total current liabilities are $1,950,000.

$$\text{Quick asset ratio} = \frac{\text{Quick assets}}{\text{Current liabilities}}$$

$$= \frac{\$2,375,000}{\$1,950,000}$$

$$= 1.22$$

An acid test ratio of 1.22 is extremely favorable in most industries; in fact, ratios of .9 to 1 are acceptable. The norm runs from .2 for shoe stores to 1 for most manufacturers.

At what value are marketable securities carried on the balance sheet?

Marketable securities represent surplus cash, that is, cash the company does not immediately need for operations. Unlike cash, the value of securities can fluctuate according to market conditions. So as not to overstate their value, they are usually carried at the lower of their cost or their present market value.

Example: Big Business carries $1,300,000 in marketable securities, which in this case are Treasury bills. They were purchased at a cost of $1,350,000 30 days ago, but since then their market value has decreased to $1,300,000. They are therefore entered on the balance sheet at their current market value.

What are "fixed" assets?

Fixed assets are those used to generate revenue for the company—the office building or warehouse, the fleet of delivery trucks, the salesperson's car, the furniture in the showroom, and so on.

What does the amount in "Property, plant, and equipment" represent?

The amount in this entry is the cost of acquisition less *depreciation*. When a company purchases an asset, cash flows out of the company. The value of the purchased asset must be reflected somewhere on the balance sheet. This value is included in the entry for "Property, plant, and equipment." Over time, however, the asset's value decreases due to wear and tear or obsolescence. For example, trucks wear out, assembly lines age and break down, automated systems go out of date. The declining value of the asset must therefore be reflected from year to year in the balance sheets.

To calculate the amount to be entered on the balance sheet (referred to as the *book value*), management needs to know two things:

- The *useful life* of the asset, that is, how long the asset will be of use to the company. Heavy equipment might be operable for up to 10 years, while a computer system may be rendered obsolete in 2 or 3 years.

- The *salvage* (or *residual*) *value,* which is the amount the company may reasonably expect as proceeds from the sale of the asset at the end of its useful life.

One formula for calculating the annual depreciation of a fixed asset is:

$$\frac{\text{Annual}}{\text{depreciation}} = \frac{\text{Acquisition cost} - \text{Salvage value}}{\text{Useful life (in years)}}$$

Example: Two years ago, Piper Mfg. Co. bought an automated assembly line for $5,000,000. Management estimated that it would be rendered "behind the times" in four years (its "useful" life), at which time it could be sold overseas for $150,000 (its salvage value) and replaced with an up-to-date system.

$$
\begin{aligned}
\frac{\text{Annual}}{\text{depreciation}} &= \frac{\text{Acquisition cost} - \text{Salvage value}}{\text{Useful life (in years)}} \\[2mm]
&= \frac{\$5,000,000 - \$150,000}{4 \text{ years}} \\[2mm]
&= \frac{\$4,850,000}{4 \text{ years}} = \$1,212,500 \text{ per year}
\end{aligned}
$$

Note: In the "real world" of business, not many companies would invest $5,000,000 in an asset with such a short useful life. We assume such a short life to keep the example brief. We also assume—for the sake of clarity—that Piper did not own any other fixed assets prior to this purchase (so that it had no entry for fixed assets).

In the first year after acquiring the system, the assets section for Piper Mfg. Co. would take on an entry for fixed assets:

Assets	
Current assets:	
Cash	$ 800,000
Marketable securities	750,000
Accounts receivable	125,000
Inventory	550,000
Total current assets	$2,225,000
Fixed Assets: Property, plant, and equipment	**$3,787,500**
Sundry assets: Prepayments	-0-
Intangibles	-0-
Total assets	$6,012,500

In the next year, the entry would be $2,575,000 (the asset cost of $5,000,000 less two years' worth of depreciation $2,425,000). Depreciation is deducted from the asset cost for each year of the useful life, until all that remains as book value is the salvage value. The schedule of depreciation would look like this:

End of Year	Asset Cost	Annual Depreciation	Accumulated Depreciation	Book Value
1	$5,000,000	$1,212,500	$1,212,500	$3,787,500
2		$1,212,500	$2,425,000	$2,575,000
3		$1,212,500	$3,637,500	$1,362,500
4		$1,212,500	$4,850,000	$ 150,000*

*Salvage value.

How many ways are there to compute depreciation?
Depreciation can be calculated in five basic ways:

- Straight-line (SL).
- Units-of-production (UOP).

- Double-declining balance (DDB).
- Sum-of-years-digits (SYD).
- Modified acceleration cost recovery system (MACRS).

What is the straight-line method?

The formula used in the preceding Piper example was the straight-line method. It is the method that most companies use to report to their stockholders and creditors.

How is the units-of-production method applied?

This approach is very similar to the straight-line method, but the useful life of the asset is measured in different terms. Whereas the straight-line method expresses useful life in terms of units of time (usually years), the UOP method expresses it in terms of units of production.

Example: One truck is driven 8 hours a day, and it is expected to last for 5 years. If another truck is driven two shifts (or 16 hours) a day, it is likely to become inoperable in much less than 5 years. Depreciating both trucks over a 5-year useful life is unrealistic. The "two-shift" truck could be depreciated on the basis of the miles it is being driven. A depreciation amount per mile is calculated and applied to the number of miles it is driven over the course of a year.

How is depreciation calculated by the units-of-production method?

The formula for the UOP method is similar to the one for straight-line:

$$\text{Annual depreciation per UOP} = \frac{\text{Acquisition cost} - \text{Salvage value}}{\text{Useful life (in UOP)}}$$

Example: Piper's new assembly line, purchased for $5,000,000 and with a salvage value of $150,000, is scheduled to run 20 out of every 24 hours, with 4 hours down for preventive maintenance and/or repair. The system's manufacturer claims (and Piper management expects) that the system can produce 1,000 widgets per 8-hour shift, and it assigns a 4-year useful life based on its running one such shift per day. But Piper plans to run it 2.5 times that (two and a half shifts) every 24-hour cycle. The 4-year useful life obviously does not apply. Piper's accountants calculate depreciation on the basis of units of production. First, the useful life in years must be translated into units of production. Piper has a 260-day work year. If it ran only one shift per day, the useful life in UOP would be:

$$
\begin{aligned}
\text{Useful life in UOP} =\ & \text{UOP per shift} \\
& \times \text{ Number of shifts per year} \\
& \times \text{ Number of years of useful life} \\
=\ & 1{,}000 \text{ UOP per shift} \\
& \times \ 260 \text{ shifts per year} \\
& \times \ 4 \text{ years of useful life} \\
=\ & 1{,}040{,}000 \text{ UOP in the useful life}
\end{aligned}
$$

Next the amount of depreciation per unit of production must be calculated:

$$
\begin{aligned}
\frac{\text{Annual depreciation}}{\text{per UOP}} &= \frac{\text{Acquisition cost} - \text{Salvage value}}{\text{Useful life (in UOP)}} \\
&= \frac{\$5{,}000{,}000 - \$150{,}000}{1{,}040{,}000 \text{ UOP}} \\
&= \frac{\$4{,}850{,}000}{1{,}040{,}000 \text{ UOP}} = \$4.66 \text{ per UOP}
\end{aligned}
$$

Finally, if Piper runs the system at a rate 2.5 times the normal in a year of use, then it will run:

$$
\begin{aligned}
\frac{\text{UOP per year}}{\text{at Piper}} &= 2.5 \ (\text{UOP per shift} \times \text{Shifts per year}) \\
&= 2.5 \ (1{,}000 \text{ UOP per shift} \times 260 \text{ shifts} \\
&\quad\ \text{per year}) \\
&= 650{,}000 \text{ UOP per year}
\end{aligned}
$$

The depreciation for the first year—and for any year in which Piper runs 2.5 shifts per day—is:

$$
\begin{aligned}
\text{Depreciation} &= 650{,}000 \text{ UOP} \times \$4.66 \\
&= \$3{,}029{,}000
\end{aligned}
$$

Piper's book value at the end of the first year of use is

therefore $1,971,000 (cost of acquisition less $3,029,000 depreciation). Its balance sheet looks like this:

Assets	
Current assets:	
Cash	$ 800,000
Marketable securities	750,000
Accounts receivable	125,000
Inventory	550,000
Total current assets	$2,225,000
Fixed Assets: Property, plant, and equipment	**$1,971,000**
Sundry assets: Prepayments	-0-
Intangibles	-0-
Total assets	$4,196,000

In the next year, the entry would be $150,000, the salvage value. The reason is that Piper is using up the life of the system at a far faster rate than was intended. Another 12 months of running 2.5 shifts uses up the depreciable value of the system before year 2 is at an end. So Piper's accountants merely bring the book value down to the salvage value. The $1,821,000 is the difference between year 1's book value ($1,971,000) and the salvage value ($150,000). The depreciation schedule is:

End of Year	Asset Cost	UOP Depreciation	Accumulated Depreciation	Book Value
1	$5,000,000	$3,029,000	$3,029,000	$1,971,000
2		$1,821,000	$4,850,000	$ 150,000

Note: In the "real world" of business, not many companies would invest $5,000,000 in an asset with such a short useful life. We assume such a short life to keep the example brief. We also assume—for the sake of clarity—that Piper did not own any other fixed assets prior to this purchase (so that it had no entry for fixed assets).

How is depreciation computed according to double-declining-balance?

The *double-declining-balance (DDB) method* is an accelerated method whereby the company writes off more of the asset's value early in its useful life than is possible with SL or UOP. This method is not used as often as straight-line.

There are four steps to this approach:

1. Compute the straight-line *rate* of depreciation per year. This is done simply by making a fraction of the number of years of useful life. For example, an asset with a useful life of 10 years is depreciated at a rate of 1/10 (or 10%) per year.

2. Double the straight-line rate to get the *DDB rate*. The 1/10 rate in our example would become 1/5 (or 20%).

   Steps 1 and 2 can be combined by use of the formula:

$$\text{DDB rate} = \frac{1}{\text{Useful life in years}} \times 2$$

3. Multiply the DDB rate by the period's beginning book value, regardless of salvage value. For example, if the asset in our example cost $1,000,000 and had a residual value of $100,000, the first-year DDB depreciation amount would be $200,000 (20%, or .20, times the full acquisition cost of $1,000,000). The first-year book value would be $800,000 ($1,000,000 less $200,000). For successive years, the rate is applied to the prior period's book value, in this case, .20 times $800,000.

4. In the last year of useful life, no calculation is made other than to bring the balance sheet entry down to the residual value.

Example: The new automated assembly line system at Piper has a price tag of $5,000,000, a useful life of 5 years, and a residual value of $150,000.

1. *Calculate the SL rate:* Given a useful life of 5 years, the SL rate is 1/5 (.20 or 20%).

2. *Calculate the DDB rate:* Double the SL rate, to arrive a DDB rate of 2/5 (.40 or 40%).

   Steps 1 and 2 combined:

$$\text{DDB rate} = \frac{1}{\text{Useful life in years}} \times 2$$
$$= \frac{1}{5 \text{ years}} \times 2 = \frac{1}{5} \times 2 = (20\% \text{ or } .20) \times 2$$
$$= 40\% \text{ or } .40$$

3. *Multiply the DDB rate by the period's beginning book value:*

First-year
depreciation $= $ Acquisition cost $\times$ DDB rate

$\qquad = \$5,000,000 \times .40 = \$2,000,000$

Piper's end-of-first-year book value is therefore $3,000,000 (cost of acquisition less $2,000,000 depreciation). Its balance sheet looks like this:

Assets	
Current assets:	
Cash	$ 800,000
Marketable securities	750,000
Accounts receivable	125,000
Inventory	550,000
Total current assets	$2,225,000
Fixed Assets: Property, plant, and equipment	**$3,000,000**
Sundry assets: Prepayments	-0-
Intangibles	-0-
Total assets	$5,225,000

In the next year, the entry would be $1,800,000:

Second year
depreciation $= $ First-year book value $\times$ DDB rate

$\qquad = \$3,000,000 \times .40 = \$1,200,000$

The accumulated depreciation of $3,200,000 ($2,000,000 plus $1,200,000), deducted from the cost of acquisition, yields a balance sheet entry of $1,800,000 ($5,000,000 less $3,200,000). The schedule of depreciation would look like this:

End of Year	Asset Cost	DDB Depreciation	Accumulated Depreciation	Book Value
1	$5,000,000	$2,000,000	$2,000,000	$3,000,000
2		$1,200,000	$3,200,000	$1,800,000
3		$ 720,000	$3,920,000	$1,080,000
4		$ 432,000	$4,352,000	$ 648,000
5		$ 498,000	$4,850,000	$ 150,000*

*Salvage value—the DDB rate is not applied. Depreciation in the last year is however much is necessary to bring the book value down to residual level.

Note: In the "real world" of business, not many companies would invest $5,000,000 in an asset with such a short useful life. We assume such a short life to keep the example brief. We also assume—for the sake of clarity—that Piper did not own any other fixed assets prior to this purchase (so that it had no entry for fixed assets).

How does the sum-of-years-digits method work?

The *sum-of-years-digits* approach is an accelerated method of depreciation by which you arrive at the annual depreciation amount by multiplying the depreciable cost by a fraction. For example, if an asset has a 5-year useful life, the first-year depreciation is figured by multiplying the depreciable cost by 5/15. Where does the fraction come from?

The *denominator* is the sum of the years' digits. For the asset with a 5-year useful life, the sum of the years' digits is:

$$\text{Sum of the years' digits} = 1 + 2 + 3 + 4 + 5$$
$$= 15$$

The denominator in this case is 15. Obviously this calculation could get unwieldy for longer useful lives. So there is a simple formula for calculating the denominator (or sum of the years' digits):

$$\text{Sum of the years' digits} = \frac{\text{Useful life (Useful life + 1)}}{2}$$

Example: In the case of the 5-year useful life, the denominator is computed as follows:

$$\text{Sum of the years' digits} = \frac{\text{Useful life (Useful life + 1)}}{2}$$
$$= \frac{5 \text{ years (5 years + 1)}}{2}$$
$$= \frac{5 \text{ years (6 years)}}{2}$$
$$= \frac{30 \text{ years}}{2} = 15 \text{ years}$$

So much for the denominator. The numerator is the number of years left in the useful life. For a 5-year useful life, the first year's numerator is 5; it is 4 in the second year, 3 in the third, and so on. The first year's depreciation amount would be the result of multiplying 5/15 by the depreciable cost. In the second year, it would be 4/15 times the depreciable cost, and so on.

Example: The newly purchased Piper assembly line system has a 4-year useful life and a salvage value of $250,000. Management elects to depreciate it by means of the sum-of-years'-digits method. The denominator is computed as follows:

$$\text{Sum of the years' digits} = \frac{\text{Useful life (Useful life + 1)}}{2}$$

$$= \frac{4 \text{ years (4 years + 1)}}{2}$$

$$= \frac{4 \text{ years (5 years)}}{2}$$

$$= \frac{20 \text{ years}}{2} = 10 \text{ years}$$

For all depreciation calculations, 10 is the denominator. The numerator depends on the year. For the first year, the depreciation amount is:

$$\text{First year's depreciation} = 4/10 \text{ (Asset cost } - \text{ Salvage value)}$$
$$= 4/10 \ (\$5,000,000 - \$250,000)$$
$$= 4/10 \ (\$4,750,000)$$
$$= \$1,900,000$$

In the second year, $4,750,000 (the depreciable amount) is multiplied by 3/10. The schedule of depreciation is as follows:

Year	Depreciable Amount	Depreciation	Accumulated Depreciation	Book Value
				$5,000,000
1 (4/10)	$4,750,000	$1,900,000	$1,900,000	$3,100,000
2 (3/10)	$4,750,000	$1,425,000	$3,325,000	$1,675,000
3 (2/10)	$4,750,000	$ 950,000	$4,275,000	$ 725,000
4 (1/10)	$4,750,000	$ 475,000	$4,750,000	$ 250,000

Note: In the "real world" of business, not many companies would invest $5,000,000 in an asset with such a short useful life. We assume such a short life to keep the example brief. We also assume—for the sake of clarity—that Piper did not own any other fixed assets prior to this purchase (so that it had no entry for fixed assets).

What is the modified accelerated cost recovery system?

The *modified accelerated cost recovery system (MACRS)* is a method of calculating depreciation *for income tax purposes.* It is very common for corporations to use book values derived by straight-line depreciation methods in their reports to stockholders and creditors, but a different method of depreciation for reporting to the IRS. Historically, the method used for the IRS allows the company to deduct more in the way of depreciation in the early years of an asset's useful life, thereby lowering current taxes. The Tax Reform Act of 1986 systematized depreciation methods used for tax purposes with the MACRS. This system assigns assets to eight classes, according to their useful lives, and requires a specific method of depreciation for each class:

Useful Life	Example	Method of Depreciation
3 years	Equipment that quickly becomes obsolete	Double-declining-balance
5 years	Cars and light trucks	Double-declining-balance
7 years	Manufacturing equipment	Double-declining-balance
10 years	Manufacturing equipment	Double-declining-balance
15 years	Telephone/data systems	150%-declining-balance
20 years	Sewer lines	150%-declining-balance
27.5 years	Residential real estate	Straight-line
31.5 years	Nonresidential property	Straight-line

How does the 150%-declining balance method work?

For 15- and 20-year assets, depreciation is taken at a rate that is 1.5 times (or 150% of) the straight-line rate.

$$\text{150\%-declining-balance rate} = \text{Straight-line rate} \times 1.5$$

Example: A $5,000,000 irrigation system has been assigned to the 20-year MACRS class. It has no salvage value. The company that constructed the system uses a straight-line method of depreciation to calculate annual depreciation and book value for the balance sheet it sends to its stockholders and creditors. For tax purposes, however, it *must* use the 150%-declining-balance method. The straight-line rate would be 1/20, or .05 or 5%. Annual depreciation would be:

$$
\begin{aligned}
\text{Straight-line annual depreciation} &= .05 \,(\text{Cost} - \text{Salvage value}) \\
&= .05 \,(\$5,000,000 - \$0) \\
&= \$250,000
\end{aligned}
$$

The book value on the stockholders' balance sheet at the end of the first year would be $4,750,000 ($5,000,000 less $250,000). Each year for 20 years, book value would be reduced by $250,000.

For income tax purposes, the annual depreciation amount is 1.5 times the straight-line rate:

$$
\begin{aligned}
\text{150\%-declining-balance rate} &= \text{Straight-line rate} \times 1.5 \\
&= .05 \times 1.5 = .075
\end{aligned}
$$

The annual depreciation would be:

$$
\begin{aligned}
\text{150\%-declining balance annual depreciation} &= .075 \,(\text{Cost} - \text{Salvage value}) \\
&= .075 \,(\$5,000,000 - \$0) \\
&= \$375,000
\end{aligned}
$$

Each year, for tax purposes, the company deducts $375,000 in depreciation. It may do so for as many years as it takes to reach the amount of the system's cost less salvage value.

What are "sundry" assets?

Sundry is another word for "miscellaneous." In this category are assets that will benefit the company in some way in the future. For example, buying raw land for future development, prepayment of expenses such as leasehold-related costs or insurance premiums, or the deferral of charges.

When a company pays cash for a sundry asset, how is the balance sheet affected?

The total asset value remains the same. Cash is reduced and the sundry asset entry is created.

Example: Piper Mfg. Co. plans to occupy a new set of offices in six months, in the next fiscal year. For tax purposes, management elects to prepay a leasehold improvement cost of $50,000. Prior to this prepayment, the balance sheet looks like this:

Assets	
Current assets:	
Cash	**$ 850,000**
Marketable securities	750,000
Accounts receivable	125,000
Inventory	550,000
Total current assets	$2,275,000
Fixed Assets: Property, plant, and equipment	$1,212,500
Sundry assets: Prepayments	**-0-**
Intangibles	$ 15,000
Total assets	**$3,502,500**

After Piper makes the prepayment, it looks like this:

	Assets	
Current assets:		
Cash		**$ 800,000**
Marketable securities		750,000
Accounts receivable		125,000
Inventory		550,000
Total current assets		$2,225,000
Fixed Assets: Property, plant, and equipment		$1,212,500
Sundry assets: Prepayments		**$ 50,000**
Intangibles		$ 15,000
Total assets		**$3,502,500**

If the check had been written to purchase unimproved property or to pay for expenses that were not yet due (that is, *deferred charges*), the effects on the balance sheet would be the same: Total assets remain the same, cash is reduced, and sundry assets increased (or, in this case, created).

What are "intangible" assets?

Intangibles are assets, usually long-lived ones, that do not exist physically, such as:

- Trademarks—the CBS "eye" or the McDonald's arches.
- Patents—the Xerox photocopying process or the Kentucky Fried Chicken recipe.
- Copyrights—a publisher's agreement with a novelist.
- Licenses—the football Giants' granting the use of the team logo on T-shirts or mugs.
- Franchises—the 7-11 or BurgerKing™ chain.
- Goodwill—the added purchase cost of a company (usually attributed to the loyalty of the clientele).

How is the value of an intangible asset arrived at?

In most cases, the acquisition cost of an intangible is spread out—that is, *amortized*—over the life of the asset. While the life of an intangible can be as short as a few years (in the case of publisher's agreement for a book that is not likely to sell beyond that time), it may not exceed 40 years. Unlike fixed assets, intangibles have no salvage or residual value. So the amount to be amortized is generally 100% of their cost.

The general formula is:

$$\text{Annual amortization} = \frac{\text{Cost of acquisition}}{\text{Useful life in years}}$$

Example: Piper Mfg. Co. pays $75,000 to patent a new assembly line device, which management expects to be "behind the times" after 5 years of use. Its useful life is therefore 5 years, even though the device itself will not have worn out. The residual, or salvage value, is zero. Piper accountants amortize the cost of acquiring the patent by dividing it evenly over the 5-year life:

$$\text{Annual amortization} = \frac{\text{Cost of acquisition}}{\text{Useful life in years}}$$
$$\text{Annual amortization} = \frac{\$75,000}{5 \text{ years}}$$
$$= \$15,000 \text{ per year}$$

Before obtaining the patent, the balance sheet looks like this:

Assets	
Current assets:	
Cash	**$ 815,000**
Marketable securities	750,000
Accounts receivable	125,000
Inventory	550,000
Total current assets	$2,240,000
Fixed Assets: Property, plant, and equipment	$1,212,500
Sundry assets: Prepayments	50,000
Intangibles	**-0-**
Total assets	**$3,502,500**

After four years of use, the balance sheet might look like this:

Assets	
Current assets:	
Cash	**$ 800,000**
Marketable securities	750,000
Accounts receivable	125,000
Inventory	550,000
Total current assets	$2,225,000
Fixed Assets: Property, plant, and equipment	$1,212,500
Sundry assets: Prepayments	$ 50,000
Intangibles	**$ 15,000**
Total assets	**$3,502,500**

The $75,000 device has been "written down" to $15,000 in its last year of useful life.

Notes: If the money had been paid for a copyright (a grant to an author), a trademark (or tradename), or a franchise or license, the amortization calculation and accounting would be the same.

The creation of the intangibles entry does not actually reduce the company's cash.

Is goodwill computed like other intangibles?

No. Goodwill does not represent an outlay of cash, as do other types of intangibles. *Goodwill,* from an accountant's viewpoint, is defined as the amount paid for an acquired company over the the value of its *net assets* (that is, total assets less total liabilities). Thus goodwill can be recorded on the balance sheet only when a company has been purchased. Goodwill is like a patent or other kind of intangible in that it is amortized over a period of not more than 40 years.

The general formula is:

$$\text{Goodwill} = \frac{\text{Purchase price} - \left(\text{Total assets} - \text{Total liabilities}\right)}{\text{Amortization period in years}}$$

Example: Three years ago, the Big Business balance looked like this:

Balance Sheet
Big Business Inc.
December 31, 19XX

Assets	
Current Assets:	
Cash	$ 650,000
Marketable securities	1,300,000
Accounts receivable	425,000
Inventory	550,000
Total current assets	$2,925,000
Fixed Assets: Property, plant, and equipment	$2,225,000
Sundry Assets: Prepayments	30,000
Intangibles	-0-
Total assets	**$5,180,000**

Liabilities	
Current Liabilities:	
Accounts payable	$ 680,000
Accrued expenses	945,000
Accrued taxes	325,000
Total current liabilities	$1,950,000
Fixed Liabilities:	
Bonds—7%, due 2006	$ 830,000
Total liabilities	$2,780,000

Stockholders' Equity	
Preferred stock—7% (Par: $100)	$ 750,000
Common stock	1,330,000
Capital surplus	100,000
Retained earnings	220,000
Total stockholders' equity	**$2,400,000**
Total liabilities and stockholders' equity	**$5,180,000**

MegaHoldings Corp. acquired Big Business for $3,000,000. There was no reason to believe that the acquired company would not carry on business indefinitely—that is, it had not been set up for a one-time venture and was in an industry with a future. The company's goodwill was calculated as follows:

$$\text{Goodwill} = \frac{\text{Purchase price} - \left(\text{Total assets} - \text{Total liabilities}\right)}{\text{Amortization period in years}}$$

$$= \frac{\$3,000,000 - (\$5,180,000 - \$2,780,000)}{40 \text{ years}}$$

$$= \frac{\$3,000,000 - \$2,400,000}{40 \text{ years}}$$

$$= \frac{\$600,000}{40 \text{ years}} = \$15,000 \text{ per year}$$

From the year of sale through the fortieth year of operation after the sale, MegaHoldings Corp. carries $60,000 of goodwill, reduced by $15,000 each year, in its intangible asset entry.

Liabilities

How are liabilities categorized?

Current liabilities consist of anything that the company owes and is obligated to pay within a year:

* *Accounts payable* are monies owed to creditors—suppliers of raw materials, the local utility, the phone company, and the like.

* *Accrued expenses* include salaries, wages, commissions, interest on short-term loans, and any costs that are accumulating but that do not have to be paid until some time in the future.

* *Accrued taxes* are not strictly expenses, but they do have to be paid, on a quarterly or annual basis. Between payment dates, the tax amounts are accumulating.

Fixed liabilities are longer-term. They might include a debt issue maturing in fifteen years, a ten-year loan from a commercial bank, a mortgage on business-owned real estate, and so on.

How do you arrive at the amounts in the equity section?

The total par values shown for *preferred* and *common stock* are "on the company books," not calculated. They represent the actual capital taken in from individuals who bought company stock.

Example: Growth has issued preferred stock, which is stock that pays a fixed dividend. The dividend is 7% of the par value, $100, or $7 per share annually. The amount received on the sale of this stock is entered as $750,000. If the par value of each share is $100, then Growth sold 7,500 shares of preferred ($750,000 divided by $100).

Example: The firm's common stock may be trading at a market value well above its par value, but it is carried on the books at par, because that is all the company received on its sale. The difference between par (usually a nominal amount) and market value belongs to the stockholders, and they may take their profits by selling their shares in the open market. The company, of course, sees none of this profit.

On the Growth balance sheet, 266,000 shares are in the hands of holders, and $1,330,000 was received for their sale. From this information you can calculate the par value of the common stock:

$$\frac{\$1,330,000}{266,000 \text{ shares}} = \$5 \text{ per share par value}$$

Correspondingly, given the par value and capital for the common stock, you could calculate the number of shares.

What is capital surplus?

Capital surplus (*paid-in* or *contributed capital*) represents the money received *over* the par value of the stock. Generally, when a company first offers its stock, in what is called an *initial public offering (IPO),* the shares are sold at more than par value. After the initial public offering, the common stock entry on the balance sheet would contain an amount equal to the number of shares sold times the par value per share, and the capital surplus (or paid-in capital) item would reflect the difference between par value and the actual sale price.

Example: In an initial offering when it first went public, Big Business offered 200,000 shares of common stock at $5 par value. The initial offering was a success, all shares were sold, and the company received $1,000,000:

Common stock = Par value × Number of shares sold

= $5 × 200,000

= $1,000,000

After the IPO, the Big Business balance sheet equity section would look like this:

Stockholders' Equity	
Preferred stock—7% (Par: $100)	$ 750,000
Common stock	1,330,000
Capital surplus	100,000
Retained earnings	-0-
Total stockholders' equity	$2,180,000

If a company sells its common stock shares for more than par value, that additional capital is reflected in the capital surplus entry.

Example: In its IPO, Big Business is able to sell 200,000 shares at $6.51, $1.51 over the par value of $5.00. After the IPO, the Stockholders' Equity section of the balance sheet would look like this:

Stockholders' Equity	
Preferred stock—7% (Par: $100)	$ 750,000
Common stock	1,000,000
Capital surplus	302,000
Retained earnings	-0-*
Total stockholders' equity	$2,052,000

*For simplicity, retained earnings have been entered as zero.

Common stock is entered at par value: $1,000,000 (200,000 shares at $5). Capital surplus represents the excess capital, that is, the difference between par value and actual sale price: $302,000 (200,000 shares times $1.51).

If capital surplus reflects the stock's performance, how are operating profits reported in the balance sheet?

Operating profitability is reflected in *retained earnings* (also known as *earned surplus*), which contains the amount of profit "retained" by the company after it pays dividends to common stockholders (if it so chooses).

Example: In 19X0, Big Business is still a "young" business, striving to show some profit. At the end of the year, its balance sheet looks like this:

Balance Sheet
Big Business Inc.
December 31, 19X0

Assets	
Current Assets:	
Cash	**$ 415,000**
Marketable securities	1,300,000
Accounts receivable	425,000
Inventory	550,000
Total current assets	**$2,690,000**
Fixed Assets: Property, plant, and equipment	$2,225,000
Sundry Assets: Prepayments	30,000
Intangibles	15,000
Total assets	**$4,960,000**

Liabilities	
Current Liabilities:	
Accounts payable	$ 680,000
Accrued expenses	945,000
Accrued taxes	325,000
Total current liabilities	$1,950,000
Fixed Liabilities:	
Bonds—7%, due 2006	$ 830,000
Total liabilities	$2,780,000

Stockholders' Equity	
Preferred stock—7% (Par: $100)	$ 750,000
Common stock	1,330,000
Capital surplus	100,000
Retained earnings	**-0-**
Total stockholders' equity	**$2,180,000**
Total liabilities and stockholders' equity	**$4,960,000**

In the next year of operation, they begin to make profits. Management elects not to pay dividends on the common stock; rather the additional funds are kept in a cash account. The aim is to avoid the type of cash flow shortages experienced in 19X0 and the consequent interest payments on the short-term notes from a commercial bank. By the end of 19X1, an additional $235,000 is available to the company for operations.

Balance Sheet
Big Business Inc.
December 31, 19X1

Assets	
Current Assets:	
Cash	**$ 650,000**
Marketable securities	1,300,000
Accounts receivable	425,000
Inventory	550,000
Total current assets	**$2,925,000**
Fixed Assets: Property, plant, and equipment	$2,225,000
Sundry Assets: Prepayments	30,000
Intangibles	15,000
Total assets	**$5,195,000**

Liabilities	
Current Liabilities:	
Accounts payable	$ 680,000
Accrued expenses	945,000
Accrued taxes	325,000
Total current liabilities	$1,950,000
Fixed Liabilities:	
Bonds—7%, due 2006	$ 830,000
Total liabilities	$2,780,000

Stockholders' Equity	
Preferred stock—7% (Par: $100)	$ 750,000
Common stock	1,330,000
Capital surplus	100,000
Retained earnings	**235,000**
Total stockholders' equity	**$2,415,000**
Total liabilities and stockholders' equity	**$5,195,000**

Theoretically, if Big Business management were to halt operations and liquidate everything at the end of 19X1, it would have $235,000 left over in profit, after the share-holders had recovered their original investment. In over-simplified terms, the liquidation would look like this:

"Cashing in" all assets	+$5,195,000
Paying off all current liabilities	− 1,950,000
Paying off the 7% '06 bond	− 830,000
Then paying off the preferred and common stockholders (including capital surplus	− 2,180,000
Retained earnings	=$ 235,000

Note: It is easy to think of retained earnings as a cash item, when in actuality it is a balancing item. When all other items are weighed in the accounting equation, retained earnings is increased or decreased to make the equation balance. The actual cash may or may not be available to the company depending on many factors. In fact, it is possible to have a *deficit* in the retained earnings entry if a negative figure is needed to make the equation balance.

What is a company's "capitalization"?

Capitalization is the corporation's "seed money," the capital with which it starts up and operates. It is the money that shareholders have invested in the corporation, along with the money that bondholders have lent it. Capitalization is equal to the total of the amounts on the balance sheet for preferred stock, common stock, and bonds.

How is capitalization calculated?

Capitalization is the sum of:

Bonds (fixed liabilities)
+ Preferred stock
+ Common stock
+ Capital surplus (if any)
+ Retained earnings (if any)
= Capitalization

Example: Big Business's capitalization is calculated as follows:

Balance Sheet
Big Business Inc.
December 31, 19XX

. . .

Liabilities

Current Liabilities:	
Accounts payable	$ 680,000
Accrued expenses	945,000
Accrued taxes	325,000
Total current liabilities	$1,950,000
Fixed Liabilities:	
Bonds—7%, due 2006	**$ 830,000**
Total liabilities	$2,780,000

Stockholders' Equity

Preferred stock—7% (Par: $100)	**$ 750,000**
Common stock	**1,330,000**
Capital surplus	**100,000**
Retained earnings	**235,000**
Total stockholders' equity	$2,415,000
Total liabilities and stockholders' equity	$5,195,000

Bonds (fixed liabilities)	$ 830,000
Preferred stock	750,000
Common stock	1,330,000
Capital surplus	100,000
Retained earnings	235,000
Capitalization	$3,245,000

Big Business's capitalization is $3,245,000.

What are capitalization ratios?

Does it make a difference whether a corporation is capitalized through stock or bond issues? It does. For example,
companies that rely heavily on bond (debt) and preferred
stock issues are said to be "highly leveraged," a condition
that some consider not very sound financially. *Capitalization ratios* are used to quantify the proportions of stock,
debt, and other components in a company's capitalization.
These are:

$$\text{Bond (debt) ratio} = \frac{\text{Bonds}}{\text{Capitalization}}$$

$$\text{Preferred stock ratio} = \frac{\text{Preferred stock}}{\text{Capitalization}}$$

$$\text{Common stock ratio} = \frac{\text{Common stock} + \text{Capital surplus} + \text{Retained earnings}}{\text{Capitalization}}$$

Example: Big Business's capitalization ratios are calculated as follows (refer to the balance sheet in Figure 1-1, page 8):

$$\text{Bond (debt) ratio} = \frac{\text{Bonds}}{\text{Capitalization}}$$

$$= \frac{\$830,000}{\$3,245,000} = .2558 = 25.6\%$$

$$\text{Preferred stock ratio} = \frac{\text{Preferred stock}}{\text{Capitalization}}$$

$$= \frac{\$750,000}{\$3,245,000} = .2311 = 23.1\%$$

$$\text{Common stock ratio} = \frac{\text{Common stock} + \text{Capital surplus} + \text{Retained earnings}}{\text{Capitalization}}$$

$$= \frac{\$1,330,000 + \$100,000 + \$235,000}{\$3,245,000}$$

$$= \frac{\$1,665,000}{\$3,245,000} = .5131 = 51.3\%$$

Note: These three ratios must total 100% (25.6%, 23.1%, 51.3%).

Unless Big Business is a bank or a public utility, either of which uses a lot of borrowed money, it is very highly leveraged; that is, the bond and preferred stock ratios well exceed a third of its capitalization. For one thing, it makes the company's profitability very vulnerable to interest rate fluctuations.

How do I know what Big Business's balance sheet is telling me as a prospective or current investor in a company?

A company's balance sheet can be compared to the "standard" balance sheet for its industry. Each item on these standard balance sheets is expressed as a percentage of total assets. The general formula is:

$$\text{Industry ratio} = \frac{\textbf{Entry on the balance sheet}}{\textbf{Total assets}}$$

Note: Industry ratios are available from most financial publishing companies, such as Moody's or Standard & Poor's. In addition, Robert Morris Associates publishes *Annual Statement Studies*, containing ratios and other information for over 200 industries.

Example: Big Business is in the "food and related products" industry, for which the standard ratio of current assets is 34.3. That is, current assets should be 34.3% of total assets. Or:

$$\text{Industry ratio} = \frac{\substack{\text{Entry on the} \\ \text{balance sheet}}}{\text{Total assets}} = .343 \text{ or } 34.3\%$$

If the company's balance sheet entry is better than the standard, the company is said to be *outperforming* the standard; if worse, it is *underperforming*.

How is the corporation's ratio calculated (so that it can be compared to industry standards)?

The items on a corporation's balance sheet have to be converted from dollar values to ratios. The general formula is a slight modification of the industry formula:

$$\text{Corporation's ratio} = \frac{\textbf{Entry on the balance sheet}}{\textbf{Total assets}}$$

Example: Big Business's current assets are $2,925,000, and its total assets are $5,195,000. Its current assets ratio is calculated using the same formula as the one for the industry standard:

$$\text{Current assets ratio} = \frac{\text{Current assets}}{\text{Total assets}}$$

$$= \frac{\$2,925,000}{\$5,195,000} = .563 \text{ or } 56.3\%$$

Big Business is greatly outperforming the industry standard.

Can a corporate balance sheet be compared to an industry standard as a whole?

Yes. In fact, "typical" balance sheets are issued for most industries annually. These balance sheets can be related item by item to that of a particular company.

Note: Industry ratios are available from most financial publishing companies, such as Moody's or Standard & Poor's. In addition, Robert Morris Associates publishes *Annual Statement Studies*, containing ratios and other information for over 200 industries.

Example: The Big Business balance sheet, integrated with the typical balance sheet for its industry (food and related products), is as follows:

Balance Sheet
Big Business Inc.
December 31, 19X1

	Big Business ($)	Big Business Ratios	Industry Ratios
Assets			
Current Assets:			
Cash	$ 650,000		
Marketable securities	1,300,000	25.0%	5.4%
Accounts receivable	425,000	8.2%	11.5%
Inventory	550,000	10.6%	15.4%
Total current assets	$2,925,000	56.3%	35.6%
Fixed Assets: Property, plant, and equipment	$2,225,000	42.8%	34.3%

	Big Business ($)	Big Business Ratios	Industry Ratios
	Assets		
Sundry Assets:			
Prepayments	30,000		
Intangibles	15,000		
Total assets	**$5,195,000**	**100.0%**	**100.00%***
	Liabilities		
Current Liabilities:			
Accounts payable	$ 680,000		
Accrued expenses	945,000		
Accrued taxes	325,000		
Total current liabilities	$1,950,000		
Fixed Liabilities:			
Bonds—7%, due 2006	$ 830,000		
Total liabilities	$2,780,000	53.5%	60.7%
	Stockholders' Equity		
Preferred stock—7% (Par: $100)	$ 750,000		
Common stock	1,330,000		
Capital surplus	100,000		
Retained earnings	235,000		
Total stockholders' equity	$2,415,000	46.5%	30.3%
Total liabilities and stockholders' equity	$5,195,000		

*Not all ratios are shown.

Can other ratios, such as the current ratio, be compared to industry standards?

Yes. Since balance sheet analysis is done largely through such ratios, industry standards are issued every year for these too. These ratios can also be related to a corporation's ratios to determine whether it is operating within the financial guidelines of its industry.

Example: Some of Big Business's key ratios are compared to those of the food and related products industry:

	Big Business	Industry
Current ratio	1.50	1.46
Quick asset ratio	1.22	.22

KEY TERMS

Accounting equation: The formula that summarizes the financial status of a company and that underlies the balance sheet:

Assets = Liabilities + Stockholders' equity

Accounts payable: Money that a corporation owes to its creditors on a short-term basis (as opposed to long-term debt, such as bonds).

Accounts receivable: Money owed to a corporation in return for goods sold or services rendered.

Accrued expenses: Accumulated expenses that a company will have to pay in the future, such as salaries or interest on short-term loans.

Accrued taxes: Tax obligations that accumulate as a corporation earns revenues but that are not yet due.

Acid test ratio (quick asset ratio, liquidity ratio): The ratio of quick assets to current liabilities, which tells whether a company could readily pay all its current obligations if they were to come due immediately.

Allowance for bad debt: A percentage that a company routinely deducts from accounts receivable on the assumption that it will not be collectible.

Asset: An economic resource, owned by a business, that is of value or that is expected to be of value in the future.

Balance sheet (statement of financial condition): A financial document that itemizes a corporation's assets, liabilities, and equity at a particular point in time, usually at the end of the company's fiscal (or accounting) year.

"Big Board": The New York Stock Exchange.

Book value: The entry on the balance sheet for property, plant, and equipment, representing the depreciated value of the asset.

Capitalization: The sum of the par value of a company's outstanding bonds and preferred stock, as well as the value of its common stock, capital surplus, and retained earnings.

Capitalization ratios: Ratios that quantify the proportions of a company's stock, debt, and other capital components to total capitalization.

Capital surplus (paid-in capital): Money received by a corporation for its common stock in excess of the stock's par value.

Cash: Bank deposits and other currency.

Common stock: A form of capital stock representing ownership in the business.

Current asset: Any resource of a corporation that is cash or that can be converted into cash within a year.

Current liability: Any obligation of a corporation that has to be met within a year.

Current ratio: The ratio of current assets to current liabilities.

Depreciation: The value of a major asset, such as a machine tool, spread out over its useful life.

Double-declining-balance method: A method of depreciating a major asset in which the annual depreciation is greater in the early years of an asset's useful life than it is when the straight-line method is used.

Earned surplus: See *Retained Earnings.*

Equity: A valid claim to the assets of a business; a share in ownership.

Fixed assets: A resource of a company that is not expected to be converted into cash within one year.

Goodwill: The amount of acquisition cost in excess of net assets.

Initial public offering (IPO): The first offering of capital stock to the investing public.

Inventory: Any resource that a company needs to provide a service or goods.

Intangible asset: A long-lived, nonphysical asset, such as a patent, trademark, or goodwill.

Liability: An economic obligation of a company that is payable to someone outside the company or to another firm.

Liquidity ratio: See *Acid test ratio*.

Marketable securities: Usually short-term securities, in which a corporation invests its surplus cash.

Market value: The price at which a share of stock is trading in the open market, subject to the forces of supply and demand.

Net current assets: See *Working capital*.

Net working capital: See *Working capital*.

Paid-in capital: See *Capital surplus*.

Par value: The value assigned to common or preferred stock upon issuance.

Plant, property, and equipment: Fixed assets of a corporation, such as real estate, heavy machinery, vehicles, computer systems, and the like.

Preferred stock: A form of capital stock that offers advantages over common stock, such as the right to fixed dividends and a claim to the company's assets before common stockholders.

Prepayments: An asset consisting of an obligation that has been prepaid by the corporation.

Quick assets: All of a company's current assets that can be quickly converted into cash, that is, within days or weeks.

Quick asset ratio: See *Acid test ratio*.

Residual value: See *Salvage value*.

Retained earnings (earned surplus): The earnings retained by the corporation after all dividends are paid out.

Salvage (residual) value: The anticipated sale value of a major asset at the end of its useful life.

Shareholders' (stockholders') equity: The portion of a corporation's assets on which holders of the company's stock have legal claim, in proportion to the number of shares held.

Shares (of stock): Certificates evidencing ownership in a corporation.

Statement of financial condition: See *Balance sheet*.

Straight-line depreciation: A method of depreciating a major asset by dividing its acquisition value, less salvage value, by the number of years in its useful life.

Sum-of-years-digits method: A method of depreciating a major asset in which the annual amount of depreciation is calculated by multiplying the acquisition cost by a fraction. The numerator is the number of years left in the asset's useful life: the denominator is the sum of the digits in the asset's useful life.

Sundry asset: An asset that is expected to benefit the corporation in the future.

Useful life: The term during which a major asset, such as a vehicle, is expected to be useful to the corporation.

Working capital (net working capital, net current assets): The excess of current assets over current liabilities.

2

Analyzing
the Income Statement

YOU WILL LEARN...

- How an income statement is constructed.
- What methods are used to analyze the income statement.
- How entries on the income statement relate to, and affect, the value of the corporation's stock.

INTRODUCTION

The balance sheet is a financial "snapshot" of a company at a point in time. It demonstrates a firm's "accounting equation" at the end of a year, a quarter, or any time management wants to look at a balance sheet. The outcome of the balance sheet is the company's "net worth."

The *income statement* covers a period, such as three months or a year, and it shows what most investors are looking for—how much money the company made during that period. The final figure, called *net income (loss)* or *earnings available for common stock,* tells the story. That's why it is sometimes called the *earnings report* or *profit and loss (P&L) statement.*

CONSTRUCTION

What does an income statement look like?

A typical income statement (earnings report, profit and loss statement) follows:

Income Statement
Hitech Corp.
January 1–December 31, 19XX

Net sales (operating revenues)	$ 3,000,000
Operating costs:	
Cost of goods sold (COGS)	−2,170,000
Selling, general, and administrative (G&A)	− 212,000
Depreciation	− 198,000
Total operating costs	$−2,580,000
Operating income	$ 420,000
Other income:	
Dividend income	+ 9,500
Less interest on bonds	− 50,000
Total other income	$− 40,500
Total income	$ 379,500
Taxes (30% rate)	− 113,850
Net income (net profit)	$ 265,650
Preferred dividends	− 8,000
Earnings available for common stock (net earnings)	$ 257,650

This is a *multiple step* format, in which subtotals are drawn.
A *single step* format enters all the same figures but draws
only one grand total at the bottom of the statement. As you
might expect, the "bottom line" is the one investors look at
first. There is more of a story to the income statement,
however. Many of the other entries contain valuable, in-
vestment-related information.

How are net sales recorded?

Net sales are the revenues that the company actually took in
as a result of their operations—goods sold, services rendered, etc. They are "net" because this figure excludes any
revenues lost due to returned goods or uncollectible
accounts receivable. Net sales are sometimes called *operating revenues* when the income statement is for a service
company (as opposed to a manufacturing, or goods, company).

Example: If a company's income statement shows exclu-
sions from revenue, it might look like this:

Net sales (operating revenues)	$3,100,000
Less returns and allowances	− 100,000
Total	$3,000,000

· · ·

What is operating income?

Operating income, at one time known as *factory income*, is equal to the difference between net sales and operating costs. It represents the margin of profit based only on revenues and costs directly related to operations; it disregards nonoperating income (such as interest on securities, royalties, or rents from real estate holdings) and nonoperating expenses (like interest on loans or bonds).

What types of expenses does operating income include?

Included in operating income are three types of costs:

- *Cost of goods sold (COGS):* These are costs directly related to the product or service offered by the company. In a computer manufacturing firm, COGS might be raw materials like silicon or semiconductors made by another company. In service-oriented businesses, COGS are usually much lower than in product companies.

- *Depreciation and amortization:* These are the "noncash" amounts that are "written off" on property, plant, and equipment (depreciation) or on intangible assets (amortization).

- *Selling, general, and administrative (G&A) expenses:* The general costs of running a business are included in this category. Selling costs might include sales commissions, advertising, and discounts. General and administrative expenses are things like phone bills, utility costs, rent on office space, legal fees, and so on.

All three types of expenses must be incurred in order to *operate* a business.

How is operating income calculated?

To arrive at operating income, deduct operating costs from net sales:

Operating income = Net sales − Operating costs

Example: Hitech had net sales of $3,000,000 (after deducting an amount for returns and allowances) and operating costs of:

Operating costs:	
Cost of goods sold (COGS)	−2,170,000
Selling, general, and administrative (G&A)	− 212,000
Depreciation	− 198,000
Total operating costs	$2,580,000

Operating income is calculated as follows:

$$\text{Operating income} = \text{Net sales} - \text{Operating costs}$$
$$= \$3,000,000 - \$2,580,000$$
$$= \$420,000$$

What is ''other income'' and why isn't it included with operating revenues?

Other income reflects income the company receives from sources that are not related to the nature of its business: interest on bonds, dividends on other companies' stock, rent on real estate, sale of an asset, and so on. This income is separate from operating income because it is not an indication of management's ability to run a business. Including it with—that is, failing to distinguish it from—operating revenues could lead would-be investors to erroneous conclusions about the company's profit-making ability.

Sometimes interest paid out by the company to service its own bonds is used to offset this kind of income. Other income can also stand by itself; in this case, interest paid is not introduced until total income is computed.

Example: Hitech's income statement lists interest paid as an offset against dividends earned, as shown in Figure 2–1. It could have also listed this expense as shown in Figure 2–2. When interest is reported in this way, total income is also referred to as *earnings before interest and taxes (EBIT).* As you can see, although total income changes, net income is unaffected by the reporting format.

Figure 2–1   *Income Statement*
Hitech Corp.
January 1–December 31, 19XX

Net sales (operating revenues)	$ 3,000,000
Operating costs:	
Cost of goods sold (COGS)	− 2,170,000
Selling, general, and administrative (G&A)	− 212,000
Depreciation	− 198,000
Total operating costs	$ − 2,580,000
Operating income	$ 420,000
Other income:	
Dividend income	+ 9,500
Less interest on bonds	**− 50,000**
Total other income	$ − 40,500
Total income	**$ 379,500**
Taxes (30% rate)	− 113,850
Net income (net profit)	**$ 265,650**
Preferred dividends	− 8,000
Earnings available for common stock (net earnings)	$ 257,650

Figure 2–2   *Income Statement*
Hitech Corp.
January 1–December 31, 19XX

Net sales (operating revenues)	$ 3,000,000
Operating costs:	
Cost of goods sold (COGS)	− 2,170,000
Selling, general, and administrative (G&A)	− 212,000
Depreciation	− 198,000
Total operating costs	$ − 2,580,000
Operating income	$ 420,000
Other income:	
Dividend income	+ 9,500
Total income (EBIT)	**$ 429,500**
Less interest on bonds	**− 50,000**
Taxes (30% rate)	− 113,850
Net income (net profit)	**$ 265,650**
Preferred dividends	− 8,000
Earnings available for common stock (net earnings)	$ 257,650

How is total income computed?

Total income is computed only one way, but the resultant figure depends on how other income is represented on the income statement:

Total income = Operating income + Other income

Example: In the income statement in Figure 2–1, Hitech has operating income of \$420,000 and other income of −\$40,500.

$$\text{Total income} = \text{Operating income} + \text{Other income}$$
$$= \$420,000 + (-\$40,500)$$
$$= \$379,500$$

In the second example (Figure 2–2), Hitech has the same operating income, but other income becomes a positive figure, \$9,500.

$$\text{Total income} = \text{Operating income} + \text{Other income}$$
$$= \$420,000 + \$9,500$$
$$= \$429,500$$

How are corporate taxes computed?

The relevant tax rate is applied to total income after interest costs have been deducted. The formula varies, depending on how interest expense is represented on the income statement, but the results are the same.

Taxes = Tax rate × Total income

or

Taxes = Tax rate (Total income − Interest expense)

Example: If Hitech elects to deduct interest on its own bond issue from other income (see Figure 2–1), taxes are calculated as follows:

$$\text{Taxes} = \text{Tax rate} \times \text{Total income}$$
$$= .30 \times \$379,500$$
$$= \$113,850$$

If the company chooses to include interest paid as an expense against total income (see Figure 2–2), then the second formula applies:

Taxes = Tax rate × Total income
  = .30 × ($429,500 − $40,500)
  = .30 × $379,500
  = $113,850

Note: The tax rate used throughout these examples is fictitious. When corporate state and local taxes are added to federal obligations, the actual rates may be higher. The formulas apply regardless of the rates.

How does net income differ from total income?

Net income is the difference between *all* income (operating or other) and *all* expenses (including interest payments on debt issues and taxes). It is the amount left over after *all* inflows and outflows are put in the balance. Total income does not include taxes (and sometimes interest payments; compare Figures 2–1 and 2–2). For this reason, net income is also sometimes called *net profit.*

Why are preferred dividend payments deducted from total income, just like interest payments?

Interest payments are expenses; they show up on the balance sheet as a liability. Preferred dividend payments represent a portion of the owners' interest in the corporation, not a cost of doing business. They appear as part of the equity portion of the balance sheet.

How do net earnings differ from net income?

Also known as *earnings available for common stock, net earnings* consist of the amount available for distribution among common stockholders, if the management chooses to distribute any of it. At this point in the income statement, all revenues have come in and all expenses have been paid. The utility company, the phone service, the office supplies distributor, the ad agency, the bondholders, the tax collector, and the preferred stockholders have all gotten what is coming to them. And there is money left over. The company has operated at a profit—"in the black." This is the so-called *bottom line,* the figure that common stockholders examine to see how well their investment is faring.

ANALYSIS

Income statements are analyzed primarily by means of applying ratios, that is, by comparing one entry against another.

What is the operating (expense) ratio?

Also known as the *expense ratio*, the operating ratio compares costs to net sales—how much is it costing the company to make those sales? It reflects how well the company's management oversees its costs, that is, how "efficient" it is. Expense ratios that are higher than the industry norm or that increase from year to year may indicate poor controls by management. Decreasing operating costs may mean increasing efficiency, inasmuch as revenues may be going up, expenses may be getting cut, or both.

How is the operating ratio calculated?

To calculate the operating ratio, compare operating costs to net sales.

$$\text{Operating ratio} = \frac{\text{Operating costs}}{\text{Net sales}}$$

Example: To calculate Hitech's operating ratio, refer to the income statement, specifically the operating costs and net sales:

Net sales (operating revenues)	**$ 3,000,000**
Operating costs:	
Cost of goods sold (COGS)	−2,170,000
Selling, general, and administrative (G&A)	− 212,000
Depreciation	− 198,000
Total operating costs	**$−2,580,000**

. . .

$$\text{Operating ratio} = \frac{\text{Operating costs}}{\text{Net sales}}$$

$$= \frac{\$2,580,000}{\$3,000,000}$$

$$= .86 \text{ or } 86\%$$

What is the margin of profit ratio?

Sometimes referred to as the *operating margin of profit ratio* or *gross margin*, this comparison reflects the part of the net sales dollar that is *not* paid out to meet expenses. The margin of profit ratio is the complement of the expense ratio, the two of which add up to 1.00 (or 100%).

How is the margin of profit ratio computed?

Divide operating income by net sales:

$$\textbf{Margin of profit ratio} = \frac{\textbf{Operating income}}{\textbf{Net sales}}$$

Example: Hitech's net sales and operating income are as follows:

Net sales (operating revenues)	**$ 3,000,000**
Operating costs:	
Cost of goods sold (COGS)	−2,170,000
Selling, general, and administrative (G&A)	− 212,000
Depreciation	− 198,000
Total operating costs	$−2,580,000
Operating income	**$ 420,000**

. . .

$$\text{Margin of profit ratio} = \frac{\text{Operating income}}{\text{Net sales}}$$

$$= \frac{\$420,000}{\$3,000,000}$$

$$= .14 \text{ or } 14\%$$

Compare this result with the Hitech expense (operating) ratio in the preceding section:

$$\begin{array}{cccc} & & \text{Margin of} & \\ \text{Expense ratio} & + & \text{profit ratio} & = 1.00 \ (100\%) \\ .86 \ (86\%) & + & .14 \ (14\%) & = 1.00 \ (100\%) \end{array}$$

What is the net profit ratio?

The *net profit ratio* indicates what the company was able to "walk away with" after all expenses were paid. It relates the "walk-away" amount—earnings available for common stock—to net sales. In effect, it compares the top and bottom lines.

$$\text{Net profit ratio} = \frac{\text{Net profit}}{\text{Net sales}}$$

Example: Hitech had net sales of $3,000,000 (the top line on the income statement) and net earnings of $257,650 (the bottom line).

$$\begin{aligned} \text{Net profit ratio} &= \frac{\text{Net profit}}{\text{Net sales}} \\ &= \frac{\$257,650}{\$3,000,000} = .0858 \text{ or } 8.6\% \end{aligned}$$

In other words, for every $1.00 that Hitech took in as sales revenue, 8.6 cents turned up as profit.

Is that good? Given that the industry standard net profit ratio for manufacturing firms is 5%, Hitech is doing very well.

Industry Standards

How do I know whether a company's bottom line is high or low?

You can compare a company's bottom line to the *industry standard,* which is usually expressed in terms of percentages of the net revenues (the top line).

Example: If net revenues are assumed to be 100%, net earnings may be expressed as a part of that percentage. For makers of transportation equipment, net earnings average 5.5% to 6.0%. A company whose earnings are better, percentagewise, than this standard are said to be *outper-*

forming its industry. If its earnings are lower than the industry standard, it is *underperforming*.

How are the dollar values of net earnings converted to a ratio?

To compare a company's earnings to the industry standard, divide the entry by net revenues.

$$\text{Net earnings ratio} = \frac{\text{Net earnings}}{\text{Net revenues}}$$

Example: Hitech's net revenues are $3,000,000 and its net earnings are $257,650. Its net earnings ratio is calculated as follows:

$$\text{Net earnings ratio} = \frac{\text{Net earnings}}{\text{Net revenues}}$$

$$= \frac{\$257,650}{\$3,000,000} = .085 \text{ or } 8.5\%$$

Hitech's net earnings ratio is 8.5%. The industry standard for net earnings ratio for manufacturers of electrical and electronic equipment is 5.2%. Hitech is outperforming the industry standard.

Can other items on the income statement be compared to industry standards?

Yes. Standards are published for all industries for most entries on the income statement. To compare a particular company to the industry, divide the entry of interest by net revenues.

$$\text{Ratio} = \frac{\text{Entry from income statement}}{\text{Net revenues}}$$

Example: Hitech's operating income is $420,000 and its net revenues are $3,000,000. The operating income ratio formula is adapted from the general formula:

$$\text{Ratio} = \frac{\text{Entry from income statement}}{\text{Net revenues}}$$

$$\begin{aligned} \frac{\text{Operating}}{\text{income ratio}} &= \frac{\text{Operating income}}{\text{Net revenues}} \\ &= \frac{\$420,000}{\$3,000,000} = .014 \text{ or } 1.4\% \end{aligned}$$

Hitech's operating income ratio is 14%. The industry standard for makers of electrical and electronic equipment is 6.4%. Hitech is greatly outperforming the industry in this category.

The same general formula can be applied to any item on the P&L, so that Hitech's statement can be laid side by side with the "industry standard" statement.

Income Statement
Hitech Corp.
January 1–December 31, 19XX

	Hitech	Hitech Ratios	Standard Ratios
Net sales (operating revenues)	$ 3,000,000	100.0%	100.0%
Operating costs:			
Cost of goods sold (COGS)	−2,170,000 ⎫		
Selling, general, and administrative (G&A)	− 212,000 ⎬	79.4%	89.8%
Depreciation	− 198,000	6.6%	3.8%
Total operating costs	$−2,580,000	86.0%	93.6%
Operating income	$ 420,000	14.0%	6.4%
Other income:			
Dividend income	+ 9,500		
Less interest on bonds	− 50,000		
Total other income	$− 40,500	<1.4%>	.9%
Total income	$ 379,500	12.7%	7.3%
Taxes (30% rate)	− 113,850	3.8%	2.0%
Net income (net profit)	$ 265,650	8.9%	5.2%
Preferred dividends	− 8,000		
Earnings available for common stock (net earnings)	$ 257,650	8.5%	6.0%

Hitech seems to be outperforming the industry in most categories. The one exception is in total other income, in which it has a negative flow, that is, an outflow of funds. Hitech's management could present this in a better light by rearranging the entries in Figure 2–2. Interest on bonds is deducted from total income, not from other income, thereby making both entries positive (as shown in Figure 2–3).

Figure 2–3

Income Statement
Hitech Corp.
January 1–December 31, 19XX

	Hitech	Hitech Ratios	Standard Ratios
Net sales (operating revenues)	$ 3,000,000	100.0%	100.0%
Operating costs:			
Cost of goods sold (COGS)	−2,170,000 ⎫		
Selling, general, and administrative (G&A)	− 212,000 ⎬	79.4%	89.8%
Depreciation	− 198,000	6.6%	3.8%
Total operating costs	$− 2,580,000	86.0%	93.6%
Operating income	$ 420,000	14.0%	6.4%
Other income:			
Dividend income	+ 9,500	.3%	.9%
Total income	$ 429,500	14.3%	7.3%
Less interest on bonds	− 50,000		
Taxes (30% rate)	− 113,850	3.8%	2.0%
Net income (net profit)	$ 265,650	8.9%	5.2%
Preferred dividends	− 8,000		
Earnings available for common stock (net earnings)	$ 257,650	8.5%	6.0%

Hitech's other income ratio comes closer to the industry standard, *and* there are no negative ratios in the statement.

When analysts talk about a company's "cash flow," what do they mean?

Among investment analysts, *cash flow* has a very specific and quantifiable meaning: It refers to the actual dollars available to the corporation *after* generating revenue from its operations and paying expenses but *before* paying dividends to preferred or common stockholders. Extraordinary revenues, such as sales proceeds from a divestiture or the sale of common stock, should not be included; if such revenues are in the statement, they should be deducted before net income is computed.

Since the emphasis is on "actual dollars," nondollar assets, specifically depreciation, may not be counted as a real dollar outlay. Since depreciation is not an outflow of cash, the investment analyst adds depreciation back into net income when calculating cash flow:

Cash flow = Net income + Depreciation

Example: Hitech includes $198,000 worth of depreciation in its income statement as a charge against net sales. To calculate Hitech's cash flow, that amount has to be added to its net income:

Net sales (operating revenues)	$ 3,000,000
Operating costs:	
Cost of goods sold (COGS)	−2,170,000
Selling, general, and administrative (G&A)	− 212,000
Depreciation	**− 198,000**
Total operating costs	$−2,580,000
Operating income	$ 420,000
Other income:	
Dividend income	+ 9,500
Less interest on bonds	− 50,000
Total other income	$− 40,500
Total income	$ 379,500
Taxes (30% rate)	− 113,850
Net income (net profit)	**$ 265,650**

. . .

Cash flow = Net income + Depreciation
         = $265,650 + $198,000
         = $463,000

Hitech's cash flow is $463,000.

What is "interest coverage"?

Many corporations carry long-term debt (that is, one or more bond issues) on their books. These corporations must make interest payments, usually twice a year, to their bondholders. *Interest coverage* tells the analyst how well the company is able to cover these payments, sometimes referred to as its *debt service*. Interest coverage is expressed in terms of how many times total income is greater than the interest paid out on bonds.

How is interest coverage calculated?

The formula is:

$$\text{Interest coverage} = \frac{\text{Total income}}{\text{Interest on bonds}}$$

Example: Hitech pays $50,000 a year in debt service on a bond issue of several years ago. Its total income (or earnings before interest and taxes, EBIT) is $379,500.

Operating income	$	420,000
Other income:		
Dividend income	+	9,500
Less interest on bonds	**−**	**50,000**
Total other income	$−	40,500
Total income	**$**	**379,500**

$$\text{Interest coverage} = \frac{\text{Total income}}{\text{Interest on bonds}}$$
$$= \frac{\$379,500}{\$50,000} = 7.6 \text{ times}$$

This means that Hitech is capable of meeting its debt service obligations over seven and a half times. Interest coverage of four times or more is generally regarded as adequate.

What is "preferred dividend coverage"?

Preferred stocks are categorized as *fixed income investments,* along with debt instruments, such as corporate bonds. The reason is that, although preferred stock represents ownership and not a debt, it does obligate the issuer (the company) to make periodic payments, not of interest, but of dividends. The effect on the income statement is the same: Dividends *and* interest payments represent outflows of cash that are up to the discretion of management. Investors who hold preferred stock are very interested in the capability of the issuer to make those payments. Like interest coverage, preferred dividend coverage is a measurement of that capability, expressed as a multiple. In this case, however, net income is used instead of total income.

How is preferred dividend coverage computed?

Divide net income the preferred dividend interest:

$$\text{Preferred dividend coverage} = \frac{\text{Net income}}{\text{Preferred dividends}}$$

Example: Hitech pays $8,000 in preferred dividends every year, against a net income in 19XX of $265,500.

	...	
Net income (net profit)	**$**	**265,650**
Preferred dividends	**−**	**8,000**
	...	

$$\text{Preferred dividend coverage} = \frac{\text{Net income}}{\text{Preferred dividends}}$$
$$= \frac{\$265,650}{\$8,000} = 33.2$$

Hitech's earnings cover the preferred dividend obligation by over 33 times.

What are the earnings per share?

Earnings per (common) share is the amount of earnings (as reflected on the bottom line of the income statement) divided by the number of shares of common stock *that are held by investors*. The earnings per share indicate the profits available for distribution to common stockholders. It is probably the most widely used measurement of a company's investment-worthiness.

Given earnings (from the income statement), how do you find out the number of shares held by investors?

When a business incorporates, its state-bestowed *charter* allows the new corporation to issue a specific number of common shares. This number is the *authorized stock*. Management may actually elect to *issue* only a portion of the authorized amount; the shares that are actually offered to investors (in an initial public offering or through subsequent offerings) are considered to be *issued and outstanding* (or just *outstanding*). Shares that are issued and outstanding and that are available for trading (that is, not closely held by major investors) make up a company's *float*. Management can also create a third category of stock, called *treasury stock*, when it repurchases shares from investors. (Treasury stock decreases the float.)

Example: Hitech's corporate charter authorizes 500,000 shares of common stock. Five years ago it offered 300,000 shares at $5 par value, and the offering was a success—all shares were sold out. One year ago, Hitech's directors voted to buy back 50,000 shares in the open market at the then current value of $11.50. Before the repurchase of the stock, the disposition of Hitech's common stock was as follows:

Issued and outstanding	300,000
Authorized but unissued	200,000
Authorized	500,000

After the repurchase, it looked like this:

Issued and outstanding	250,000*
Treasury	50,000
Authorized but unissued	200,000
Authorized	500,000

*There are still 300,000 "issued."

This number—the number of shares issued and outstanding—is used in the calculation of the earnings per share. Excluded are authorized but unissued shares and treasury stock.

This number is sometimes found in the income statement itself, but more likely it will be found in the "Notes" to the statement.

How are earnings per share computed?

Net earnings are divided by the number of shares issued and outstanding:

$$\text{Earnings per share} = \frac{\text{Net earnings}}{\text{Number of shares issued and outstanding}}$$

Example: Hitech's earnings (available for common stock) are $257,650.

. . .	
Earnings available for common stock (net earnings)	$ 257,650

As of 19XX, it has 250,000 shares issued and outstanding.

$$\text{Earnings per share} = \frac{\text{Net earnings}}{\text{Number of shares issued and outstanding}}$$

$$= \frac{\$257,650}{250,000} = \$1.03$$

How does the number of shares issued and outstanding affect earnings per share:

As the number of shares issued and outstanding increases, earnings per share decreases.

Example: Suppose Hitech's board had not reacquired the 50,000 shares of outstanding stock. The earnings per share would then be lower:

$$\text{Earnings per share} = \frac{\text{Net earnings}}{\substack{\text{Number of shares issued} \\ \text{and outstanding}}}$$

$$= \frac{\$257,650}{300,000} = \$.86$$

The earnings per share dropped below the $1 mark, to $.86 from $1.03, when the 50,000 shares of treasury stock were included in the computation.

What is the difference between "primary earnings per share" and "diluted earnings per share"?

Primary earnings per share is the calculation described in the preceding section, that is, it uses only the number of shares *actually* in the hands of stockholders. *Diluted* (or *fully diluted*) *earnings per share* calculations use the same formula but they include the number of shares that *would be* in the hands of investors if certain "common stock equivalents" were exercised. *Common stock equivalents* are financial instruments that give their owners the right to buy common stock sometime in the future, usually at what is expected to be a favorable price. For example, investors may be holding warrants to buy the common stock, or they may own convertible bonds, which can be "traded in" to the issuer for common stock. If holders of common stock equivalents were to exercise their rights and trade in their warrants and convertibles (bonds or preferred stock) for common stock, the number of shares issued and outstanding would increase, in some cases dramatically.

The formula for calculating common stock equivalent shares is:

Common stock equivalent shares = **Common stock equivalent** × **Number of shares per common stock equivalent**

The formula for calculating diluted earnings per share is:

$$\text{Earnings per share} = \frac{\text{Net earnings}}{\substack{\text{Number of shares issued} \\ \text{and outstanding after} \\ \text{conversion}}}$$

Example: To "sweeten" the original offering of stock, Hitech awarded warrants to the original investors. Each warrant enabled the holder to buy an additional 25 shares at $15. Hitech awarded 230 warrants.

The computation of earnings per share did not include the shares represented by the warrants. The figuration of *primary* earnings per share does include them.

To calculate primary earnings per share, the common stock represented by the warrants has to be included:

$$\substack{\text{Common stock} \\ \text{equivalent} \\ \text{shares}} = \substack{\text{Common} \\ \text{stock} \\ \text{equivalent}} \times \substack{\text{Number of shares} \\ \text{per common stock} \\ \text{equivalent}}$$

$$\substack{\text{Equivalent} \\ \text{shares} \\ \text{for warrants}} = 230 \text{ warrants} \times 25 \text{ shares per warrant}$$

$$= 5,750$$

Add the two groups of common stock equivalents to the number of shares issued and outstanding:

Issued and outstanding	250,000
Warrant equivalents	5,750
Total shares after conversion	255,750

To calculate primary earnings per share:

$$\text{Earnings per share} = \frac{\text{Net earnings}}{\substack{\text{Number of shares issued} \\ \text{and outstanding after} \\ \text{conversion}}}$$

$$= \frac{\$257,650}{\substack{255,750 \\ \text{shares}}} = \$1.01 \text{ per share}$$

To an investor, earnings per share is less representative of the company's investment-worthiness than primary earnings per share. Most corporations now include primary earnings per share in their financial statements. For those that do not, look for information in the notes for common stock equivalents.

If bonds are converted to common stock, what effect does that have on the income statement?

Conversion of bonds to stock eliminates the debt service entry, freeing up more revenue for total income. The increased earnings *may* boost primary earnings per share depending on how big the tax bite is and how many additional shares are outstanding.

Example: Hitech floated a *convertible* bond issue; that is, it included in the bond's *trust agreement* a clause that enables the bondholder to turn in the bond for 50 shares of common. Hitech sold 500 $1,000 par value bonds in that offering, each representing a potential 50 shares issued and outstanding in the future. To recalculate primary earnings per share on a fully diluted basis, the additional shares have to be accounted for:

$$\begin{matrix} \text{Common stock} \\ \text{equivalent} \\ \text{shares} \end{matrix} = \begin{matrix} \text{Common} \\ \text{stock} \\ \text{equivalent} \end{matrix} \times \begin{matrix} \text{Number of shares} \\ \text{per common stock} \\ \text{equivalent} \end{matrix}$$

$$\begin{matrix} \text{Convertible} \\ \text{bonds} \\ \text{equivalent} \\ \text{shares} \end{matrix} = 500 \text{ bonds} \times 50 \text{ shares per bond}$$

$$= 25,000 \text{ shares}$$

These shares must be added to the others issued and outstanding:

Issued and outstanding	250,000
Warrant equivalents	5,750
Convertible bond equivalents	25,000
Total shares after conversion	280,750

But converting the bonds has an additional effect: It eliminates the $50,000 entry for interest on bonds from the income statement. Hitech's 19X1 statement looks like this:

Income Statement
Hitech Corp.
January 1–December 31, 19X1

Net sales (operating revenues)	$ 3,000,000
Operating costs:	
Cost of goods sold (COGS)	−2,170,000
Selling, general, and administrative (G&A)	− 212,000
Depreciation	− 198,000
Total operating costs	$−2,580,000
Operating income	$ 420,000
Other income:	
Dividend income	+ 9,500
Less interest on bonds	-0-
Total other income	$ 9,500
Total income	$ 429,500
Taxes (30% rate)	− 128,850
Net income (net profit)	$ 300,650
Preferred dividends	− 8,000
Earnings available for common stock (net earnings)	$ 292,650

To calculate primary earnings per share:

$$\text{Full diluted primary earnings per share} = \frac{\text{Net earnings}}{\substack{\text{Number of shares issued} \\ \text{and outstanding after} \\ \text{conversion}}}$$

$$= \frac{\$292,650}{280,750 \text{ shares}} = \$1.04 \text{ per share}$$

Assuming Hitech has not issued any other common stock equivalents, the earnings per share can be considered fully diluted.

STATEMENT OF CHANGES IN FINANCIAL POSITION

What purpose is served by the statement of changes in financial position?

The balance sheet presents a company's net worth and the income statement its net income. The *statement of changes in financial position* (also called *sources and uses of funds, cash flow,* or *funds flow*) sheds light on the funds available for paying dividends or reinvestment in operations. Its purpose is to clarify how much free cash the corporation really has.

One would think that the income statement supplies that information in the form of net earnings, the "bottom line." That is not so, for a couple of reasons.

One has to do with how a corporation accounts for its business transactions. If a company were on a cash system of accounting, net earnings would very closely reflect available cash. In a *cash* system, revenue is recorded and reported when it is received, and expenses when they are paid. For example, a company on a cash basis would record revenue for goods sold when the customer sends in the check, not when the billing is sent out. Given a cash system, therefore, the income statement could also serve as a fairly accurate statement of cash flow.

But rarely does a corporation operate on a cash basis. Almost all of them use an accrual accounting system. In an *accrual* system, expenses and revenues are matched so as to reflect the business activities underlying the accounting transactions. For example, a company may bill customers for goods and services in one fiscal period but not receive payment until the following period. Nevertheless, the billing is recorded as an asset (an account receivable). Or, if a company buys a major piece of equipment, the accountant does not record 100% of the cost as a cash outflow. Instead, the equipment hits the balance sheet as an asset, and the acquisition cost is recorded over a number years (as a depreciated asset, "plant, property, and equipment").

Another reason that income statements fall short as indicators of cash flow is that a corporation can have sources of income other than operations. The income statement—also known as the *earnings statement*—does not always provide for reporting other types of income. Interest on bonds or dividends on preferred stock may be entered as other income, but proceeds from a new debt or stock issue would not be. The sale of a capital asset may bring in a large sum of cash, but only the net gain or loss over the book value may be recorded on the income statement.

Hence the need for some brief statement that shows investors how much cash, or working capital, is really at hand—the statement of changes in financial position.

What should investors look for in the statement of financial change?

There is really only one thing to look for: the cash balance at the bottom of the statement. In many cases, the company's annual report will include a comparison between the current and prior years' statuses.

Example: All-Star Brand's statement of cash flows is:

Statement of Cash Flows
All-Star Brand Corp.
December 31, 19XX

Cash flows from operations:	
Receipts:	
Payments by customers	$3,000,000
Dividends on preferred stock	50,000
Total cash receipts	$3,050,000
Payments:	
Suppliers	$2,170,000
Payroll	212,000
Interest on bonds	50,000
Taxes	113,850
Total cash payments	$2,545,850
Net operating cash flows	$ 504,150
Cash flows from investments:	
Purchase of truck fleet	<$ 75,000>
Loan to sister company	< 20,000>
Proceeds from sale of old truck fleet	5,000
Net cash outflow	<$ 90,000>
Cash flows from capitalization:	
Preferred dividends	<$ 8,000>
Net increase in cash	**$ 406,150**

KEY TERMS

Amortization: The prorating of an asset's value over its useful life.

Authorized shares: The number of shares a corporation is authorized to issue by the state in which it is incorporated.

"Bottom line": See *Net earnings*.

Cash flow: The actual dollars available to a corporation after generating revenues and paying all expenses, but before paying dividends.

Common stock equivalents: Securities, such as warrants or convertible bonds, that may be converted to common stock.

Cost of goods sold (COGS): Costs directly related to the product or service offered by a company.

Diluted earnings per share: Earnings per share with all common stock equivalents assumed to be converted.

Dilution: The reduction of earnings per share by increasing the number of shares issued and outstanding.

Earnings available for common stock: See *Net earnings*.

Earnings before interest and taxes (EBIT): Net sales after deducting cost of goods sold and general and administrative expenses, but before deducting interest on long-term debt (the corporate bonds), and taxes.

Earnings per (common) share: Earnings available for common stock divided by the number of common shares outstanding.

Earnings report: See *Income statement*.

Expense ratio: Expenses expressed as a ratio of net sales.

Factory income: See *Operating income*.

Float: The number of shares that a corporation has issued and outstanding and that are available for trading (that is, not held closely by insiders).

Income statement (earnings report, profit and loss statement, statement of operations): A listing of a corporation's revenues, expenses, and net income over a given period, usually a fiscal year.

Industry standards: Average ratios or percentages of similar companies within an industry.

Interest coverage: The comparison, expressed as a ratio, of total income to the interest paid out on bonds.

Issued and outstanding: Stock that has been issued to stockholders and that has not been reacquired.

Margin of profit ratio: The portion of net sales that is not paid out for expenses (the complement of the expense ratio).

Net earnings (earnings available for common stock or bottom line): Income available for distribution to common stockholders after preferred stock dividends are paid.

Net income (net profit): The excess of all income over all expenses.

Net profit: See *Net income.*

Net profit ratio: Net income (profit) expressed as a ratio of net sales.

Net sales (top line): All revenues "net" of returns and allowances.

Operating income (factory income): The excess of net sales over operating costs.

Operating ratio: Operating costs expressed as a ratio of net sales.

Preferred dividend coverage: The comparison, expressed as a ratio, of total income to preferred dividends paid out by the corporation.

Primary earnings per share: See *Earnings per (common) share.*

Profit and loss statement: See *Income statement.*

Selling, general, and administrative (G&A) expenses: The expenses of running a company that are not directly related to the product or service—overhead.

Statement of changes in financial position: An attachment to the income statement that indicates how much free cash a corporation really has.

Statement of operations: See *Income statement.*

"Top line": See *Net sales.*

Total income: The sum of income from all sources.

Treasury stock: Shares that were issued and that were repurchased by, or given back to, the corporation.

Trust agreement: The statement on a bond certificate listing the terms of the debt.

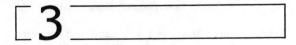

3

Stock Calculations

YOU WILL LEARN...

- How to compute ratios using information from both the income statement and balance sheet.
- How cash and stock dividends, as well as stock splits, affect a company's "financials."
- What determines the value of a common stock share, including mutual fund shares.
- The value of a rights offering certificate.
- How to prepare comparative financial statements.

INTRODUCTION

Analyzing a company's financial statements is actually only one of the many steps taken before making an investment in stocks or bonds. In addition to the investor's general knowledge about the issuing company, the industry, and the market itself, a number of other calculations should be made before deciding on the purchase or sale of a stock.

STOCK QUOTATIONS

How are stocks quoted?

Stocks are usually quoted in eighths (1/8s), with each eighth equal to $.125. Most trades occur in multiples of eighths. Some low-priced stocks (under $5 per share) may be transacted in sixteenths (1/16s).

Table 3–1

*Multiples of a Dollar in
Eighths (1/8s) and
Sixteenths (1/16s)*

1/16	$ .0625
1/8	$ .125
3/16	$ .1875
2/8 (1/4)	$ .250
5/16	$ .3125
3/8	$ .375
7/16	$ .4375
4/8 (1/2)	$ .500
9/16	$ .5625
5/8	$ .625
11/16	$ .6875
6/8 (3/4)	$ .750
13/16	$ .8125
7/8	$ .875
15/16	$ .9375
8/8 ($1)	$1.000

Example: A stock that trades in eighths may trade successively at $50.000, $50.125, $50.250, $50.125, $50.500, $50.375, and so on. All these prices are multiples of an eighth (see preceding table). The stock may *not* trade at $50.080, $50.005, $50.150, and so on. These are not multiples of one-eighth.

How can a price quoted in eighths or sixteenths be converted to dollars?

Quotes in eighths or sixteenths can be converted to dollar figures in two ways: One is to look up the eighth or sixteenth in Table 3–1 for the corresponding dollar value and then add that amount to the whole dollar value.

$$\begin{array}{c}\text{Dollar}\\\text{value}\end{array} = \begin{array}{c}\text{Whole}\\\text{dollar}\end{array} + \begin{array}{c}\text{Corresponding value}\\\text{of } n\text{-eights or}\\n\text{-sixteenths}\end{array}$$

Example: Convert 5⅞ to its dollar equivalent. The whole dollar value is, of course, $5. To this add $.875, which is the dollar equivalent of 7/8 in the table.

$$\begin{aligned}
\text{Dollar value} &= \text{Whole dollar value} + \text{Corresponding value of} \\
&\quad \text{n-eighths/sixteenths} \\
&= \$5 + \$.875 \\
&= \$5.875
\end{aligned}$$

The other method, if the table is unavailable, is to use the following formula:

$$\textbf{Dollar value} = \textbf{Dollars} + (\textbf{\textit{n}} \times \textbf{\$.125})$$

where

n = the number of eighths

Dollars = whole dollar value of the quote

Example: Convert 5⅞ to its dollar equivalent.

$$\begin{aligned}
\text{Dollar value} &= \text{Dollars} + (n \times \$.125) \\
&= 5 + (7 \times \$.125) \\
&= 5 + \$.875 = \$5.875
\end{aligned}$$

KEY RATIOS

Dividend Payout Ratio

What is the dividend payout ratio?

Investors buy stock with the expectation that they will share in the company's success. That expectation is fulfilled partly when other would-be owners of the stock bid its price up in the stock market; that is, the stock appreciates in value as the company proves its ability to be profitable. Another way for investors to share in profitability is through dividends. Most companies pay their common stockholders some portion of their net earnings. That portion is known as the *dividend payout ratio*. Young companies on a growth track may have a ratio of 10% or less, while more mature corporations, particularly manufacturers, may pay up to 50%.

How is the payout ratio computed?

Divide the dividends on common stock by net earnings:

$$\text{Payout ratio} = \frac{\text{Common stock dividends}}{\text{Net earnings}}$$

Example: In 19XX, Hitech's directors vote to pay a common stock dividend of $.10 per share. If 280,750 shares are issued and outstanding, then the total dollar value of the dividend is:

$$
\begin{aligned}
\text{Total dividend} &= \text{Dividend per share} \\
&\quad \times \text{Shares outstanding} \\
&= \$.10 \times 280{,}750 = \$28{,}075
\end{aligned}
$$

Hitech's net earnings are available from its income statement:

Income Statement
Hitech Corp.
January 1–December 31, 19XX

Net sales (operating revenues)	$ 3,000,000
Operating costs:	
Cost of goods sold (COGS)	−2,170,000
Selling, general, and administrative (G&A)	− 212,000
Depreciation	− 198,000
Total operating costs	$−2,580,000
Operating income	$ 420,000
Other income:	
Dividend income	+ 9,500
Less interest on bonds	− 50,000
Total other income	$− 40,500
Total income	$ 379,500
Taxes (30% rate)	− 113,850
Net income (net profit)	$ 265,650
Preferred dividends	− 8,000
Earnings available for common stock (net earnings)	**$ 257,650**

The payout ratio is:

$$
\begin{aligned}
\text{Payout ratio} &= \frac{\text{Common stock dividends}}{\text{Net earnings}} \\
&= \frac{\$28{,}075}{\$257{,}650} = .108 \text{ or } 11\%
\end{aligned}
$$

Current Yield

What is current yield?

Current yield is the percentage represented by dividing a (common or preferred) stock's annual dividends by its market price. The result reflects the return to the investor based on the purchase price. The formula is:

$$\textbf{Current yield} = \frac{\textbf{Annual dividend}}{\textbf{Market value}}$$

Example: Hitech's board votes on a \$.10-per-share dividend when the company's stock is trading at \$7.25. The current yield is:

$$\text{Current yield} = \frac{\text{Annual dividend}}{\text{Market value}}$$
$$= \frac{\$.10}{\$7.25} = .014 \text{ or } 1.4\%$$

Current yield can also be calculated for preferred stock.

Example: Hitech's preferred stock is trading at \$94.50 and pays an annual per-share dividend of \$8. The current yield on the preferred stock is:

$$\text{Current yield} = \frac{\text{Annual dividend}}{\text{Market value}}$$
$$= \frac{\$8}{\$94.50} = .0846 \text{ or } 8.5\%$$

Cash Dividends

When is a stockholder eligible for receiving a cash dividend?

To be entitled to dividends on common stock, a stockholder must be the owner on the books of the issuing corporation as of the "record date." To know this date, you need to understand what is known as the *dividend cycle*.

For *cash dividends,* this cycle involves four dates:

1. The *declaration date* is the day on which the board announces the dividend.

2. The *ex-dividend date* is the first day after the declaration date on which investors who buy the stock are no longer eligible for the dividend. Since most trades are on a *regular way* (or *five-day*) *settlement* basis, this date is usually four business days before the record date.

3. On the *record date,* the corporation asks its transfer agent (the keeper of the stockholders records) to supply a list of the shareholders as of that day.

4. The *payment date,* usually about ten business days after the record date, is the day on which dividend checks are issued.

Example: In September of 19XX, Big Business votes for a $1.50 cash dividend on its common stock. The decision is not made public until October 2, Monday. The dividend cycle (a typical one) is as follows:

- *Declaration date:* October 2, Monday
- *Ex-dividend date:* October 17, Tuesday
- *Record date:* October 23, Monday
- *Payment date:* November 6, Monday

October						
Sun.	*Mon.*	*Tues.*	*Wed.*	*Thurs.*	*Fri.*	*Sat.*
1	2	3	4	5	6	7
8	9	10	11	12	13	14
15	16	17	18	19	20	21
22	23	24	25	26	27	28
29	30	31				

November						
Sun.	*Mon.*	*Tues.*	*Wed.*	*Thurs.*	*Fri.*	*Sat.*
			1	2	3	4
5	6	7	8	9	10	11
12	13	14	15	16	17	18
19	20	21	22	23	24	25
26	27	28	29	30		

Why is the ex-dividend date four business days before the record date? The reason is that most stock transactions are settled the "regular way," which is five business days after the trade date. A trade on October 13 is settled on October 20 (five *business* days later). The significance is that the purchaser is not on the registrar's books until settlement. Someone who purchases the stock on October 16 or sooner is said to be purchasing the stock *cum dividend* (*with dividend*). Anyone who buys it on the 17th or thereafter will not be recorded as the owner until after the record date; the purchase is considered *ex-dividend* (or *without the dividend*).

Note: Those who purchase the stock up to and/or on the record date and who settle in *cash* are entitled to the dividend. The reason is that cash transactions settle on the same day as the trade.

Does it make any difference whether stock is purchased within the period of the dividend cycle?

It does. The price declines approximately by the amount of the dividend on the ex-dividend date, on which day knowledgeable would-be purchasers know that they are no longer entitled to the dividend; the market value backs off to whatever it would be without the dividend included.

Example: With its common stock trading at $20.25 on October 2 (after the close of trading for the day), Big Business declares a cash dividend of $1.50, for payment on November 6. The stock continues to trade more or less at that level (given the normal market fluctuations), until October 17, the ex-dividend date. On that day, in theory, the stock will then sell for $1.50 less, or a little under $19 per share ($20.25 less $1.50).

What effects does declaring a cash dividend have on the issuing corporation's balance sheet?

If a balance sheet were done after the declaration date but before the payment date, current liabilities increase by the total dollar amount of the dividend, and retained earnings decrease by that amount.

Example: Big Business has 100,000 shares of common

stock issued and outstanding, and it declares a $1.50 per-share dividend. The total dollar amount represented by this dividend is $150,000 ($1.50 per share times 100,000 shares). The company now has a current liability of $150,000 that it did not have before. The balance sheet changes from this (note the boldface entries):

Balance Sheet
Big Business Inc.
December 31, 19XX

Assets	
Current Assets:	
Cash	$ 650,000
Marketable securities	1,300,000
Accounts receivable	425,000
Inventory	550,000
Total current assets	$2,925,000
Fixed Assets: Property, plant, and equipment	$2,225,000
Sundry Assets: Prepayments	30,000
Intangibles	$ 15,000
Total assets	$5,195,000

Liabilities	
Current Liabilities:	
Accounts payable	$ 680,000
Accrued expenses	945,000
Accrued taxes	325,000
Total current liabilities	**$1,950,000**
Fixed Liabilities:	
Bonds—7%, due 2006	$ 830,000
Total liabilities	**$2,780,000**

Stockholders' Equity	
Preferred stock—7% (Par: $100)	$ 750,000
Common stock	1,330,000
Capital surplus	100,000
Retained earnings	**235,000**
Total stockholders' equity	**$2,415,000**
Total liabilities and stockholders' equity	$5,195,000

To this:

Balance Sheet
Big Business Inc.
December 31, 19XX

Assets

Current Assets:	
Cash	$ 650,000
Marketable securities	1,300,000
Accounts receivable	425,000
Inventory	550,000
Total current assets	$2,925,000
Fixed Assets: Property, plant, and equipment	$2,225,000
Sundry Assets: Prepayments	30,000
Intangibles	$ 15,000
Total assets	$5,195,000

Liabilities

Current Liabilities:	
Accounts payable	$ 680,000
Accrued expenses	945,000
Accrued taxes	325,000
Dividends payable	**150,000**
Total current liabilities	**$2,100,000**
Fixed Liabilities:	
Bonds—7%, due 2006	$ 830,000
Total liabilities	**$2,930,000**

Stockholders' Equity

Preferred stock—7% (Par: $100)	$ 750,000
Common stock	1,330,000
Capital surplus	100,000
Retained earnings	**85,000**
Total stockholders' equity	**$2,265,000**
Total liabilities and stockholders' equity	$5,195,000

Note the changes:

- A new entry for dividends payable ($150,000) is created in current liabilities, which increases total liabilities to $2,930,000.

● Retained earnings is decreased by $150,000, to $85,000, which lowers total stockholders' equity to $2,265,000.

But the accounting equation can never be out of balance. The total of liabilities and stockholders' equity remains the same and is equal to total assets ($5,195,000). Before declaring the dividend, the equation looks like this:

$$\text{Total assets} = \begin{array}{l} \text{Total liabilities} \\ + \text{ Stockholders' equity} \end{array}$$

$$\$5,195,000 = \$2,780,000 + \$2,415,000$$

After the declaration date, it is:

$$\text{Total assets} = \begin{array}{l} \text{Total liabilities} \\ + \text{ Stockholders' equity} \end{array}$$

$$\$5,195,000 = \$2,930,000 + \$2,265,000$$

What effects does paying a cash dividend have on a company's balance sheet?

After the dividend is paid, the balance sheet changes again. This time cash decreases and the current liability is taken off the balance sheet. Thus both sides of the accounting equation are reduced by equal amounts.

Balance Sheet
Big Business Inc.
December 31, 19XX

Assets	
Current Assets:	
Cash	**$ 500,000**
Marketable securities	1,300,000
Accounts receivable	425,000
Inventory	550,000
Total current assets	$2,775,000
Fixed Assets: Property, plant, and equipment	$2,225,000
Sundry Assets: Prepayments	30,000
Intangibles	$ 15,000
Total assets	**$5,045,000**

	Liabilities	
Current Liabilities:		
Accounts payable		$ 680,000
Accrued expenses		945,000
Accrued taxes		325,000
Total current liabilities		**$1,950,000**
Fixed Liabilities:		
Bonds—7%, due 2006		$ 830,000
Total liabilities		**$2,780,000**

	Stockholders' Equity	
Preferred stock—7% (Par: $100)		$ 750,000
Common stock		1,330,000
Capital surplus		100,000
Retained earnings		85,000
Total stockholders' equity		$2,265,000
Total liabilities and stockholders' equity		**$5,045,000**

The accounting equation is satisfied:

$$\text{Total assets} = \begin{array}{l}\text{Total liabilities}\\ +\text{ Stockholders' equity}\end{array}$$

$$\$5,045,000 = \$2,780,000 + \$2,265,000$$

Stock Dividends

How do stock dividends differ from cash dividends?

When a company pays a stock dividend, it does nothing more than issue more of its authorized stock to current stockholders at no charge. No cash is paid out. Since no cash "leaves" the asset section of the balance sheet, it is not altered. Since the company incurs no obligation to pay out cash, the liability segment remains the same also. The formula is:

$$\text{Stock dividend} = \frac{\text{Additional shares}}{\text{Shares held}}$$

Example: A company decides to give each of its common stockholders two additional shares for every six that he or she now holds:

$$\text{Stock dividend} = \frac{\text{Additional shares}}{\text{Shares held}}$$
$$= \frac{2}{6} = .333 \text{ or } 33.3\%$$

Is the dividend cycle for a stock dividend different from that for a cash dividend?

Yes. The order of dates in the stock dividend cycle is:

- Declaration date.
- Record date.
- Payment date.
- Ex-distribution date (not ex-dividend date).

Example: Dynamic Corp. declares a stock dividend on October 2 for a payment date of October 24. The stock will then trade ex-distribution on October 25. Someone who purchases the stock so as to take delivery before or on October 24 is entitled to the dividend.

October						
Sun.	*Mon.*	*Tues.*	*Wed.*	*Thurs.*	*Fri.*	*Sat.*
1	2	3	4	5	6	7
8	9	10	11	12	13	14
15	16	17	18	19	20	21
22	23	**24**	**25**	26	27	28
29	30	31				

Why does a corporation issue a stock dividend rather than a cash dividend?

A company awards stock dividends, in lieu of cash dividends, for basically two reasons:

1. *To conserve cash:* Since no cash leaves the company, the assets remain intact.
2. *To reduce the market value of the issued and outstanding shares:* When a corporation is prospering, the value of its shares normally rises in the stock market. If the per-share price goes too high, some investors may be

dissuaded from purchasing the stock. Stock dividends have the effect of diminishing the per-share price.

What is a "small" or "large" stock dividend?

A stock dividend is *small* if it represents 25% or less of the company's issued stock. A *large* stock dividend is 25% or more of the corporation's issued stock. The stock dividend percentage is calculated as follows:

$$\text{Stock dividend percentage} = \frac{\text{Dividend shares}}{\text{Shares issued and outstanding}}$$

Once this percentage is ascertained, the number of additional shares to be distributed in the stock dividend can be calculated:

$$\text{Stock dividend shares} = \frac{\text{Shares issued and outstanding}}{} \times \text{Stock dividend percentage}$$

Example: General Entertainment, Inc. is authorized 50,000 shares and has issued 20,000 shares, with a $10 par value and a market value of $16. The board votes to issue 1 new share for every 10 currently issued and outstanding.

$$\text{Stock dividend percentage} = \frac{\text{Dividend shares}}{\text{Shares issued and outstanding}}$$
$$= \frac{1}{10} = .10 \text{ or } 10\%$$

This is a small stock dividend, less than 25%. The number of shares in stock dividend may be calculated next:

$$\text{Stock dividend shares} = \frac{\text{Shares issued and outstanding}}{} \times \text{Stock dividend percentage}$$
$$= 20,000 \times .10$$
$$= 2,000 \text{ additional shares}$$

Example: If General Entertainment had elected to issue 2

new shares for each 5 shares issued and outstanding, the calculation would be:

$$\text{Stock dividend percentage} = \frac{\text{Dividend shares}}{\text{Shares issued and outstanding}}$$

$$= \frac{2}{5} = .40 \text{ or } 40\%$$

This would be considered a large stock dividend, over 25%. The number of additional shares in the dividend is:

$$\text{Stock dividend shares} = \frac{\text{Shares issued and outstanding}}{} \times \text{Stock dividend percentage}$$

$$= 20,000 \times .40$$

$$= 8,000 \text{ additional shares}$$

How do stock dividends affect the issuing corporation's balance sheet?

Stock dividends affect only the equity section of the balance sheet. Since no cash is promised to stockholders, no liability is created. And, since no cash is ever paid out, assets are not affected. How the equity section is affected depends on whether the dividend is small or large.

How does declaring a small stock dividend affect the balance sheet?

There are a number of ways to account for stock dividends. A common way is to create an entry for "common stock dividend distributable." That entry is equal to the number of shares in the dividend times par value:

Common stock dividend distributable = **Dividend shares × Par value**

But the total liabilities and equity amount may not change, because in so doing it would upset the accounting equation underlying the balance sheet. So the amount for common stock dividend distributable must come from somewhere. Thus retained earnings is decreased by this amount.

Example: Big Business's board decides to issue 1 new share for every 10 now issued and outstanding. Big Business has issued 266,000 shares with a par value of $5. This is a small stock dividend (less than 25%):

$$\text{Stock dividend percentage} = \frac{\text{Dividend shares}}{\text{Shares issued and outstanding}}$$

$$= \frac{1}{10} = .10 \text{ or } 10\%$$

This percentage indicates that 26,600 additional shares will be distributed:

$$\text{Stock dividend shares} = \frac{\text{Shares issued and outstanding}}{} \times \text{Stock dividend percentage}$$

$$= 266,000 \times .10$$

$$= 26,600 \text{ additional shares}$$

Before the declaration date, Big Business's equity section looked like this:

Stockholders' Equity	
Preferred stock—7% (Par: $100)	$ 750,000
Common stock (266,000 issued and outstanding)	1,330,000
Capital surplus	100,000
Retained earnings	**235,000**
Total stockholders' equity	$2,415,000
Total liabilities and stockholders' equity	$5,195,000

On the declaration date, the entry called "common stock dividend distributable" is created:

$$\text{Common stock dividend distributable} = \text{Dividend shares} \times \text{Par value}$$

$$= 26,600 \times \$5 = \$133,000$$

Now the equity section is:

Stockholders' Equity	
Preferred stock—7% (Par: $100)	$ 750,000
Common stock (266,000 issued	
and outstanding)	1,330,000
Common stock dividend distributable	
(26,600 shares)	**133,000**
Capital surplus	100,000
Retained earnings	**102,000**
Total stockholders' equity	$2,415,000
Total liabilities and stockholders' equity	$5,195,000

The new entry has been created, and retained earnings have
been decreased to account for it.

*When a small stock dividend is distributed, what
happens to the balance sheet?*

Upon distribution of a small stock dividend:

- Retained earnings is decreased for the market value of
  the additional shares.

$$\begin{matrix} \textbf{Decrease in retained} \\ \textbf{earnings} \end{matrix} = \begin{matrix} \textbf{Dividend} \\ \textbf{shares} \end{matrix} \times \begin{matrix} \textbf{Market} \\ \textbf{value} \end{matrix}$$

- Common stock is increased by the par value of the
  additional stock.

$$\begin{matrix} \textbf{Increase in common} \\ \textbf{stock} \end{matrix} = \begin{matrix} \textbf{Dividend} \\ \textbf{shares} \end{matrix} \times \begin{matrix} \textbf{Par} \\ \textbf{value} \end{matrix}$$

- Capital surplus (paid-in capital) is increased by the difference between the market value and par value.

$$\begin{matrix} \textbf{Increase in} \\ \textbf{capital surplus} \end{matrix} = \textbf{Market value} - \textbf{Par value}$$

Example: Refer to the small stock dividend declared by
Big Business in the preceding section. The common stock
was selling at $7.50 on the declaration date, which is the
date on which market value is recorded.
  Retained earnings is decreased for the market value of
the additional shares.

$$\begin{array}{c} \text{Decrease in retained} \\ \text{earnings} \end{array} = \begin{array}{c} \text{Dividend} \\ \text{shares} \end{array} \times \begin{array}{c} \text{Market} \\ \text{value} \end{array}$$

$$= 26{,}600 \times \$7.50 = \$199{,}500$$

Common stock is increased by the par value of the additional stock.

$$\begin{array}{c} \text{Increase in common} \\ \text{stock} \end{array} = \begin{array}{c} \text{Dividend} \\ \text{shares} \end{array} \times \begin{array}{c} \text{Par} \\ \text{value} \end{array}$$

$$= 26{,}600 \times \$5 = \$133{,}000$$

Capital surplus (paid-in capital) is increased by the difference between the market value and par value.

$$\begin{array}{c} \text{Increase in} \\ \text{capital surplus} \end{array} = \text{Market value} - \text{Par value}$$

$$= \$199{,}500 - \$133{,}000$$

$$= \$66{,}500$$

The equity section now looks like this:

Stockholders' Equity	
Preferred stock—7% (Par: $100)	$ 750,000
Common stock (292,600 shares issued	
and outstanding)	1,463,000
Capital surplus	166,500
Retained earnings	35,500
Total stockholders' equity	$2,415,000
Total liabilities and stockholders' equity	$5,195,000

- Common stock increased to $1,463,000: $1,330,000 plus $133,000.
- Capital surplus increased to $166,500: $100,000 plus $66,500.
- Retained earnings drops to $35,500: $235,000 less $199,500.

Because of the way they hit the balance sheet, small stock dividends are regarded as *distributions of earnings*. Here's why. Given the small size of the dividend, the market value of the stock is not likely to be greatly affected.

So investors wind up with a greater number of shares that have, for the most part, the same market value as they did before the dividend. In effect, they have increased the overall value of their position in the stock.

How does a large stock dividend affect the balance sheet?

Like small dividends, large stock dividends do not alter the asset or liability section at all. Only the equity section is affected. (See the preceding section on small stock dividends.) They simply transfer funds from retained earnings to capital surplus (paid-in capital). For small dividends, accountants use the market value to make that transfer.

For large dividends, they use par value. The reason is that, of the two types of stock dividends, a large dividend is more likely to have a decreasing influence on the market value of the stock. Large stock dividends are therefore sometimes referred to as *capitalized retained earnings*.

When a large stock dividend is declared, what happens to the balance sheet?

The effects on the balance sheet of declaring a large stock dividend are basically the same as for a small dividend. On the declaration date, an entry is created for "common stock dividend distributable." That entry is equal to the number of shares in the dividend times par value:

$$\text{Common stock dividend distributable} = \text{Dividend shares} \times \text{Par value}$$

Since the total liabilities and equity amount may not change (a change would "unbalance" the balance sheet), the amount for common stock dividend distributable must come from somewhere else in the equity section. Specifically, retained earnings is decreased for the par value of the additional shares.

$$\text{Decrease in retained earnings} = \text{Dividend shares} \times \text{Par value}$$

• Common stock is increased by the par value of the additional stock.

$$\begin{array}{c}\text{Increase in common}\\\text{stock}\end{array} = \begin{array}{c}\text{Dividend}\\\text{shares}\end{array} \times \begin{array}{c}\text{Par}\\\text{value}\end{array}$$

Hence:

$$\begin{array}{c}\text{Common stock dividend}\\\text{distributable}\end{array} = \begin{array}{c}\text{Decrease in retained}\\\text{earnings}\end{array}$$

Example: General Business Corp. declares a stock dividend of 2 shares for every 5 issued and outstanding—a 40% dividend (2 divided by 5). Since 300,000 shares are issued and outstanding (with a par value of $4), this percentage indicates that 120,000 additional shares will be distributed:

$$\begin{array}{c}\text{Stock dividend}\\\text{shares}\end{array} = \begin{array}{c}\text{Shares issued}\\\text{and}\\\text{outstanding}\end{array} \times \begin{array}{c}\text{Stock dividend}\\\text{percentage}\end{array}$$

$$= 300,000 \times .40$$

$$= 120,000 \text{ additional shares}$$

Before the declaration date, General's equity section looked like this:

. . .	
Stockholders' Equity	
Preferred stock—7% (Par: $100)	$ 950,000
Common stock (266,000 issued and outstanding)	2,350,000
Capital surplus	1,000,000
Retained earnings	635,000
Total stockholders' equity	$4,935,000
. . .	

On the declaration date, the common stock dividend distributable entry is created:

$$\begin{array}{c}\text{Common stock}\\\text{dividend}\\\text{distributable}\end{array} = \text{Dividend shares} \times \text{Par value}$$

$$= 120,000 \times \$4 = \$480,000$$

Also:

$$\begin{matrix} \text{Decrease in retained} \\ \text{earnings} \end{matrix} = \begin{matrix} \text{Dividend} \\ \text{shares} \end{matrix} \times \begin{matrix} \text{Par} \\ \text{value} \end{matrix}$$

$$= 120,000 \times \$4 = \$480,000$$

Hence:

$$\begin{matrix} \text{Common stock dividend} \\ \text{distributable} \end{matrix} = \begin{matrix} \text{Decrease in retained} \\ \text{earnings} \end{matrix}$$

$$\$480,000 = \$480,000$$

Now the equity section is:

· · · *Stockholders' Equity*	
Preferred stock—7% (Par: $100)	$ 950,000
Common stock (266,000 issued and outstanding)	2,350,000
Common stock dividend distributable	**480,000**
Capital surplus	1,000,000
Retained earnings	**155,000**
Total stockholders' equity	$4,935,000
· · ·	

The new entry has been created ($480,000 for distributable dividends), and retained earnings has been decreased to account for it ($635,000 less $480,000).

When a large stock dividend is distributed, what happens to the balance sheet?

Upon the declaration date, the common stock entry is increased by the amount of the common stock distributable dividend, and the latter entry is taken off the sheet. Retained earnings (already decreased) and capital surplus remain the same.

Example: After General Business Corp. distributes its stock dividend, the equity section looks like this:

. . .

Stockholders' Equity

Preferred stock—7% (Par: $100)	$ 950,000
Common stock (266,000 issued and outstanding)	**2,830,000**
Capital surplus	1,000,000
Retained earnings	155,000
Total stockholders' equity	$4,935,000

. . .

Common stock has absorbed the amount of the dividend, calculated at par value (the original amount of $2,350,000 plus $480,000 in dividends).

Stock Splits

What does it mean when a stock "splits"?

A *split* is a distribution of additional authorized stock to current shareholders. A split serves the same purpose as a stock dividend: It decreases the market value of a stock by increasing the number of shares outstanding. A split, however, can have a greater impact on price than a dividend because, in a stock split, the issuing corporation often awards its stockholders one or more shares for every one held. Notice that a stock dividend usually is expressed as a percentage—such as a "25% dividend"—because the number of shares awarded is usually lower than the number of shares already held by the stockholder—for instance, "one for four." A stock split is expressed as a ratio—"two for one," for example—because the number of shares awarded is sometimes greater than the number of shares owned. Three-for-two (3/2), four-for-three (4/3), and five-for-four (5/4) splits are probably as common as two-for-ones or three-for-ones.

A corporation splits its stock for several reasons. In the long term, the common stock price is lowered, but more likely the purpose is either to increase the number of issued shares for listing or to lessen the concentration of institutional stockholders in the issue.

How does a stock split affect the issuer's balance sheet?

Not much changes on the balance sheet as the result of a stock split. Assets and liabilities are unaltered, but the equity section will change. Just as in the case of a stock dividend, the additional shares come out of the authorized but unissued portion of the corporation's stock. So the number of shares outstanding increases, and that number may be so noted in the statement. But, if the common stock entry is the amount resulting from multiplying the number of shares outstanding with the par value, then shouldn't that increase? In turn, if assets and liabilities do not change, doesn't changing the equity total throw the balance sheet off?

The answer is that, in a stock split, the par value of the stock is adjusted downward so that the common stock entry remains the same.

$$\text{New par value} = \frac{\text{Old par value}}{\text{Shares awarded per each share held}}$$

Example: MegaCorp. has issued 266,000 out of its 1,500,000 authorized shares (with a par value of $15). With each share trading at the $90 level, the corporate directors decide that the stock is being priced out of the range of many investors. A stock dividend is considered, but it will not bring the market price down to the $30-to-$50 range that the board feels will broaden the appeal of Mega-Corp. stock among investors. Instead, they vote for a 3-for-1 stock split.

Before the stock split, the balance sheet looks like this:

. . .	
Stockholders' Equity	
Preferred stock—8% (Par: $100)	$1,250,000
Common stock (266,000 shares at $15 par)	3,990,000
Capital surplus	1,980,000
Retained earnings	995,000
Total stockholders' equity	$8,215,000
. . .	

With the stock split, the new par value must be computed:

$$\text{New par value} = \frac{\text{Old par value}}{\text{Shares awarded per each share held}}$$

$$= \frac{\$15}{3} = \$5$$

Once the new shares are distributed—3 for every 1 issued—the number of shares outstanding is tripled: 3 times 266,000 equals 798,000. When that number is multiplied by the new par value, the same common stock entry results:

$$\frac{\text{Common}}{\text{stock entry}} = \text{Shares outstanding} \times \text{New par value}$$

$$= 798,000 \times 5 = \$3,990,000$$

The equity section now looks like this:

. . .
Stockholders' Equity

Preferred stock—8% (Par: $100)	$1,250,000
Common stock (798,000 shares at $5 par)	**3,990,000**
Capital surplus	1,980,000
Retained earnings	995,000
Total stockholders' equity	$8,215,000

. . .

Inventory Turnover Ratio

How do you evaluate the effectiveness of a company in selling its goods?

The *inventory turnover ratio* is a determinant of a company's effectiveness in distributing its product. The calculation reflects how many times it sells out its inventory within the accounting period reflected by the financial statement. The simplest formula is:

$$\text{Inventory turnover ratio} = \frac{\text{Net sales}}{\text{Year-end inventory}}$$

Example: Big Business's income statement (not shown) indicates that it had net sales of $4,000,000 in 19XX, with year-end inventories of $550,000 (see its balance sheet).

Assets	
Current Assets:	
Cash	$ 650,000
Marketable securities	1,300,000
Accounts receivable	425,000
Inventory	**550,000**
Total current assets	$2,925,000

. . .

Its inventory turnover ratio is:

$$\text{Inventory turnover ratio} = \frac{\text{Net sales}}{\text{Year-end inventory}}$$

$$= \frac{\$4,000,000}{\$550,000} = 7.3$$

The result of 7.3 means that Big Business has sold the amount of inventory equal to its year-end level over 7 times.

What is a valid inventory turnover rate?

Inventory turnover rates vary from one industry to the next. Farm equipment makers might turn inventory over almost 3 times a year, while a department store will sell out its goods 3.5 times a year, and a seller of building materials almost 5 times a year.

Example: Big Business's ratio of 7.3 is extremely high. Ordinarily, a high ratio is an indicator of brisk sales, but some questions must be asked. Is Big Business really doing great business, or is management not keeping enough inventory on hand to meet demand? If inventory is low most of the time, is the company losing sales? Also, is the year-end inventory representative of inventory levels throughout the year? Could the annual average inventory actually be much higher (or lower)?

Is the end-of-year inventory level in balance sheet accurate?

Not usually. The formula presented in the preceding section is easy because it requires only the information from the company's balance sheet and income statement. It is also not as accurate as it should be. A more precise formula is:

$$\text{Inventory turnover ratio} = \frac{\text{Cost of goods sold}}{\text{Average inventory}}$$

What is the *average* inventory? One way of determining this is to find out the ending inventories of all 12 months covered by the P&L, adding them up, and dividing by 12. This information, however, may be hard to obtain. A nearly as accurate method is to add the beginning and ending inventories for the year and dividing by 2. The formula is:

$$\text{Average inventory} = \frac{\text{Beginning inventory} + \text{Ending inventory}}{2}$$

The beginning inventory might be mentioned in the "Notes" section of the company's financial statements, or it might be taken from the ending inventory of the preceding year when two years are represented on one statement.

Example: Hitech's 19X0 income statement contains an amount for cost of goods sold of $2,170,000. Its balance sheets of 19X0 and 19X1, when placed side by side, look like this:

Hitech Corp.
Balance Sheet
December 31

	19X1	19X0
Assets		
Current Assets:		
Cash	$ 650,000	$ 540,000
Marketable securities	1,300,000	1,100,000
Accounts receivable	425,000	350,000
Inventory	550,000	425,000
Total current assets	$2,925,000	$2,415,000

. . .

$$\text{Average inventory} = \cfrac{\text{Beginning inventory} + \text{Ending inventory}}{2}$$

$$= \cfrac{\$550,000 + \$425,000}{2}$$

$$= \cfrac{\$975,000}{2} = \$487,500$$

Cost of goods sold can be taken from the Hitech income statement:

Net sales (operating revenues)	$ 3,000,000
Operating costs:	
Cost of goods sold (COGS)	**−2,170,000**
Selling, general, and administrative (G&A)	− 212,000
Depreciation	− 198,000
Total operating costs	$−2,580,000

. . .

$$\text{Inventory turnover ratio} = \cfrac{\text{Cost of goods sold}}{\text{Average inventory}}$$

$$= \cfrac{\$2,170,000}{\$487,500} = 4.5$$

Rate of Return on Net Sales

What is the rate of return on net sales?

The *rate of return on net sales,* or simply *return on sales,* is a measurement of the company's profitability, expressed as a percentage or ratio. This percentage/ratio is created by comparing net income to sales (both amounts taken from the income statement).

$$\text{Return on sales} = \cfrac{\text{Net income}}{\text{Net sales}}$$

Example: According to its 19XX income statement, Hitech's "top line" was $3,000,000, with net income of $265,650.

Net sales (operating revenues)	**$ 3,000,000**
Operating costs:	
Cost of goods sold (COGS)	−2,170,000
Selling, general, and administrative (G&A)	− 212,000
Depreciation	− 198,000
Total operating costs	$−2,580,000
Operating income	$ 420,000
Other income:	
Dividend income	+ 9,500
Less interest on bonds	− 50,000
Total other income	$− 40,500
Total income	$ 379,500
Taxes (30% rate)	− 113,850
Net income (net profit)	**$ 265,650**

. . .

$$\text{Return on sales} = \frac{\text{Net income}}{\text{Net sales}}$$

$$= \frac{\$265,650}{\$3,000,000} = .0885 \text{ or } 8.9\%$$

This rate is fairly good. Rates of return on sales vary widely among industries, from as low as 4% to as high as the midteens.

Rate of Return on Total Assets

How is the rate of return on total assets calculated?

Another measurement of profitability, the *rate of return on total assets* (or just *return on assets*) indicates how management is using the company's assets to earn profits. Expressed as a percentage or ratio, this measurement is derived from comparing net income *plus* interest expense (from the income statement) to total assets (from the balance sheet).

$$\textbf{Return on assets} = \frac{\textbf{Net income + Interest expense}}{\textbf{Total assets}}$$

Example: Hitech's 19XX net income and interest expense, according to the balance sheet, were $265,650 and $50,000, respectively:

. . .

Operating income	$	420,000
Other income:		
Dividend income	+	9,500
Less interest on bonds	**−**	**50,000**
Total other income	$−	40,500
Total income	$	379,500
Taxes (30% rate)	−	113,850
Net income (net profit)	**$**	**265,650**

. . .

Hitech's balance sheet showed total assets of $4,737,000:

Assets	
Current Assets:	
Cash	$1,920,000
Marketable securities	400,000
Accounts receivable	712,000
Inventory	313,000
Total current assets	$3,345,000
Fixed Assets: Property, plant, and equipment	$1,345,000
Sundry Assets: Prepayments	25,000
Intangibles	$ 22,000
Total assets	**$4,737,000**

. . .

$$\text{Return on assets} = \frac{\text{Net income + Interest expense}}{\text{Total assets}}$$

$$= \frac{\$265,650 + \$50,000}{\$4,737,000}$$

$$= \frac{\$315,650}{\$4,737,000} = .067 \text{ or } 6.7\%$$

Given an average return on assets of 5% among most industries, Hitech's return is better than average. It also compares favorably with the return of General Motors (about 10%) or Superior Oil (about 8%). Other, large corporations can have returns on assets in the low to mid-teens.

Return on Equity

What does return on equity indicate about a company?

Return on equity (or *rate of return on common stockholders' equity*), as the phrase suggests, is a measurement of how much management is making on the use of the company's equity. Net income, less preferred dividends, is considered the "return." High rates of return reflect efficient and effective use of the equity. Net income is taken from the income statement, stockholders' equity from the balance sheet.

$$\text{Return on equity} = \frac{\text{Net income} - \text{Preferred dividends}}{\text{Stockholders' equity}}$$

Example: In 19XX, Hitech Corp. had $265,650 in net income (before deducting dividends on preferred stock):

	. . .	
Total income	$	379,500
Taxes (30% rate)	−	113,850
Net income (net profit)	**$**	**265,650**
Preferred dividends	−	8,000
Earnings available for common stock (net earnings)	$	257,650

In the same year, its common stockholders' equity was $2,925,000:

STOCK CALCULATIONS **103**

$$\overset{\cdot \; \cdot \; \cdot}{\textit{Stockholders' Equity}}$$

Preferred stock—8% (Par: $100)	$ 100,000
Common stock	1,550,000
Capital surplus	400,000
Retained earnings	875,000
Total stockholders' equity	**$2,925,000**

$\cdot \; \cdot \; \cdot$

Hitech's rate of return on equity is:

$$\text{Return on equity} = \frac{\text{Net income} - \text{Preferred dividends}}{\text{Stockholders' equity}}$$

$$= \frac{\$265,650 - \$8,000}{\$2,925,000}$$

$$= \frac{\$257,650}{\$2,925,000} = .088 \text{ or } 8.8\%$$

This rate is a little low. Management is going to have to work harder to bring Hitech's return on equity up to and above 10%, which is the average for most industries. (Some of the major companies, such as IBM or General Motors, enjoy rates of return of 20% or better.)

Note: In this example net income is equal to net earnings once preferred dividends are deducted. Net earnings was *not* used because, on some statements, other deductions may be taken out of net income to arrive at net earnings.

Some analysts prefer to use *average* stockholders' equity. That is, they add the equity amounts from two or more successive balance sheets and then divide by the average.

$$\text{Average equity} = \frac{\text{Period 1 equity} + \text{Period 2 equity} \ldots + \text{Period } n \text{ equity}}{n}$$

Example: If Hitech's equity was $2,925,000 in 19X1 and $3,240,000 in 19X2, the average equity would be:

$$\text{Average} \atop \text{equity} = \frac{\text{Period 1 equity + Period 2 equity} \ldots + \text{Period } n \text{ equity}}{n}$$

$$= \frac{\$2,925,000 + \$3,240,000}{2}$$

$$= \frac{\$6,165,000}{2} = \$3,082,500$$

Hitech's average common stockholder's equity would be $3,082,500. This same formula could be used for quarterly balance sheets: The numerator would contain four amounts and the denominator would be 4 (for 4 quarters).

Return on Invested Capital

What does the return on invested capital say about a company?

Return on invested capital indicates how well management is using the total capitalization of the corporation. Expressed as a percentage or as a ratio, this measurement compares net income and interest on debt (both from the income statement) with total capitalization (from the balance sheet).

$$\text{Return on} \atop \text{invested capital} = \frac{\text{Net income + Interest on debt}}{\text{Total capitalization}}$$

Example: Hitech's net income, in 19XX, was $265,650, and its interest expense was $50,000:

Operating income	$	420,000
Other income:		
Dividend income	+	9,500
Less interest on bonds	**−**	**50,000**
Total other income	$−	40,500
Total income	$	379,500
Taxes (30% rate)	−	113,850
Net income (net profit)	**$**	**265,650**

Hitech's total capitalization, according to the 19XX balance sheet, was $2,925,000:

. . .	
Stockholders' Equity	
Preferred stock—8% (Par: $100)	$ 100,000
Common stock	1,550,000
Capital surplus	400,000
Retained earnings	875,000
Total stockholders' equity	**$2,925,000**

$$\text{Return on invested capital} = \frac{\text{Net income} + \text{Interest on debt}}{\text{Total capitalization}}$$

$$= \frac{\$265,650 + \$50,000}{\$2,925,000}$$

$$= \frac{\$315,650}{\$2,925,000} = .108 \text{ or } 10.8\%$$

Price/Earnings (P/E) Ratio

What is the price/earnings ratio?

The *price/earnings* (or *P/E*) *ratio* relates a corporation's profitability (that is, its earnings per share) to the price of the common stock in the stock market (its market value). The ratio expresses market value as a multiple of earnings per share; hence it is sometimes called the *price multiple*. This ratio is so widely used that it appears in the stock quotations of *The Wall Street Journal* and in most financial stock listings.

$$\textbf{Price/earnings ratio} = \frac{\textbf{Market value}}{\textbf{Earnings per share}}$$

Example: Hitech's common stock is selling at $4.75 at a time that its primary earnings per share are $1.01.

$$\text{Price/earnings ratio} = \frac{\text{Market value}}{\text{Earnings per share}}$$

$$= \frac{\$4.75}{\$1.01} = 4.70$$

Each share of Hitech common is selling for 4.70 times the earnings generated per share.

Net Asset Value

What is net asset value?

Net asset value, also known as *book value*, reflects the amount of assets backing a corporation's securities—bonds and stock. The net assets are equal to total assets less total liabilities. In this calculation, assets are stated "conservatively"; that is, intangible assets are removed from total assets.

$$\text{Net assets} = (\text{Total assets} - \text{Intangible assets}) - \text{Total liabilities}$$

Example: What is Big Business's net asset value? The balance sheet provides the information we need:

Assets	
Current Assets:	
Cash	$ 650,000
Marketable securities	1,300,000
Accounts receivable	425,000
Inventory	550,000
Total current assets	$2,925,000
Fixed Assets: Property, plant, and equipment	$2,225,000
Sundry Assets: Prepayments	30,000
Intangibles	**$ 15,000**
Total assets	**$5,195,000**

Liabilities	
Current Liabilities:	
Accounts payable	$ 680,000
Accrued expenses	945,000
Accrued taxes	325,000
Total current liabilities	$1,950,000
Fixed Liabilities:	
Bonds—7%, due 2006	$ 830,000
Total liabilities	**$2,780,000**

. . .

$$\begin{array}{c} \text{Net} \\ \text{assets} \end{array} = \begin{array}{c} (\text{Total} \\ \text{assets} \end{array} - \begin{array}{c} \text{Intangible} \\ \text{assets}) \end{array} - \begin{array}{c} \text{Total} \\ \text{liabilities} \end{array}$$

$$= (\$5,915,000 - \$15,000) - \$2,780,000$$

$$= \$5,900,000 - \$2,780,000 = \$3,120,000$$

The net asset (or book) value of Big Business is $3,120,000.

What is net asset value (or book value) per share (or bond)?

To arrive at the per-share or per-bond net asset value, the *appropriate* portion of net assets must be divided by the number of shares or bonds outstanding.

$$\begin{array}{c} \textbf{Net asset value} \\ \textbf{per share} \end{array} = \frac{\textbf{Net assets}}{\textbf{Shares (bonds) outstanding}}$$

Example: Big Business has outstanding:

- 266,000 shares of common stock.
- 7,500 shares of preferred.
- 830 bonds: $830,000 in fixed liabilities divided by $1,000 (the value of each bond).

. . . Stockholders' Equity	
Preferred stock—7% (Par: $100)	$ 750,000
Common stock	1,330,000
Capital surplus	100,000
Retained earnings	235,000
Total stockholders' equity	$2,415,000
Total liabilities and stockholders' equity	$5,195,000

To arrive at the "appropriate" portion of net assets, you must understand the priority of claims among bond owners, preferred stockholders, and common shareholders. In the event of liquidation, a company must pay its creditors first. Among the creditors are the bond owners. They *lent* the company money; they are not owners. Next, preferred

stockholders are paid, then the common stockholders.
Therefore:

- For common stockholders, fixed liabilities (the debt to
  bondholders) and preferred stock have to be deducted
  from total assets.
- For preferred stockholders, only fixed liabilities need to
  be deducted.
- For bondholders, the full amount of net asset value is
  applied.

Example: Calculate the net asset value per bond or share
for Big Business.
  Bonds:

$$\text{Net asset value per bond} = \frac{\text{Net assets}}{\text{Bonds outstanding}}$$

$$= \frac{\$3,120,000}{830 \text{ bonds}} = \$3,759.04 \text{ per bond}$$

Each \$1,000 Big Business bond is backed by \$3,759 in net
assets.
  Preferred stocks:

$$\text{Net asset value per preferred stock} = \frac{\text{Net assets} - \text{Fixed liabilities}}{\text{Stocks outstanding}}$$

$$= \frac{\$3,120,000 - \$830,000}{7,500 \text{ shares}}$$

$$= \frac{\$2,290,000}{7,500 \text{ shares}} = \$305.33 \text{ per share}$$

Each \$100 Big Business preferred share is backed by \$305
in net assets.
  Common stocks:

$$\text{Net asset value per common stock} = \frac{\text{Net assets} - \text{Fixed liabilities} - \text{Preferred stock}}{\text{Stocks outstanding}}$$

$$= \frac{\$3,120,000 - \$830,000 - \$750,000}{266,000 \text{ shares}}$$

$$= \frac{\$1,540,000}{266,000 \text{ shares}} = \$5.79 \text{ per share}$$

Each Big Business common share is backed by $5.79 in net assets.

How is net asset value applied to mutual fund shares?

In the investment company industry, *net asset value per share* (or just *NAV*) is used to describe the value of shares in a mutual fund. A mutual fund does not manufacture things or offer a service; its business purpose is to make a profit by investing pools of funds from many investors. That's why it is called an "investment company" (or "open-end investment company"). It is an "open-end" company because, unlike most corporations, a mutual fund issues and redeems shares all the time as its shareholders buy more stock or sell it back to the fund.

In the daily newspaper's financial listings for stocks other than mutual funds, the *bid* price is the price that buyers are willing to pay for the stock. Next to the bid is the *offer*, or price at which sellers are willing to sell. When mutual fund stockholders buy stock, they pay the offer price; when they sell the stock back to the fund, it is at the bid price.

How is a mutual fund's net asset value per share calculated?

The phrase "net asset value" is just another name for shareholders' equity. "Net asset value per share" is another way of saying "shareholders' equity per share." The mutual fund prospectus describes how this value is figured, but the fundamental formula is:

$$\begin{array}{c}\text{Net asset}\\\text{value}\\\text{per share}\end{array} = \begin{array}{c}\text{Market}\\\text{value per}\\\text{share}\end{array} + \frac{\begin{array}{c}\text{Value of all}\\\text{other assets}\end{array} - \begin{array}{c}\text{Total}\\\text{liabilities}\end{array}}{\text{Shares outstanding}}$$

Mutual funds must calculate the net asset value (NAV) at least once a day.

Example: Faithful Mutual Fund has 1,000,000 shares outstanding. The value of all its assets is $14,500,000, and its total liabilities add up to $3,800,000. What is the net asset value (NAV)?

$$\begin{aligned}\text{Net asset value per share} &= \frac{\text{Value of all other assets} - \text{Total liabilities}}{\text{Shares outstanding ("float")}}\\[4pt]&= \frac{\$14,500,000 - \$3,800,000}{1,000,000 \text{ shares}}\\[4pt]&= \frac{\$10,700,000}{1,000,000 \text{ shares}} = \$10.70 \text{ per share}\end{aligned}$$

Faithful funds is redeeming its shares at NAV, $10.70 each.

COMPARATIVE STATEMENTS

Does a company's past performance indicate how it will do in the future?

In investing, there are no guarantees as to what a company will do, but past performance is one indicator of how a corporation *may* perform in the future. Partly for this reason, most companies prepare *comparative* financial statements each year. That is, they position the preceding year's figures next to the those for the current year, to show shareholders and prospective investors how the corporation has fared over the prior twelve months.

Example: Hitech's income statement for 19X1 might look like this (19X0 is the prior year):

Income Statement
Hitech Corp.
January 1–December 31, 19X1

	19X1	19X0
Net sales (operating revenue)	$ 3,000,000	$ 2,800,000
Operating costs:		
Cost of goods sold (COGS)	−2,170,000	−1,953,000
Selling, general, and administrative (G&A)	− 212,000	− 184,440
Depreciation	− 198,000	− 198,000
Total operating costs	$−2,580,000	$−2,335,440

	19X1		19X0	
Operating income	$	420,000	$	464,560
Other income:				
Dividend income	+	9,500	+	9,500
Less interest on bonds	−	50,000	−	50,000
Total other income	$−	40,500	$−	40,500
Total income	$	379,500	$	424,060
Taxes (30% rate)	−	113,850	−	127,218
Net income (net profit)	$	265,650	$	296,842
Preferred dividends	−	8,000	−	8,000
Earnings available for common stock (net earnings)	$	257,650	$	288,842

Note that, while Hitech's top line was lower last year (19X0), its operating income, total income, and earnings available for common stock were all higher. Why? Apparently, in 19X1, management let operating costs rise to a higher proportion of net sales. In other words, Hitech's operating (cost) ratio rose in 19X1.

$$\frac{19\text{X0}}{\text{operating ratio}} = \frac{19\text{X0 operating costs}}{19\text{X0 net sales}}$$

$$= \frac{\$2,335,440}{\$2,800,000} = .834 \text{ or } 83.4\%$$

$$\frac{19\text{X1}}{\text{operating ratio}} = \frac{19\text{X1 operating costs}}{19\text{X1 net sales}}$$

$$= \frac{\$2,580,000}{\$3,000,000} = .860 \text{ or } 86\%$$

Less than a 3% rise in operating costs (86% less 83.4%) meant a significant decrease in net earnings. Does this mean that Hitech's net earnings will continue to erode in the coming year (19X2)? The comparison of two years' worth of data is simply not sufficient to make such a prediction. Perhaps the company is deliberately staffing up (with the related increase in G&A) or purchasing inventory (with concomitantly higher COGS) in anticipation of filling orders on hand in 19X2. If so, the increase in operating ratio can be taken to mean *not* that management is not watching costs, but rather that the company's top line next year should be greatly increased.

This is just one example of the types of things investors should be analyzing in year-to-year financial comparisons. In general, analyzing financial statements for just one or two years of operation does not provide enough information for prudent investment decision making. Most sophisticated investors gather data on five to ten years of operating activity.

Given five to ten years' worth of a company's financial statements, what do I look for?

The wealth of information in many years' worth of financial statements must be summarized for ease of analysis. Generally, investors should watch trends in:

- Net sales in dollars (the "top line" on the income statement).
- Net earnings in dollars (the "bottom line" on the income statement).
- Net earnings as a percentage of sales.
- Return on capital.
- Primary earnings per share of common stock.
- Yield on preferred and common shares—the dividend policy of the company.

Trends can also be detected in ratios or other calculations, such as current ratio, working capital, P/E ratio, and the like.

Example: A five-year financial summary for Hitech might look like this (individual investors may want to include other data or exclude some found here):

All data in $000,000*

	19X0	19X1	19X2	19X3	19X4
From the income statement:					
Net sales	$2.80	$3.00	$3.33	$3.76	$4.01
Operating income	.46	.42	.56	.60	.85
Net earnings	.29	.26	.35	.42	.55

	19X0	19X1	19X2	19X3	19X4
From the balance sheet:					
Working capital	1.55	1.76	1.89	2.02	2.30
Property, plant, and equipment	1.35	1.35	1.35	—	—
Fixed liabilities	.22	.22	—	—	—
Capital surplus	.22	.22	.22	.22	.22
Retained earnings	.76	.88	1.23	1.30	1.64
Net assets	2.70	2.93	3.31	3.40	3.76

*For example, $2.80 = $2,800,000.

Only by compiling relevant financial information, whether in the form of dollars, percentages, or ratios, can investors determine whether a company's managers are efficient and effective as stewards of the firm's fortunes.

Are dollars the only way to express financial information?

No. In fact, most year-to-year financial information is expressed in percentages, using one year (selected for whatever reasons) as the base year. The base year data is pegged at 100%, and the data from all other years is expressed as greater or lesser percentages.

$$\text{Percentage of base year} = \frac{\text{Dollar value of subsequent year}}{\text{Dollar value of base year}}$$

Example: In the preceding example, make 19X0 the base year. All data in that column is expressed as 100%.

	19X0
From the income statement:	
Net sales	100.00
Operating income	100.00
Net earnings	100.00
From the balance sheet:	
Working capital	100.00
Property, plant, and equipment	100.00
Fixed liabilities	100.00
Capital surplus	100.00
Retained earnings	100.00
Net assets	100.00

All the dollar figures for subsequent years are then calculated as percentages of the base year (19X0). For example, the net sales for 19X1 ($3,000,000) is divided by the net sales of 19X0 ($2,800,000):

$$\text{Percentage of base year} = \frac{\text{Dollar value of subsequent year}}{\text{Dollar value of base year}}$$

$$= \frac{\$3,000,000}{\$2,800,000} = 1.071 \text{ or } 107.1\%$$

All other figures in the table are put through the same computation to produce the following results (19X1 net sales are in boldface):

	19X0	19X1	19X2	19X3	19X4
From the income statement:					
Net sales	100.00	**107.1**	118.9	134.2	143.2
Operating income	100.00	91.3	121.7	130.4	184.8
Net earnings	100.00	89.6	120.7	161.5	189.7
From the balance sheet:					
Working capital	100.00	113.5	121.9	130.3	148.4
Property, plant, and equipment	100.00	100.0	100.0	0	0
Fixed liabilities	100.00	100.0	0	0	0
Capital surplus	100.00	100.0	100.0	100.0	100.0
Retained earnings	100.00	115.8	161.8	171.1	215.8
Net assets	100.00	108.5	122.6	125.9	139.3

Over the five years in this summary, Hitech has shown itself to be a growing company, capable of boosting sales, operating income, net earnings, working capital, retained earnings, and net assets each year after its "get ready" year of 19X1. Also in this period, it reduced its fixed liabilities to zero (its bond issue came due), doing so the year after property, plant, and equipment was fully depreciated. (Time for a new bond issue for a major purchase of plant or equipment?)

This is only one kind of summary that can be put together in analyzing a company. Each investor has to devise the kind of summary that best suits his or her individual needs.

SUBSCRIPTION PRIVILEGES

What is a "subscription privilege"?

When a corporation is preparing to offer more of its authorized shares to the public (to raise additional capital), its charter may require it to issue a *subscription privilege* (also known as a *preemptive right* or *rights offering*) to its current stockholders. This privilege, which is a kind of option, entitles current stockholders to submit a specified number of the rights certificates in return for additional shares. Most corporate charters oblige the issuer to make the offering first to recorded stockholders, who must exercise the option before a predetermined deadline or lose the right altogether.

Example: Quickfood, Inc. has 200,000 issued and outstanding shares, out of 600,000 authorized. The directors vote for a rights offering. A right will be issued for each issued and outstanding share, 200,000 in all. Further, with Quickfood common trading at $75 a share, the board decides on a *subscription price* of $70. That is, current stockholders may turn in 4 rights and $70 for 1 additional share of common.

A Quickfood stockholder who owns 100 shares will receive 100 rights, one for each share held. That stockholder may turn in all 100 rights and $1,750 for 25 additional shares:

$$25 \text{ additional shares} = 25 \, (4 \text{ rights} + \$70)$$
$$= 100 \text{ rights} + \$1,750$$

Does the right certificate have any value of its own?

It does. A subscription privilege is worth some fraction of the related stock's market value. In fact, a right can be traded like a stock or other security, once it is issued by the corporation. But before its issuance, its market value is considered "theoretical" because, when the value is calculated, the right is not yet trading in the open market. Many investors, not realizing that the right has a value of its own and not wishing to submit it for additional shares, discard the certificate. When they do, they are simply throwing away money. The approximate *theoretical value* of the right can be calculated by means of the formula:

$$\text{Theoretical value} = \frac{\text{Market price of stock} - \text{Subscription price}}{\text{Number of rights for subscription} + 1}$$

Since the theoretical value is computed before the shares trade without the rights (that is, "ex-rights"), the price of the right is embedded in the price of the stock. Hence the "+1" in the denominator.

Example: Assume that, as in the preceding example, 4 rights can be turned in for 1 share of a stock at a subscription price of $70, and that the stock is trading at $75.

$$\begin{aligned}\text{Theoretical value} &= \frac{\text{Market price of stock} - \text{Subscription price}}{\text{Number of rights for subscription} + 1} \\ &= \frac{\$75 - \$70}{4 + 1} \\ &= \frac{\$5}{5} = \$1.00\end{aligned}$$

When the owner of 100 shares of Quickfood common received 100 rights, the theoretical value is $100 (100 rights times a theoretical value of $1.00).

Note: This same formula can be applied to warrants. Like rights, warrants entitle their holders to purchase stock at a specific price (usually one that is expected to be lower than market value sometime in the future). Unlike rights, warrants are much longer term, generally good for five to ten years—and sometimes perpetually.

SALE AND LEASEBACK AGREEMENTS

What is a sale and leaseback agreement?

Sometimes a corporation will sell a fixed asset, such as a piece of real estate or equipment, with the understanding that the purchaser will lease it back to the company. This type of arrangement is called a *sale and leaseback agreement*.

Example: Big Business sells some of its plant equipment to American Financing for $125,000. American Financing arranges a 5-year lease, by which Big Business continues to use the equpment and thereby incurs a monthly lease payment of $2,500. The two companies have engaged in a sale-leaseback arrangement.

How does a sale and leaseback agreement affect the balance sheet?

In a sale and leaseback agreement, the seller exchanges a fixed asset (property, plant, or equipment) for a current asset (cash). The effect on the balance sheet depends on whether the exchange was made for more or less than the value at which the property was being carried (that is, its book value). If the sales proceeds are greater than the book value, the company makes a profit, which is reflected in retained earnings. If the book value is greater than the sale price (the usual situation), a loss is taken in retained earnings.

Example: In the preceding example, the book value of the sold equipment was $70,000. Given the sale price of $125,000, Big Business made a profit of $55,000. Before the sale, the P&L looked like this:

Balance Sheet
Big Business Inc.
December 31, 19XX

Assets	
Current Assets:	
Cash	$ 650,000
Marketable securities	1,300,000
Accounts receivable	425,000
Inventory	550,000
Total current assets	$2,925,000
Fixed Assets: Property, plant, and equipment	$2,225,000
Sundry Assets: Prepayments	30,000
Intangibles	$ 15,000
Total assets	$5,195,000

Liabilities	
Current Liabilities:	
Accounts payable	$ 680,000
Accrued expenses	945,000
Accrued taxes	325,000
Total current liabilities	$1,950,000
Fixed Liabilities:	
Bonds—7%, due 2006	$ 830,000
Total liabilities	$2,780,000

Stockholders' Equity	
Preferred stock—7% (Par: $100)	$ 750,000
Common stock	1,330,000
Capital surplus	100,000
Retained earnings	235,000
Total stockholders' equity	$2,415,000
Total liabilities and stockholders' equity	$5,195,000

After the sale, current assets (cash) increase by $125,000 (the sales proceeds), and fixed assets (property, plant, and equipment) decrease by $70,000 (the book value). That means that total assets must increase by $55,000 (the profit differential between $125,000 on the sale and the $70,000 book value). If one side of the balance sheet changes, so must the other; the additional $55,000 in total assets is "balanced" by an equal increase in retained earnings, which rise to $290,000.

Balance Sheet
Big Business Inc.
December 31, 19XX

Assets	
Current Assets:	
Cash	**$ 775,000**
Marketable securities	1,300,000
Accounts receivable	425,000
Inventory	550,000
Total current assets	**$3,050,000**
Fixed Assets: Property, plant, and equipment	**$2,155,000**
Sundry Assets: Prepayments	30,000
Intangibles	$ 15,000

Liabilities	
Current Liabilities:	
Accounts payable	$ 680,000
Accrued expenses	945,000
Accrued taxes	325,000
Total current liabilities	$1,950,000
Fixed Liabilities:	
Bonds—7%, due 2006	$ 830,000
Total liabilities	$2,780,000

Stockholders' Equity	
Preferred stock—7% (Par: $100)	$ 750,000
Common stock	1,330,000
Capital surplus	100,000
Retained earnings	**290,000**
Total stockholders' equity	**$2,470,000**
Total liabilities and stockholders' equity	**$5,250,000**

What purpose does a sale and leaseback arrangement serve?

By increasing current assets, management enhances the firm's working capital and current ratio.

Example: Before the sale and leaseback, Big Business's working capital and current ratio were:

$$\text{Working capital} = \text{Current assets} - \text{Current liabilities}$$
$$= \$2,925,000 - \$1,950,000$$
$$= \$975,000$$

$$\text{Current ratio} = \frac{\text{Current assets}}{\text{Current liabilities}}$$
$$= \frac{\$2,925,000}{\$1,950,000} = 1.50$$

After the arrangement is made, both computations put the company in a better light:

$$\text{Working capital} = \text{Current assets} - \text{Current liabilities}$$
$$= \$3,050,000 - \$1,950,000$$
$$= \$1,100,000$$

$$\text{Current ratio} = \frac{\text{Current assets}}{\text{Current liabilities}}$$

$$= \frac{\$3,050,000}{\$1,950,000} = 1.56$$

KEY TERMS

Book value: See *Net asset value.*

Capitalized retained earnings: A phrase to describe large stock dividends since stock dividends deplete the capital surplus potential but leave retained earnings unaltered.

Cash dividends: A cash distribution of retained earnings among stockholders.

Comparative statement: A financial statement that contains more than one year's information.

Current yield: The comparison, expressed as a percentage, of dividends to the market price of the stock (common or preferred).

Declaration date: The day on which a dividend is declared by a corporation.

Dividend payout ratio: The portion of a corporation's net earnings, expressed as a ratio, that are paid out in dividends on common stock.

Eighth: Unit of trading for stocks, equal to $.125. Most U.S. stock transactions generally take place at increments of this unit value, although low-priced shares, particularly those below $5, often trade in units of 1/16 ($.0625).

Ex-dividend date: The first day on which a stock no longer trades with a dividend attached to it.

Inventory turnover ratio: A ratio of net sales to inventory that expresses how quickly a company "turns inventory over" into sales.

Net asset value: (1) In mutual funds, expressed as NAV, the value of all assets, less liabilities, divided by the number of shares outstanding. (2) Or *book value*, total assets less intangibles and total liabilities.

Net asset value per share: (1) The value of a mutual fund share. (2) Net asset (or book) value divided by the number of shares outstanding. (May also be calculated per bond.)

Payment date: The day on which cash dividend checks are issued by the paying corporation.

Payout ratio: See *Dividend payout ratio.*

Preemptive right: See *Subscription privilege.*

Price/earnings (P/E) ratio: A ratio in which market value is compared to earnings per share.

Rate of return on common stockholders' equity (return on equity): A ratio that compares net income less preferred dividends with stockholders' equity.

Rate of return on net sales (return to sales): A ratio in which net income is compared to net sales.

Rate of return on total assets (return on assets): A ratio in which net income plus interest expense are compared to net sales.

Record date: The day on which a corporation prepares a list of registered shareholders for the payment of dividends.

Return on assets: See *Rate of return on total assets.*

Return on equity: See *Rate of return on common stockholders' equity.*

Return on invested capital: A ratio that compares net income plus interest on debt to total capitalization.

Return on sales: See *Rate of return on net sales.*

Regular-way settlement: Settlement of a securities transaction five business days after the trade is made.

Rights offering: See *Subscription privilege.*

Sale and leaseback agreement: An agreement in which a company sells an asset on the assumption that the purchaser will lease it back to the company.

Stock dividends: An issuance of additional authorized shares to current stockholders.

Stock split: The distribution of additional authorized shares to current stockholders, in proportions that are usually larger than those of a stock dividend.

Subscription privilege (preemptive right, rights offering): A right offered to current stockholders by the issuing corporation to acquire additional authorized shares.

Theoretical value of a right: The computed value of a right before it is actually traded in the open market.

II
INVESTING IN
SECURITIES

4

Fixed Income Investments

YOU WILL LEARN TO...

- Arrive at simple and compound interest amounts.
- Read and interpret bond listings.
- Convert bond price listings into dollar values.
- Calculate the coupon rate, current yield, and yield to maturity of a bond.
- Use the "basis point" system.
- Compute accrued interest when selling or buying a bond.
- Read the yield curve and compare yields on short-, intermediate-, and long-term bonds.
- Estimate when a callable bond might be called.
- Know when to sell or convert a convertible bond.

INTRODUCTION

While stockholders are owners of a corporation, bondholders are creditors. Common stock pays dividends, which depend on the success of the company. Bonds are loans to the company, and as such they pay interest to holders at a fixed rate, regardless of the company's profitability. Because the flow of income from bonds is unvarying, they are considered one of a category of securities known as *fixed income instruments*. This category also includes notes, bills, commercial paper, many other forms of "loan"-type securities, and, somewhat surprisingly, preferred stock. Although preferred stock, like common stock, represents a share of equity, like bonds, it pays dividends at a fixed rate. Hence its inclusion the fixed-income category.

Also included are *floaters*, which are bonds that pay a floating, or adjustable, rate. Even though the rate is not fixed, it is still considered an interest-bearing security and is therefore a debt instrument.

Corporations are not the only issuers of debt securities. Every year, bonds—as well as shorter-term debt instruments—are issued by the United States Treasury, federal agencies, state and local governments, and by foreign governments.

Note: Many computations related to fixed income investing may be performed with simple handheld calculators (or by means of the bond yield tables, which are available from Financial Publishing Company [Boston, MA] and are found in the larger bookstores at moderate cost). Other calculations, however, require the use of more sophisticated calculators, such as the Hewlett-Packard 12C or 7B.

THE INTEREST EQUATION

What is interest?

Money is a commodity, like prime steak, pork bellies, or corn. Like any commodity, when it is in short supply, the price of money goes up; when the market is flooded, the price goes down. *Interest* is the "cost" of borrowing money. If there is little money available for all borrowers (or, in a sense, "buyers"), demand for it rises and interest rates (prices) go up. Mortgage rates rise, car loans become more expensive, and consumer credit is harder to get. When there is plenty of money for lending, demand drops and so do interest rates. The "rates" on loans of all types come down.

Interest is usually expressed as an *interest rate*, that is, an annual percentage of the amount loaned, called the *principal*. The equivalent dollar value of the interest rate is a function of the rate applied to the principal over the period of time the money is out on loan, the *term*. At the end of the term, the loan *matures*, and the principal must be repaid.

$$\text{Interest} = \text{Principal} \times \text{Rate} \times \text{Time}$$

This is the interest equation, and it is the basis for most of the calculations in this and the next two chapters.

Example: A bank extends a one-year, $1,000 loan to a

patron at an annual rate of 12%. The principal is $1,000, the term (or time) is 1 year, and the rate is 12%.

$$\text{Interest} = \text{Principal} \times \text{Rate} \times \text{Time}$$
$$= \$1,000 \times .12 \times 1 = \$120$$

Interest on the loan is $120. If the loan were for two years:

$$\text{Interest} = \text{Principal} \times \text{Rate} \times \text{Time}$$
$$= \$1,000 \times .12 \times 2 = \$240$$

What if a loan is for part of a year?

If the loan is extended for part of a year, then the time may be expressed as a fraction—that is, as the number of days over 365, the number of weeks over 52, or the number of months over 12.

Example: The $1,000, 12% loan of the previous example is extended for nine months.

$$\text{Interest} = \text{Principal} \times \text{Rate} \times \text{Time}$$
$$= \$1,000 \times .12 \times \frac{9 \text{ months}}{12 \text{ months}}$$
$$= \$120 \times \frac{9}{12} = \$90$$

The interest for a nine-month term is $90.

What is the difference between "simple" interest and "compound" interest?

Simple interest is interest only on the original principal, or amount loaned. The calculation assumes that interest is paid to the lender and not included with the principal.

Example: Ernest Knewitz puts $1,000 into a 5-year time deposit that pays 12% annual simple interest. The bank pays Knewitz $120 every year for the use of his money. Knewitz is, in effect, lending the bank money. The principal of the loan is $1,000, the time 5 years, and the interest rate 12%. The interest payment on this account for each of the 5 years is the same:

$$\text{Interest} = \text{Principal} \times \text{Rate} \times \text{Time}$$
$$= \$1,000 \times .12 \times 1 = \$120$$

This arrangement is an example of simple interest.

In actuality, compound interest is more typical of time deposits. *Compound interest* results when interest is left to accumulate with the principal, so that the borrower is paying interest on interest.

Example: Knewitz deposits his $1,000 in another bank's time deposit. The terms are the same—5-year maturity and 12% interest rate—but interest is "compounded annually." In year 1 the interest is the same as in a simple interest arrangement:

$$\text{Year 1 interest} = \text{Principal} \times \text{Rate} \times \text{Time}$$
$$= \$1,000 \times .12 \times 1 = \$120$$

The $120, however, is not withdrawn; it is left in the time deposit account, which now contains $1,120 ($1,000 principal plus $120 first year's interest). In the second year, the interest rate for the account is applied to the $1,120.

$$\text{Year 2 interest} = \text{Principal} \times \text{Rate} \times \text{Time}$$
$$= \$1,120 \times .12 \times 1 = \$134.40$$

The $134.40 in interest is added to the account for a total of $1,254.40. Each year the interest accumulates in the account and interest is paid on the interest (in addition to the principal):

$$\text{Year 3 interest} = \text{Principal} \times \text{Rate} \times \text{Time}$$
$$= \$1,254.40 \times .12 \times 1 = \$150.53$$
$$\text{Year 4 interest} = \text{Principal} \times \text{Rate} \times \text{Time}$$
$$= \$1,404.93 \times .12 \times 1 = \$168.59$$
$$\text{Year 5 interest} = \text{Principal} \times \text{Rate} \times \text{Time}$$
$$= \$1,573.52 \times .12 \times 1 = \$188.82$$

When the time deposit matures, the total compounded interest is $762.34.

How does simple interest compare to compound interest?

Compound interest accumulates more rapidly than simple interest and is therefore always more beneficial to lenders. The longer interest is permitted to compound, the greater the benefits to the lender.

Example: Refer to the two preceding examples. Compare Knewitz's return in the simple interest and compound interest accounts:

Year	Simple Interest	Compound Interest
1	$120.00	$120.00
2	$120.00	$134.40
3	$120.00	$150.53
4	$120.00	$168.59
5	$120.00	$188.82
	$600.00	$762.34

Can compounding occur more often than annually?

Yes. It can occur as often as daily. And the more often interest is compounded, the greater the benefit to the lender. The interest calculation is simply adjusted for the compounding period.

$$\textbf{Interest} = \textbf{Principal} \times \textbf{Rate} \times \frac{\textbf{Compounding}}{\textbf{period (time)}}$$

Example: Knewitz goes to a third bank and places $1,000 in a 5-year, 12% time deposit. In this account, however, interest is compounding quarterly. The interest equation applies, but the time component is adjusted to reflect the portion of the year during which simple interest is paid.

Quarter 1
$$\text{Interest} = \text{Principal} \times \text{Rate} \times \frac{\text{Compounding}}{\text{period (time)}}$$

$$= \$1,000 \times .12 \times \frac{3 \text{ months}}{12 \text{ months}}$$

$$= \$120 \times \frac{3}{12} = \$30$$

The interest for a 3-month term is $30. The $30 interest is now included with principal, and the account's interest rate is applied to the total, $1,030 ($1,000 principal plus $30 interest).

Quarter 2

$$\text{interest} = \text{Principal} \times \text{Rate} \times \begin{array}{l}\text{Compounding}\\ \text{period (time)}\end{array}$$

$$= \$1,030 \times .12 \times \frac{3 \text{ months}}{12 \text{ months}}$$

$$= \$123.60 \times \frac{3}{12} = \$30.90$$

Interest is again added to principal and the computation repeated for the remaining two quarters of the year.

Quarter 3

$$\text{interest} = \text{Principal} \times \text{Rate} \times \begin{array}{l}\text{Compounding}\\ \text{period (time)}\end{array}$$

$$= \$1,060.90 \times .12 \times \frac{3 \text{ months}}{12 \text{ months}}$$

$$= \$127.31 \times \frac{3}{12} = \$31.83$$

Quarter 4

$$\text{interest} = \text{Principal} \times \text{Rate} \times \begin{array}{l}\text{Compounding}\\ \text{period (time)}\end{array}$$

$$= \$1,092.73 \times .12 \times \frac{3 \text{ months}}{12 \text{ months}}$$

$$= \$131.13 \times \frac{3}{12} = \$32.78$$

With interest compounding quarterly, Knewitz earns $125.51 in the first year. Compare the following first-year returns:

Simple	Annual Compounding	Quarterly Compounding
$120.00	$120.00	$125.51

If interest were compounded "faster"—that is, more frequently per year—the total interest would be even higher. For example, $1,000 earning 12% compounded *daily* yields $129.40 in the first year. So an account that offers a slightly lower rate but faster compounding might offer a greater return than one with a higher rate but slower compounding. Computations must be done to determine which offers the greater dollar return.

Is there a simpler way to calculate compound interest?

Yes. There is a formula for calculating compound interest for any interest rate and for any number of periods. For short periods and relatively infrequent compounding, it might be useful. However, for most "real-world" situations, a calculator should be used, or compound interest tables consulted. These tables contain the total amount of principal and interest an investor would have at the end of a given period, at a given rate, for each dollar of principal invested. The values in the table are factors, which represent the *future value* of each dollar, given the rate, time, and frequency of compounding. The factor is then multiplied by the principal. Finding the total of principal and interest at the end of a given period involves a couple of simple steps:

1. Go to the table with the applicable compounding period—quarterly, monthly, etc.
2. Go to the column headed by the relevant interest rate.
3. Run down the column to the row at the end of the period.
4. Multiply the factor there by the principal.

Future value = Principal × Factor

Example: Refer to the previous example. Knewitz invests $1,000 in a time deposit at 12%, compounded quarterly for 5 years. He wants to know how much the account will hold at maturity.

1. Go to the table with the applicable compounding period. He consults the following Quarterly Compounding table:

Quarterly Compounding

Future Value of $1			
Quarter	*Annual Interest Rates*		
11%	11.5%	12%	12.5%
1	1.0275000	1.0287500	1.0300000	1.0312500
2	1.0557562	1.0583266	1.0609000	1.0634766
3	1.0847895	1.0887535	1.0927270	1.0967102
4	1.1146213	1.1200551	1.1255088	1.1309824
	. . .		
19	1.6743829	1.7135119	1.7535061	1.7943835
20	1.7204284	1.7627753	**1.8061112**	1.8504580
	. . .		
Year			
10	2.9598740	3.1073769	3.2620378	3.4241948
11	3.2991385	3.4804334	3.6714523	3.8727040
12	3.6772899	3.8982772	4.1322519	4.3799601
	. . .		

2. Go to the column for the relevant interest rate: He goes to the 12% column (heading in boldface).

3. Run down the column to the end of the compounding period: In this case, the compounding period ends in 5 years, or 20 quarters (5 years times 4 quarters per year). (See the boldface entry in the row for "20.")

4. Multiply that factor by the principal:

Future value = Principal × Factor
= $1,000 × 1.8061112 = $1,806.11

Knewitz will have $1,806.11 in his account at the end of five years.

Note: Refer to the previous example, in which the first year's interest ($125.51) was calculated for this account. If you follow the same procedure with the preceding table, you come up with the same amount.

Future value = Principal × Factor
= $1,000 × 1.1255088 = $1,125.51

CORPORATE BONDS

Primary Market

What is a bond?

A bond is a *debt instrument* (or *debt security*), issued by a corporation. This type of security reflects a lender-borrower agreement between the company and the bondholder. The bond is the certificate that reflects the loan. In fact, on the back of the bond certificate is the *indenture*, which specifies the loan's terms and conditions.

Corporate bonds are issued in an *initial public offering (IPO)*, like stock. The industry-wide denomination is $1,000, which represents a portion of the principal and is called the *par*, or *face, value*. The rate of interest that the bond pays is the *coupon*, or *nominal, rate*. And the term of the loan is the time between issuance and the *maturity date*. The issuer generally makes interest payments twice a year and repays the principal at maturity.

Example: General Production issues $10,000,000 of 9% bonds maturing in 20 years. Investors who purchase the bonds become creditors of the company. For each bond they purchase, they extend a loan of $1,000 (the par or face value). For 20 years, the company pays interest to the bondholders (at the coupon or nominal rate). At maturity, it repays bondholders their $1,000 principal.

How does a corporation benefit by issuing bonds?

In most cases, the corporate managers expect to earn enough profits on the borrowed money to make the interest payments and have earnings left over. To put it another way, they expect to use borrowed money to make more than the money costs, which is a form of *leverage*.

Example: General Production uses the proceeds of the issue to construct a new plant with which it intends to increase net earnings by $1,500,000 a year. If it can do so, it will earn $600,000 more than it is paying in interest on the bond issue.

Interest = Principal × Rate × Time
= $10,000,000 × .09 × 1 year = $900,000

The increased earnings of $1,500,000, less the interest payments of $900,000, gives General Production $600,000 more in retained earnings a year. If it puts a percentage of those retained earnings away each year into some interest-earning investment and allows the interest to compound for 20 years, it will have enough to repay the principal. (Alternatively, it could issue another $10,000,000 worth of bonds to repay, or *refund*, the first issue.)

How do bond owners benefit by "lending money" to a corporation?

Investors who buy corporate bonds are generally looking for a flow of income in the form of the semiannual interest payments. In addition, they are willing to trade off the possibility of greater returns, such as they might enjoy if the issuer's stock should increase dramatically in value, for the certainty of the steady return.

Example: Each year for 20 years, holders of General Production 9%, 20-year bonds will receive semiannual interest payments at a rate of 9%.

$$\text{Annual interest (\$)} = \text{Face value} \times \text{Coupon (nominal)} \\ \text{rate (\%)} \\ = \$1,000 \times .09 = \$90 \text{ per year}$$

Since corporate bond interest payments are made twice a year, each payment would be $45 ($90 divided by 2).

At maturity, they are repaid their $1,000 principal.

Note: The semiannual payments on bonds are a form of simple interest. The interest is not added to principal for compounding.

Do all bonds make their semiannual payments at the same times of the year?

No. Payments can be made in any two months of the year. Usually payments are made on the 1st or the 15th day of the payment months, but other days are possible. The months in which payments are to be made are generally indicated by their first initials.

J&J	January and July
F&A	February and August
M&S	March and September
A&O	April and October
M&N	May and November
J&D	June and December

Types of Bonds

Is there only one type of corporate bond?

No, there are basically two types:

- *Unsecured* bonds are backed only by the promise of the issuing corporation. There is no specific security. Some unsecured bonds, called *notes*, may be issued for terms of 1 to 10 years. Others, known as *debentures*, may be issued for as much as 30 or 40 years. For this type of bond, the biggest factor for investors to consider is the issuer's creditworthiness.

- *Secured* bonds are backed by some sort of collateral—the company's plant and equipment, for instance. *Mortgage bonds* are backed by real estate owned by the corporation. *Equipment trust certificates* are secured by the company's equipment, perhaps a fleet of aircraft or rolling stock. The key factor for secured bonds is the true value of the security: What is it worth if it has to be sold to honor the debt?

Secondary Market

How are corporate bonds quoted once they start trading in the secondary market?

The market price of a corporate bond is quoted as a percentage of face value, which is assumed to be $1,000 unless otherwise stated.

Price ($) = Face value × Quote (%)

Example: General Production bonds are trading at "92½," that is, at 92½% of face value ($1,000).

$$\text{Price (\$)} = \text{Face value} \times \text{Quote (\%)}$$
$$= \$1,000 \times .925 = \$925$$

Can corporate bonds trade at market prices above or below their face value?

Yes. They can trade below, at, or above their face value. When the price of corporate bond is below face value, it is said to be trading at a *discount*. When trading at face value, it is *at par*. Above face value, the price is called a *premium*.

Example: In the preceding example, General Production bonds were trading at a discount. Another corporate bond is trading at a premium, 101½.

$$\text{Price (\$)} = \text{Face value} \times \text{Quote (\%)}$$
$$= \$1,000 \times 1.015 = \$1,015$$

Example: A third corporate bond is trading at par, 100. In this case, the market value is equal to face value ($1,000).

What is the unit of price variation in corporate bond trading?

As in the stock market, the trading variation for bonds is ⅛-point. Unlike trading in stocks, however, a full point is equal to $10, not $1. So ⅛-point is equal to $1.25, not to $.125. See Figure 4–1.

Figure 4–1

Values of ⅛-points in Corporate Bond Trading

⅛	$ 1.25
²⁄₈ (¼)	$ 2.50
⅜	$ 3.75
⁴⁄₈ (½)	$ 5.00
⅝	$ 6.25
⁶⁄₈ (¾)	$ 7.50
⅞	$ 8.75
⁸⁄₈ (1)	$10.00

All trades in corporate bonds take place at increments of $1.25.

Example: Trading in General Production bonds may take place at 92½ ($950), 92⅜ ($923.75), or 92⅞ ($928.75). They do not take place at 92⁷⁄₁₆, 92⁵⁄₃₂, and so on; these are not multiples of ⅛ ($1.25).

How is a corporate bond quote with a fraction converted to a dollar value?

Converting the quote to a dollar amount takes two steps:

1. Make the whole number in the quote a decimal.
2. Add the equivalent dollar value of the fraction to the decimal, with the decimal dropped.

Example: A trade in General Production bonds takes place at the discount price of 92⅜.

1. Make the whole number in the quote a decimal. The whole number, 92, becomes .92 (the price is less than 100% of par).

2. Add the equivalent dollar value of the fraction to the decimal, with the decimal dropped. The equivalent dollar value of ⅜ is $3.75. Drop the decimal, to make it 375, and add it to the whole number decimal: .92 plus 375 = .92375.

This decimal can then be used in the price formula.

$$\text{Price (\$)} = \text{Face value} \times \text{Quote (\%)}$$
$$= \$1,000 \times .92375 = \$923.75$$

Example: Another corporate bond trades at the premium price of 104⅝.

1. Make the whole number in the quote a decimal. The whole number, 104, becomes 1.04 (the price is greater than 100% of par).

2. Add the equivalent dollar value of the fraction to the decimal, with the decimal dropped. The equivalent dollar value of ⅝ is $6.25. Drop the decimal, to make it 625, and add it to the whole number decimal: 1.04 plus 625 = 1.04625.

This decimal can then be used in the price formula.

$$\text{Price (\$)} = \text{Face value} \times \text{Quote (\%)}$$
$$= \$1,000 \times 1.04625 = \$1,046.25$$

Quotations

How are corporate bonds quoted in the news?

Corporate bonds are identified by their coupon (or nominal) rate and date of maturity. The financial listings contain:

- Current yield.
- Volume of trading.
- Closing price.
- Net change from the close of the last trading session.

Example In the following listing:

Bonds	Cur Yld	Vol	Close	Net Chg.
GMA 8¾ 01	8.8	10	99½	+ 1

- *GMA 8¾ 01* is a General Motors 8¾% bond that matures in 2001.
- *8.8* is the current yield.
- *Vol* means that $10,000 worth of this bond were traded today.
- *Close* indicates that the GMA bond ended trading at a price of 99½ ($995).
- *Net Chg.* is the difference between the closing price of the quoted session and that of the prior session. In this case, the change is positive. The closing price is up one point, or $10, per bond from the price on the previous day.

Yield

What is "yield"?

Yield is the return on an investment, normally expressed as a percentage. In fixed income investing, the factors affecting yield are the amount of the investment, the interest rate, and the length of time to maturity. A bond's coupon, or nominal, rate (the fixed annual rate at which it pays interest) is one type of yield, but there are two other types of yields, each of which is calculated a little differently:

- Current yield.
- Yield to maturity.

How do I know the nominal yield of a bond?

Nominal yield is found in the financial listings as part of the identification of the bond. This rate is applied to the face value of the bond, which is $1,000 unless otherwise stated.

Annual interest ($) = Face value × Coupon (nominal)
rate (%)

Example The nominal (or coupon) yield is boldfaced in the following listing:

Bonds	Cur Yld	Vol	Close	Net Chg.
GMA 8¾ 01	8.8	10	99½	+ 1

Annual interest ($) = Face value × Coupon (nominal)
rate (%)

= $1,000 × .0875 = $87.50

The holder of a GMA 8¾ 01 bond will receive two semi-annual interest payments of $43.75 each ($43.75 plus $43.75 equals $87.50).

How is the "current yield" on a corporate bond calculated?

Current yield is the yield that you get, expressed as a percentage, when you divide the fixed interest payments by the purchase price (not face value). The bondholder receives the fixed interest payment (which is a percentage of the face value), regardless of how much the bond cost. Yet the purchase price is the real amount of the investment, not the face value; and the actual yield should be calculated as a percentage of that investment. Because current yield is based on the fluctuating market value of the bond, it can, and usually does, change often, as the market price of the bond rises or falls in the market.

$$\text{Current yield (\%)} = \frac{\text{Interest (\$)}}{\text{Current price}}$$

Note that the relationship between current yield and price is *inverse*. That is, as price increases, current yield declines, and vice versa.

Example: A 10% Commonwealth Edison $1,000 corporate bond is purchased for 103 ($1,030). What is the current yield?

$$\text{Nominal yield (\$)} = \text{Face value} \times \text{Nominal rate (\%)}$$
$$= \$1,000 \times .10 = \$100$$

$$\text{Current yield (\%)} = \frac{\text{Interest (\$)}}{\text{Current price}}$$
$$= \frac{\$100}{\$1,030} = .0970 \text{ or } 9.70\%$$

For someone who purchased the bond for a price of $1,030, the current yield is 9.70%. For that holder, the current yield will not change because his or her purchase price will not change.

Note that the current yield is less than the nominal yield because the investor paid more than face value for the bond, which was trading at a premium. So the fixed return is worth less, percentagewise, to the purchaser.

The current yield on the bond can change over its lifetime. That's why it is called the "current" yield. If the bond drops in market value to 97 ($970), its current yield changes also.

$$\text{Current yield (\%)} = \frac{\text{Interest (\$)}}{\text{Current price}}$$
$$= \frac{\$100}{\$970} = .1031 \text{ or } 10.31\%$$

Note that, as the price declines, current yield increases. For anyone purchasing this bond at 97 ($970), the current yield is 10.31%. The current yield is higher than the nominal rate because the bond is purchased at a discount. The "savings" in price from the face value is a factor in calculating the current yield.

What is "yield to maturity"?

The computation of *yield to maturity* (*YTM*), like current yield, takes the purchase price into account, but it also includes the eventual repayment of principal (face value, $1,000) if the bond is held to maturity.

● If the purchase price is lower than par (that is, discounted), then the bondholder receives more than what was paid, and this extra amount must be considered part of the overall yield.

Example: If a $1,000 face value corporate bond costs $900, the $100 difference between the price and par must be considered additional yield at maturity.

● If the price is higher (that is, at a premium), the bondholder is paid less, and the added cost lessens the yield.

Example: If a $1,000 bond is sold for $1,100, then the additional $100 in price has to be deducted from the yield at maturity.

● With a purchase price at par, yield to maturity is the same as current yield, which in turn is the same as the nominal yield.

Example: If a $1,000 bond sells for $1,000, then nothing needs to be added or deducted from the yield at maturity. And, since the purchase price (the basis of the current yield formula) equals par value, the current yield is the same as the nominal yield.

Yield to maturity is a better assessment of return than current yield because it considers all the factors affecting yield—interest rate, market price, and time to maturity.

Note: The yield to maturity is not included in the financial listings for corporate bonds.

How is a corporate bond's yield to maturity calculated?
The calculation for YTM entails two steps:

● Spread out, or *prorate*, the premium or discount over the years remaining to maturity.

$$\text{Prorated premium/discount} = \frac{\text{Difference between face value and price}}{\text{Years remaining to maturity}}$$

- Apply the YTM formula.

$$\text{Yield to maturity} = \frac{\text{Nominal rate} + \left(\begin{array}{l} + \text{ Prorated discount (\$) or} \\ - \text{ Prorated premium (\$)} \end{array}\right)}{(\text{Price} + \text{Face value})/2}$$

Note: This formula is called the *rule of thumb* because it is not as exact as the true formula, which involves the use of calculus and a computer. (That is why the yield to maturity in the financial listings is never the same as calculated by the rule of thumb method.) This method, however, serves the purpose for the individual investor, particularly if it is expressed in terms of days to maturity.

Example: A Commonwealth Edison $1,000 corporate bond is purchased at 103 ($1,030), pays 10% nominal interest ($100), and has exactly 15 years remaining to maturity. What is the yield to maturity?

- *Prorate the premium.*

$$\text{Prorated premium/discount} = \frac{\begin{array}{c}\text{Difference between} \\ \text{face value and price}\end{array}}{\text{Years remaining to maturity}}$$

$$= \frac{\$1,030 - \$1,000}{15 \text{ years}}$$

$$= \frac{\$30}{15 \text{ years}} = \$2 \text{ per year}$$

The bond is worth an additional $2 per year in yield.

- *Apply the YTM formula:*

$$\text{Yield to maturity} = \frac{\text{Nominal rate} + \left(\begin{array}{l} + \text{ Prorated discount (\$) or} \\ - \text{ Prorated premium (\$)} \end{array}\right)}{(\text{Price} + \text{Face value})/2}$$

$$= \frac{\$100 - \$2}{(\$1,030 + \$1,000)/2}$$

$$= \frac{\$98}{\$2,030/2} = \frac{\$98}{\$1,015} = 0.966 \text{ or } 9.66\%$$

If held to maturity, this bond's yield to maturity will be 9.66%. The bondholder, having bought the bond at a premium, receives a yield that is less than the nominal rate (10%).

Can yield to maturity change like current yield?

Yes. Yield to maturity can change from moment to moment in the marketplace, as a bond's price goes up or down. For two different investors who purchased the same bond at different times, the yields to maturity are probably going to be different for two reasons: The purchase prices may be different, and the times remaining to maturity will certainly be different.

- Yield increases as price decreases, and vice versa.
- Yield on a discounted bond increases as the time to maturity decreases.
- Yield on a bond selling at a premium decreases as the time to maturity decreases.

Example: Refer to the preceding example. The 10%, $1,000 corporate bond is purchased at a different price, 95 ($950), and with exactly 7 years remaining to maturity. What is the yield to maturity?

- *Prorate the discount.*

$$\begin{array}{c} \text{Prorated} \\ \text{premium/discount} \end{array} = \frac{\begin{array}{c}\text{Difference between} \\ \text{face value and price}\end{array}}{\text{Years remaining to maturity}}$$

$$= \frac{\$1,000 - \$950}{7 \text{ years}}$$

$$= \frac{\$50}{7 \text{ years}} = \$7.14 \text{ per year}$$

The bond is worth an additional $7.14 per year in yield.

- *Apply the YTM formula.*

$$\text{Yield to maturity} = \frac{\text{Nominal rate} + \left(\begin{array}{l} + \text{ Prorated discount (\$) or} \\ - \text{ Prorated premium (\$)} \end{array}\right)}{(\text{Price} + \text{Face value})/2}$$

$$= \frac{\$100 + \$7.14}{(\$950 + \$1,000)/2}$$

$$= \frac{\$107.14}{\$1,950/2} = \frac{\$107.14}{\$975.00} = .1099 \text{ or } 10.99\%$$

If held to maturity, this bond's yield to maturity will be 10.99%. The bondholder, having bought the bond at a discount, enjoys a yield that is greater than the nominal rate (10%). The YTM is higher than it was for the investor who bought the bond at $1,030 8 years earlier. In this case, both the lower (discount) price and the shorter time to maturity increased the yield. (If the bond had been bought at a premium, the shorter time to maturity would have lessened yield.)

What if the bond is not bought with an exact number of years remaining to maturity?

In the real world, bonds are usually *not* bought exactly on the date of their issuance. In these cases, the prorating and YTM formulas are restated using months, weeks, or—as is usually the case—days remaining to maturity.

$$\text{Prorated premium/discount} = \frac{\text{Difference between face value and price}}{\text{Days remaining to maturity}}$$

$$\text{Yield to maturity} = \frac{\text{Nominal rate}/365 + \left(\begin{array}{l} + \text{ Prorated discount (\$) or} \\ - \text{ Prorated premium (\$)} \end{array}\right)}{(\text{Price} + \text{Face value})/(2 \times 365 \text{ days})}$$

Example: Refer to the preceding example. The 10%, $1,000 corporate bond is purchased at 95 ($950). It is purchased so that the buyer becomes the owner of record on December 15 of 19X1, and maturity is on April 5 of 19X5. What is the yield to maturity? The first step is to determine the number of days to maturity:

19X1	
December	17 (the 15th is counted)
19X2	365
19X3	365
19X4	365
19X5	365
January	31
February	28
March	31
April	5

Total days to maturity 1,572

$$\text{Prorated premium/discount} = \frac{\text{Difference between face value and price}}{\text{Days remaining to maturity}}$$

$$= \frac{\$1,000 - \$950}{1,572 \text{ days}}$$

$$= \frac{\$50}{1,572 \text{ days}} \$.031807 \text{ per day}$$

$$\text{Yield to maturity} = \frac{\dfrac{\text{Nominal rate}}{365} + \left(\begin{array}{l}+ \text{ Prorated discount (\$) or} \\ - \text{ Prorated premium (\$)}\end{array}\right)}{(\text{Price} + \text{Face value})/(2 \times 365 \text{ days})}$$

$$= \frac{(\$100/365 \text{ days}) + \$.031807}{(\$950 + \$1,000)/(2 \times 365)}$$

$$= \frac{\$.27397 + \$.031807}{\$1,950/(730 \text{ days})} = \frac{\$.305777}{\$2.67123} = .1144 \text{ or } 11.44\%$$

If held to maturity, this bond's yield to maturity will be 11.44%. The bondholder, having bought the bond at a discount, enjoys a yield that is greater than the nominal rate (10%).

Note: This formula is called the *rule of thumb* because it is not as exact as the true formula, which involves the use of calculus and a computer. (That is why the yield to maturity in the financial listings is never the same as calculated by the rule of thumb method.) This method, however, serves the purpose for the individual investor, particularly if it is expressed in terms of days to maturity.

What is a "basis point"?

In fixed income trading and investing, the differences among yields to maturity can be slight (particularly in the Treasury and agency securities markets). Yields sometimes have to be expressed in very fine calibrations. One way to refine yield-to-maturity measurements and comparisons is to use the *basis point*, which is .01%—1/100 of 1%—of yield on a debt instrument. There are 100 basis points in 1%.

$$1.00\% = 100 \text{ basis points}$$

Example: If the price of a corporate bond changes from 9.21% to 9.20%, it changes by 1 basis point: 9.21% less 9.20% equals .01%. A change from 8.50% to 8.75% is 25 basis points: 8.75% less 8.50 equals .25%.

If the seminannual interest payments on a bond are a form of simple interest, is there any way to compound it?

The interest itself can be put into another interest-earning investment, thereby creating what is called *interest on interest*, which is different from compounding. The overall return, in terms of both dollars and percentages, may or may not be the same as it would be if interest were added to principal. Assuming an investor earns zero interest for the first half of each year (until the first interest payment is made) and then full interest on the first semiannual payment for the balance of the year, the rate at which interest is reinvested can be halved to arrive at the interest-on-interest rate.

$$\frac{\text{Interest-on-}}{\text{interest rate}} = \text{Principal} \times (\text{Rate}/2) \times \text{Time}$$

Example: Investor Ernest Knewitz purchases ten 10%, $1,000 corporate bonds and holds them for 5 years. If over that holding period, Knewitz uses interest payments for noninvestment purposes, his total simple interest is $5,000:

FIXED INCOME INVESTMENTS **147**

$$\text{Interest} = \text{Principal} \times \text{Rate} \times \text{Time}$$
$$= \$10{,}000 \times .10 \times 5 \text{ years} = \$5000$$

Suppose, however, that he reinvests each payment in a 6-month certificate of deposit (CD) that yields 8% and that matures just as he receives the next interest payment. Here's how interest on interest will accumulate:

First year's
interest-on- = Principal $\times$ (Rate/2) $\times$ Time
interest rate

$$= \$1{,}000 \times (.08/2) \times 1 \text{ year}$$
$$= \$1{,}000 \times .04 \times 1 \text{ year} = \$40$$

Add the second year's interest payment (\$1,000) and the interest from the first year (\$40) to the CD principal, for the second-year principal of \$2,040.

Second year's
interest-on- = Principal $\times$ (Rate/2) $\times$ Time
interest rate

$$= \$2{,}040 \times (.08/2) \times 1 \text{ year}$$
$$= \$2{,}040 \times .04 \times 1 \text{ year} = \$81.60$$

For each year, add the next year's interest payments and last year's earned interest.

Third year's
interest-on- = Principal $\times$ (Rate/2) $\times$ Time
interest rate

$$= \$3{,}121.60 \times (.08/2) \times 1 \text{ year}$$
$$= \$3{,}121.60 \times .04 \times 1 \text{ year} =$$
$$\$124.86$$

Fourth year's
interest-on- = Principal $\times$ (Rate/2) $\times$ Time
interest rate

$$= \$4{,}246.46 \times (.08/2) \times 1 \text{ year}$$
$$= \$4{,}246.46 \times .04 \times 1 \text{ year} =$$
$$\$169.86$$

Fifth year's
interest-on- = Principal × (Rate/2) × Time
interest rate

= $5,416.32 × (.08/2) × 1 year

= $5,416.32 × .04 × 1 year =
$216.65

When the fifth year's interest on interest ($216.65) is added to the fourth year's total ($5,416.32), the total interest is $5,632.97, considerably more than Knewitz would have earned in straight interest.

Interest on interest, however, does not earn as much as semiannually compounded interest. If the issuer of the bond were to credit Knewitz's account with the interest (adding it to principal for purposes of calculating interest) and compound the total semiannually, the total of principal and interest at the end of 5 years (according to the compound interest tables) would be $16,288.95. Compare the results:

	Simple Interest	Interest on Interest	Compound Interest
Principal	$10,000.00	$10,000.00	$10,000.00
Interest	$ 5,000.00	$ 5,632.97	$ 6,288.95

Conceivably, if the rate at which interest is reinvested is considerably higher than the coupon rate on the bond, then the dollar amount resulting from the interest on interest could approach or even exceed the amounts created by compounding at the coupon rate.

Note: The compounding of the interest on this bond is purely for the sake of comparison. In the "real world" of securities, interest on bonds is never compounded.

Accrued Interest

When investors sell a bond, do they lose some of the interest due them from the last interest payment date?

No. Bondholders are entitled to interest for every day of ownership, even if they have not actually received the interest. To put it another way, interest "accrues" to the owner on a daily basis.

What is "accrued" interest?

Accrued interest is the interest on a bond that accumulates in the owner's name between payment dates.

Example: Interest payments on a "J&J" bond are made on the 1st of January and June. Interest accrues (or accumulates) to the owner of record between payment dates. On November 31, for instance, the owner is entitled to interest that has accrued during the months of June, July, August, September, October, and November—but not December.

What happens if a bond changes owners between interest payments?

When a bond is sold between interest payment dates, the buyer must pay the seller the interest that has accrued up to, but not including, the settlement date of the trade. This amount is added to the purchase price of the bond. The new owner then collects the check for the full amount of the semiannual payment on the next interest payment date.

The accrued interest is calculated by means of a derivation of the interest formula:

$$\textbf{Interest} = \textbf{Principal} \times \textbf{Rate} \times \textbf{Time}$$

Principal is the face value of the bond, assumed to be $1,000.

Rate is the coupon (or nominal) rate.

Time is a fraction, in which the numerator consists of the number of days from the day of the transaction (when the bond changes hands) to, but not including, the day of settlement. The denominator is the number of days in the year. For purposes of calculating accrued interest on corporate bonds:

- Each month is 30 days (not the actual calendar days).
- The year (the denominator) is 360 (not the actual days in the year).

Example: Ben Sauls sells an Exxon 9.25%, $1,000 debenture to Judy Wise on Thursday, March 20, at a price of 104 ($1,040). Interest payments are made on January 1 and June 1 ("J1 and J1"). Settlement for corporate debt transactions normally takes place 5 business days, or 7 calendar days (barring holidays); this is called *regular way settle-ment*. On March 27, Sauls (the seller) is to deliver the note, and Wise (the buyer) is to make payment.

In addition to payment of the purchase price, Wise has to pay Sauls the interest that the note accrued from the last interest payment date to the day before settlement. (She will then keep the next full interest payment.) The principal is the face (or par) value of the note, $1,000, and the rate is 9.25%. But what is the time? Time is expressed in terms of 30-day months:

January	30 days
February	30 days
March	26 days (Settlement day, the 27th, is excluded.)
Total	86 days

$$\text{Interest} = \text{Principal} \times \text{Rate} \times \text{Time}$$
$$= \$1,000 \times .0925 \times \frac{86}{360}$$
$$= \$1,000 \times .0925 \times .2389 = \$22.10$$

Wise pays Sauls the purchase price of $1,040 plus the accrued interest of $22.10, for a total of $1,062.10. On January 1 of the next year, the next interest payment date, Wise will receive $46.25 (the semiannual interest payment).

THE YIELD CURVE

Why aren't all bonds purchased at face value, even in the secondary market?

After bonds are issued, they begin to trade on the exchanges and in the over-the-counter market, collectively known as the *secondary market*. Most outstanding issues trade at discounts (prices below par value) or at premiums (prices above par value). While a number of factors affect bond prices, such as their ratings, the most influential of all arises from *prevailing interest* rates, that is, the general level of rates currently available on equivalent debt instruments.

The driving principle is that every participant in the

bond market is seeking the best return, or yield. Someone trying to sell a bond with a coupon rate that is lower than the prevailing rates has to settle for a discounted price so that a buyer will have a current yield equivalent to prevailing rates. An owner selling a bond with a rate higher than what is generally available can demand a premium price. The risk that interest rates will rise, creating lesser demand for bonds already held, is known as *interest rate risk.*

How can an investor know the "right" price for a bond selling at a discount or a premium?

In general:

- *Bond prices fall when prevailing rates increase.*
- *Bond prices rise when prevailing rates drop.*

The individual investor can compute an *approximate* price for a bond selling at a discount or premium by means of the current yield formula. (The yield to maturity rule of thumb formula is more accurate. However, since the purpose is only to arrive at a rough price level, the current yield formula is easier to use.) The current yield formula is:

$$\text{Current yield (\%)} = \frac{\text{Interest (\$)}}{\text{Current price (\$)}}$$

It becomes:

$$\text{Current price (\$)} = \frac{\text{Interest (\$)}}{\text{Current yield (\%)}}$$

Example: Shelly Widmer purchases a General Motors 8% debenture at 100 ($1,000) in an initial offering. For one year, she receives seminannual interest payments of $40 ($80 annual interest divided by 2). For as long as she holds the bond, her current yield and yield to maturity are the same as the coupon rate.

Price of a discount bond: One year after she purchases the bond, rates for a "General Motors" type of bond rise to 9%. Her 8% General Motors bond is reduced in value because newly issued equivalent bonds are yielding more. If she were to sell the bond, the price would have to be reduced to a level that makes the current yield for the buyer equivalent to the coupon rates on the new bonds.

What would that price be? If the desired current yield is 9% and the annual interest payment on the old bond is $80, then:

$$\text{Current yield (\%)} = \frac{\text{Interest (\$)}}{\text{Current price (\$)}}$$

$$.09 = \frac{\$80}{\text{Current price (\$)}}$$

Or:

$$\text{Current price (\$)} = \frac{\$80}{.09} = \$888.89$$

The older bond would have to sell for about $888.89. This might translate, in terms of units of trading, into 88⅞ ($888.75) or 89 ($890).

Price of premium bond: Prevailing rates fall to 7% during the first year of ownership. The value of Widmer's GM bond would rise in the marketplace. Anyone wishing to buy the 8% bond would have to "compensate" Widmer for the better-than-available yield by paying a premium price.

$$\text{Current yield (\%)} = \frac{\text{Interest (\$)}}{\text{Current price (\$)}}$$

$$.07 = \frac{\$80}{\text{Current price (\$)}}$$

Or:

$$\text{Current price (\$)} = \frac{\$80}{.07} = \$1,142.86$$

In units of trading, this price might be 114¼ ($1,142.50) or 114⅜ ($1,143.75).

Are prevailing rates the only significant factor that determines yield?

No. Time to maturity is also a notable influence. The general principle is that, *the longer the time to maturity, the greater the return demanded by the lender for the money loaned.* Underlying this principle is interest rate risk. When money is loaned out and prevailing interest rates rise, the money is being *underutilized*; it could be earning more. If the loan is short-term, then the underutilization—and loss of interest— is not great. For long-term commitments of capital, however, the losses can be heavy. Lenders hedge loans with longer maturities by demanding higher rates than they would on shorter-term commitments.

The same is true in the debt (or fixed income) securities market. The lenders (bondholders) expect higher coupon rates for longer-term debt. For debt securities with maturities under one year, the yield is probably going to be lower than for those with maturities of from one to ten years. Both would have lower rates than bonds, which mature in 20 to 40 years. As a rule of thumb in the debt market, therefore, yields rise as maturities get longer.

This principle is depicted graphically in what is known as the *yield curve*, which is a graph that plots yields against maturities.

Example: For a group of corporate bonds, all of the highest rating but with varying maturities, the shorter maturities will yield less than the longer ones. The graph for this phenomenon is shown in Figure 4–2.

- Bonds maturing in one year provide a return of about 7.5%.
- Bonds with 5-year maturities yield 7.8%.
- Fifteen-year bonds are returning 8.50%.
- At 30 years, bonds are yielding 9.50%.
- Maturities of 40 years are associated with 10.30% returns.

Investor Gerry Hillman feels that prevailing rates will decline in the coming 5 years or so. Given that outlook, he would be best advised to purchase the very long maturities (perhaps at face value) with yields in the 10%-plus range. Assuming Hillman's prediction is correct and rates drop, his 10% bonds increase in value. He could then sell the bonds at a premium for a profit, or he could simply enjoy the higher-than-current rate of return.

Figure 4–2.

The usual relationship between short- and long-term fixed-income securities.

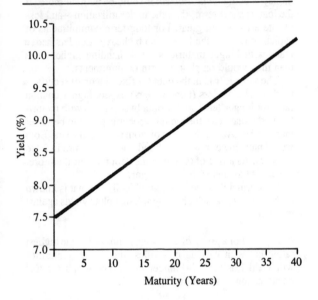

Is the angle of the yield curve always the same?

No. The yield curve angle changes according to supply and demand for the various maturities. When it comes to supply and demand, the rules are forever the same. Keeping in mind that as prices fall, yields rise, and when prices move up, yields suffer, the rules are:

● High demand (more buyers than sellers) for securities anywhere along the curve tends to drive prices up in that area and therefore to depress yields.

● Excessive supply (more sellers than takers) tends to force prices down and thereby to increase yields.

Example: If the outlook among investors changes so that they expect yields on long-term bonds to decline, there will be an aggressive push on to purchase bonds before the lower yields set in. This demand at the "long" end of the yield curve tends to "flatten" the yield curve in a couple of ways.

In the primary market, it allows corporations to offer lowered yields on their new, long-term issues; it's a "seller's" market, so to speak. In the meantime, the interest on short-term bonds would wane, and short-term issuers (in a "buyer's market") have to attract investors by assigning higher yields. Effect: decreasing yields farther out on the curve, depressed yields in the near term.

In secondary trading, the demand for long-range issues drives prices up and yields down. Short-term issues, having fallen out of favor, drop in value, with related rises in yields. Effect: lower long-term yields and increased short-range yields.

The result is shown in Figure 4–3.

Figure 4–3.

A "flattened" yield curve.

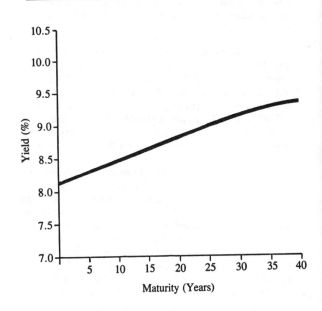

Is the yield curve always straight?

No. In fact, it is generally depicted as arched. Normally, *the yields for short- and intermediate-term instruments rise at a more rapid rate than that of the longer maturities.* Again, the underlying principle is interest rate risk. A lender who commits to a loan of two years and sees rates rise after one year loses more, percentagewise, than one who extends a loan for 30 years and sees rates rise after 28 or 29 years. The effects of underutilization at the far end of the curve are lessened by the long-term nature of the instruments involved. As a result, when lenders are determining the appropriate rate for a long-term extension of credit, the difference in exposure to risk between 28 or 30 years is little compared to that between 2 and 3 years. In the same vein, when investors are considering buying a bond with 28 or 30 years to maturity (that is, when considering lending their capital for that long), the difference between the two maturities is not as significant as it would be between a 1-year certificate of deposit or a 3-year Treasury note. The effect on the yield curve is that it rises quickly at first and then bows downward, almost flattening out completely for the longest maturities. Figure 4–4 shows what a *normal yield curve* looks like.

Example: A corporation issues 2-year, $100,000 notes at 8%. Investors who buy the notes are committing their capital for 2 years. After a year, prevailing rates are up to 10%. If the investors had the $100,000 to commit, they could earn $10,000 ($100,000 times .10) instead of $8,000 ($10,000 times .08). Their $100,000 is being underutilized by $2,000; they are earning 20% ($2,000 divided by $10,000) less than prevailing rates would permit them to now.

The same corporation issues 30-year bonds at 9.5%. For 28 years, interest rates rise and fall, averaging about 9.5%. So far, bondholders who bought the bonds and who are holding them to maturity are content that they are earning as much as can be expected, given the available rates. In the last two years before maturity, however, interest rates rise to 11%. If the investors had the capital to commit, they could be earning 11% a year, as opposed to 9.5%. When the difference between the two rates over two years is compared to the overall return over the prior 28 years, the *percentage* of underutilization is minuscule.

Figure 4–4.

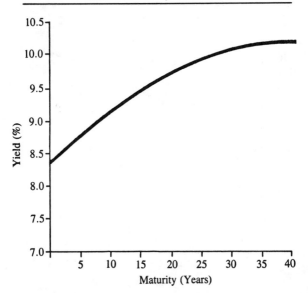

The "normal" yield curve.

From the investor's point of view, then, making long-term commitments of capital for just a few more years may not be worthwhile?

Exactly. As the increase in yields decelerates toward the "end" of the yield curve, the additional return for longer maturities diminishes. Investors should examine the real worth of committing funds for an extra 5, 10, or more years, in light of the return.

Example: Figure 4–5 shows the yield curve for AAA-rated public utility bonds. Public utilities are highly regulated "legal" monopolies—they have no competition—with exclusive rights to service a geographic area. They are less likely to go out of business than nonregulated companies that do not provide necessary services or goods. Utility bonds are therefore considered to be quite safe and favored by many investors. In comparing public utility 30-year and 40-year bonds, investor Ben Hecht notes that there is only a 10-basis-point spread between the yields (10.00% com-

Figure 4–5.

Yield curve for public 30- to 40-year utility bonds.

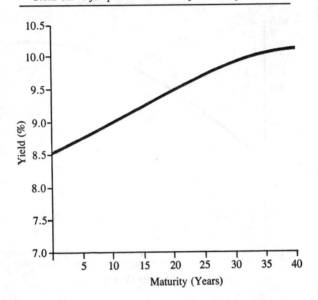

pared to 10.10%). He decides that committing funds for an additional 10 years is not worth 10 basis points. He chooses the 30-year bonds.

Can short-term yields ever be higher than long-range rates?

Yes. The yield curve can be *negative* or *inverted*. (See Figure 4–6.) The most common cause of such an inversion is the expectation among investors that short-term yields will decline. Due to the nature of short-term instruments, investors have to *roll over* their capital often. As a maturity date is reached and principal repaid, the capital has to be placed into another investment, or "rolled over." If the expectation is that short-term yields are declining, investors will shift their funds to issues with longer maturities.

The forces of supply and demand do the rest. In the primary market, corporations (and other issuers) can decrease yields in what has become a seller's market. Short-

Figure 4–6.

A negative (or inverted) yield curve.

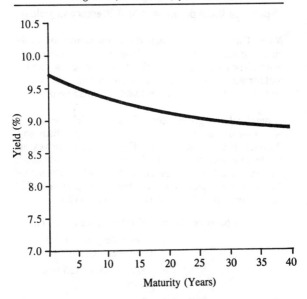

term issuers have to boost yields to attract investors. In the secondary market, the demand for longer-term issues drives prices up and yields down. The excess supply of short-term instruments causes prices to drop and yields to rise. The result is something like what you see in Figure 4–6.

Of what use are yield curves to investors?

Investors can use the yield curve to compare the investment merits of different fixed-income securities. Corporate bond curves can be compared to municipal or Treasury security curves. Yields on bonds of one industry can be related to those of another industry.

Whatever types of securities are being compared, the curves for various instruments (available from the rating services and brokerage firms) are affected by a number of factors, but the primary one is *investment quality*. Investors should particularly note the difference between yields (or the *spread*) of the compared instruments. The spread is usually expressed in terms of basis points.

Spread in basis points = 100 (Difference in yields)

Note: The yield curve is only one of the many tools available to investors when determining how to position their assets. The examples in this chapter do not deal with other tools or with other considerations, and they must be considered as having value only in that they illustrate points.

Example: U.S. government (Treasury) debt securities, which are of highest quality, carry lower yields than, say, AAA-rated corporate bonds. The two yield curves are shown in Figure 4–7. In that figure, 1-year Treasuries are yielding 7.10% and 1-year corporates 8.45%. The spread (or difference in yields) between these two securities is 135 basis points (8.45% less 7.10% equals 1.35%).

Spread in basis points = 100 (Difference in yields)
     = (Corporate yield: .0845 − Treasuries: .0710)
     = 100 × .0135 = 135 basis points

What does the spread tell investors?

If actual rates diverge from the ones anticipated on the curve charts, or if the spread widens or narrows, then investors might look for an investment opportunity.

Example: In Figure 4–7, the spread between 30-year Treasuries (yielding 8.50%) and 30-year corporates (9.80%) is 130 basis points.

Spread in basis points = 100 (Difference in yields)
     = (Corporate yield: .0980 − Treasuries: .0850)
     = 100 × .0130 = 130 basis points

If an analyst estimates that the spread should be closer to 200 basis points (2.00%), then the spread can be expected

Figure 4–7.

*Comparison of the yield curve for Treasury securities
and AAA-rated corporate bonds.**

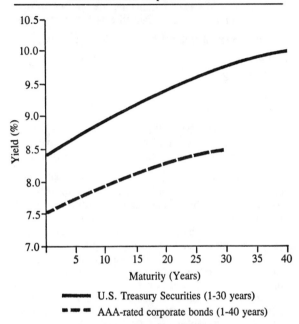

U.S. Treasury Securities (1-30 years)

AAA-rated corporate bonds (1-40 years)

*The curve for corporate bonds extends for 40 years, the one for
Treasury securities for 30. The reason is that, although the U.S. Treasury
has on occasion issued 40-year bonds, the overwhelming majority are for 30
years.

to widen sometime soon in the future. Specifically, either
prices on corporate bonds would have to decline (and yields
rise), or Treasury securities prices would have to rise (and
yields decline), or both securities would react to the ''too-
narrow'' spread. The analyst would most likely buy
Treasuries.

Why? If the spread does indeed widen, corporate bonds
are likely to decline in price or at least remain at the same
price. If anything, Treasuries are probably going to rise in
value.

RETIRING BONDS

What does it mean to "retire" a bond?

Retiring a bond means terminating the lender-borrower arrangement. A corporation can retire its debt in five ways:

- Redemption at maturity.
- Call.
- Refunding.
- Sinking fund.
- Conversion.

Redemption

How is a bond redeemed at maturity?

To redeem a bond at maturity, the corporation repays the principal to the owners of record on the maturity date.

Example: General Production issued $10,000,000 worth of 9%, 20-year bonds, and today is the day of maturity. Any bondholders on the company's records as owners of the bonds will be repaid their principal. That is, an investor holding 10 $1,000 bonds will receive a check for $10,000 (10 bonds times $1,000 face value), regardless of the price paid for the bonds. In all, the corporation will have to issue $10,000,000 worth of such checks to bondholders of record. This is in addition to the interest already paid to various bondholders, $900,000 a year (.09 times principal of $10,000,000). Over 20 years, interest amounted to $18,000,000 (20 years times $900,000 a year).

Call

What does it mean for a corporate bond to be "callable"?

When a bond is *callable*, the issuer retains the right to retire (that is, repurchase) all or some of the bonds prior to maturity—to "call" them back. The *call feature* always works to the benefit of the issuer because the bond will be called only when it is in the issuer's best interest to do so. Consequently, this feature must be clearly stated at the time of issuance.

Note: Callable corporate bonds are not identified as such in the financial listings. Investors must inquire about such features when purchasing bonds.

What are the terms of the call feature on a bond?

Corporate call features can become rather complicated, and there is no "typical" set of terms. In many cases, however, two clauses appear:

- Investors are offered *call protection*, usually for the first five years. That is, the issuer guarantees the bonds will not be called within the first five years after issuance.

- Once a bond becomes callable, the issuer may repurchase them at a premium price (that is, at a price above the $1,000 face value, not above current market price). Each year until maturity, the premium declines until, at some point close to maturity, it ceases to exist. At that point, should the bonds be called, the investors get only the face value.

Note: Under no circumstances will an investor receive less than face value in a normal call situation.

Example: General Production 9% debentures are due to mature in November 2009 and are issued in November 1989. A call protection clause in the indenture states that the bonds may be called by the issuer but *not* within the first five years of issuance. Buyers of this issue may be assured of receiving interest payments, without the bonds' being called, up to November 1994.

Thereafter the bonds become subject to repurchase at premium prices, according to the following schedule:

Call and Refunding Terms	
Year	Price
1–5	Noncallable
6	109 ($1,090)
7	108 ($1,080)
8	107 ($1,070)
9	106 ($1,060)
10	105 ($1,050)
11	104 ($1,040)
12	103 ($1,030)
13	102 ($1,020)
14	101 ($1,010)
15–19	100 ($1,000)

When a portion of an issue is called, how is the portion selected?

Bonds are generally selected at random for call. An advertisement might appear in the financial section of the newspaper listing the numbers of the bonds called. Owners would also be notified by mail. It is possible that an owner would have some of his or her bonds called, but not all.

How does an investor know whether a corporation is likely to recall an issue?

Once a bond becomes callable, the corporate issuer determines whether it would lower its debt service expense to *refund* the issue, that is, issue new bonds at a lower rate of interest and use the proceeds to call in the existing bonds. Generally, if the prevailing interest rates are lower than the coupon (or nominal) rate on the existing debt, the issuer will call the bond and issue new debt at a lower interest rate. The corporation's accountants have to figure out whether the lower debt service is worth the premium the company would have to pay to call the old debt.

Example: Refer to the preceding example. The November '09 bonds, with a coupon rate of 9%, become callable in 1995. In the 8th year after issuance, prevailing rates enable General Production to borrow money at 6%. The board of directors addresses the question as to whether $3,000,000 worth of the 9% debenture should be called in (3,000 bonds, or $3,000,000 divided by $1,000 face value). The question is whether the savings in debt service are worth the premium price. The company can save over $1,000,000 in debt serice by refunding $3,000,000 worth of the issue, that is, by issuing new bonds at 6% and using the proceeds to pay off the old 9% debt.

9% interest on $3,000,000 × 12 years	$3,240,000
6% interest on $3,000,000 × 12 years	$2,160,000
Savings in interest to maturity	$1,080,000

If the company calls the $3,000,000, it will have to pay a premium price of 107 ($1,070)—an additional $210,000 ($70 per $1,000 bond times 3,000 bonds). That $210,000 is offset many times by the savings in interest over the remaining years to maturity.

What does this mean for investors? They must watch the prevailing rates when they own or or are considering the purchase of a callable bond.

Example: Suppose an investor is about to purchase a General Production debenture at 107½ in the 8th year after its issuance, when prevailing rates are averaging 6%. That investor could buy the bond on Monday at 107½, have it called away at 107, and be out the half-point in price and commissions.

Note: These bonds do not generally trade above their call price, but the point is that, with callable bonds, investors must be aware of prevailing rates, the call price, and the market price.

Refunding

What is "refunding"?

Refunding is using the proceeds of the sale of a new issue of bonds to repurchase an older issue. Like the call feature, refunding terms must be stated in the indenture on the back of the bond certificate. These terms are usually the same as for a call:

- Investors are offered protection against refunding, usually for the first five years. That is, the issuer guarantees the bonds will not be refunded within the first five years after their initial issuance.
- Once a bond becomes refundable, the issuer may repurchase them at a premium price (that is, at a price above the $1,000 face value, not above current market price). Each year until maturity, the premium declines until, at some point close to maturity, it ceases to exist. At that point, should the bonds be refunded, the investors get only the face value.

Example: General Production 9% debentures are not callable or refundable for the first 5 years after issuance, thereafter they may be repurchased (that is, either refunded or called) at the following prices per bond:

	Call and Refunding Terms
Year	*Price*
1–5	Noncallable
6	109 ($1,090)
7	108 ($1,080)
8	107 ($1,070)
9	106 ($1,060)
10	105 ($1,050)
11	104 ($1,040)
12	103 ($1,030)
13	102 ($1,020)
14	101 ($1,010)
15–19	100 ($1,000)

They become refundable in 1995. In the 14th year after issuance, prevailing rates enable General Production to borrow money at 5%. The board of directors addresses the question as to whether the entire issue ($10,000,000) of the 9% debenture should be refunded. The question is whether the savings in debt service are worth the premium price. The company can save $2,400,000 in debt service by refunding the issue, that is, by issuing new bonds at 5% and using the proceeds to pay off the old 9% debt.

9% interest on $10,000,000 × 6 years	$5,400,000
5% interest on $10,000,000 × 6 years	$3,000,000
Savings in interest to maturity	$2,400,000

If the company refunds the issue, it will have to pay a premium price of 101 ($1,010)—an additional $100,000 ($10 per $1,000 bond times 10,000 bonds). The additional $100,000 is a small price to pay for the great savings in interest to maturity.

Note: Bonds are called or refunded only when it is in the best interests of the issuer to do so. If interest rates rise during the term of the bond, the issuer is not going to exchange bonds that will result in higher debt service expenses.

Sinking Fund

What is a "sinking fund"?

A *sinking fund* is an account into which a corporation deposits a predetermined amount of money periodically so that it will have enough funds to repurchase all or part of a bond issue in the open market or call them. Once repurchased, the bonds cease to exist as negotiable (that is, tradable) securities. The loan agreement is terminated because the principal has been repaid. The specific provisions of such a fund can vary greatly from issue to issue, but the terms are always laid out in the indenture.

Example: In the indenture for the $10,000,000 issue of 9% General Production debentures, there is a provision that the company will set aside $200,000 each year for the 20 years to maturity. This money will be used each year to repurchase the bonds in the open market. In the first year of issuance, GP buys back $200,000 worth of bonds (assuming they are trading at par). It thereby saves the $18,000 of interest that it would have had to pay on that $200,000 each year for the next 19 years.

9% interest on $10,000,000	$900,000
9% interest on $ 9,800,000	$882,000
Total savings	$ 18,000

Assuming, for the sake of simplicity, that the bonds trade at par value (or face value, $1,000) until maturity and that the company repurchases $200,000 worth of them a year, the company will save a total of $3,240,000 in interest cost. (The calculation is irrelevant to the needs of the investor.)

What effect does a sinking fund have on an investor's position?

In general, a sinking fund helps the investor. The fund makes the loan more secure by reducing the debt and the amount of interest to be paid each year. Also, since the bonds are repurchased in the open market, investors need not part with their bonds unless they choose to do so by putting in an order with their brokers. (The bonds are not "selected" for repurchase as they are for a call or refund.)

Finally, if the coupon rate on the bond is higher than prevailing rates (which is a good reason for the issuer to be repurchasing them), then their growing scarcity from year to year could even make them more valuable in the open market.

Does a sinking fund reduce the cost of redemption at maturity?

Yes. In fact, some reduce the cost of redemption to zero. These funds may be designed to retire, or *sink*, 50%, 75%, 90%, or even 100% of the issue. An *80% sinker*, for example, is a bond issue with a sinking fund designed to retire 80% of the debt before maturity.

Example: General Production issues $10,000,000 worth of bonds, with $200,000-a-year sinking fund. Over 19 years (one year short of maturity), the company will retire $3,800,000 worth of the issue (again, assuming the bonds trade at par throughout their term). The GP bond issue might be known as a "38% sinker."

Conversion

What is "conversion"?

Some bonds may be converted into shares of the issuer's common stock. This feature is called *conversion*, and the bonds are said to be *convertible*. The convertibility is usually expressed in terms of the common stock price; that is, the $1,000 face value is convertible to common stock at *$x* per share. The dollar value of the stock, or *conversion price*, is fixed. The number of shares into which the bond is convertible can be calculated:

$$\text{Number of shares} = \frac{\text{Face value}}{\text{Conversion price}}$$

Example: The General Production 9% debenture is convertible to 50 shares of GP common at $20 per share.

$$\begin{aligned}\text{Number of shares} &= \frac{\text{Face value}}{\text{Conversion price}} \\ &= \frac{\$1,000}{\$20 \text{ per share}} = 50 \text{ shares}\end{aligned}$$

A GP bond is convertible into 50 shares.

What benefits does a convertible bond offer investors?

In general, convertible bond owners have the flexibility of becoming shareholders if the stock is yielding more *income* than the bonds.

Example: Refer to the preceding example. Ellen Lichten owns 10 GP convertible bonds, yielding 9% ($90 per year per bond, or $900 for all 10 bonds). Holders of GP common stock are being paid $3.00 per share every year. Ellen can convert her 10 bonds to 500 shares and earn $1,500 in dividends per year.

$$
\begin{aligned}
\text{Number of shares} &= \frac{\text{Face value}}{\text{Conversion price}} \\
&= \frac{10 \text{ bonds} \times \$1,000}{\$20 \text{ per share}} \\
&= \frac{\$10,000}{\$20 \text{ per share}} \\
&= 500 \text{ shares } (\times \$3 \text{ per share} = \$1,500)
\end{aligned}
$$

If the common stock is not paying dividends, when does it make sense to convert a bond?

Dividends aside, convertible bondholders might *have to* convert to avoid a loss. The reason is that, without exception, *convertible bonds are also callable*, and bonds are usually callable at prices set forth in the indenture. To see how a convertible could cause a loss of money, investors must understand the concept of "parity."

What is "parity"?

Parity is the price of the common stock at which conversion results in neither a profit nor a loss.

Example: If GP common stock is trading at $18 a share, conversion would result in a loss of value to the bondholder. The investor would wind up with 50 shares of stock worth $18 apiece, or $900 total ($18 times 50 shares), in exchange for a $1,000 bond.

Even when the common stock is equal to the conversion price, the conversion does not make sense. The investor would have to exchange a guaranteed return of principal and fixed income for the possible gain in value of the stock. It is better to wait until the stock has gained value and then convert.

It would seem that, as soon as the common stock price rises far enough above the conversion price, the investor should convert. That's true, except that in the "real" world of securities markets, the price of the bond usually rises also. As the common stock appreciates in value, other investors see the value of the convertible, attempt to buy it, and thereby create a demand for it. The bond's market value is therefore on the rise too, typically in step with the common stock. It is not uncommon for convertible bond prices to rise at such a rate as to stay almost exactly at parity—that is, at a price that makes conversion neither profitable nor a loss.

$$\frac{\text{Face value}}{\text{Conversion price}} = \frac{\text{Price of convertible}}{\text{Price of common stock}}$$

Example: GP common is appreciating in market value, and its convertible bond is being bid up along with it. The following table is a history of the price activity:

Market Prices Common Stock	Bond Price
16 (× 50 shares)	80 ($800)
18 (× 50 shares)	90 ($900)
22 (× 50 shares)	110 ($1,100)
28 (× 50 shares)	140 ($1,400)
32 (× 50 shares)	160 ($1,600)

As the table shows, the GP convertible's price rises to stay at parity with the price of the common stock. To demonstrate this, calculate the price of the convertible, given the common stock market value:

$$\frac{\text{Face value}}{\text{Conversion price}} = \frac{\text{Price of convertible}}{\text{Price of common stock}}$$

$$\frac{\$1,000}{\$20} = \frac{x}{\$16}$$

$$\$20\,x = \$16,000$$

$$x = \$80$$

This price, $800, is exactly what the GP convertible was selling for. (The other prices meet the requirements of the formula also.)

How do rising stock and bond prices lead to a loss of money for the investor?

The potential for loss arises from the fact that the issuer can call all or part of the issue at a price specified in the trust agreement.

Example: General Production 9% debentures are callable after the first 5 years. Thereafter, they may be called at the following prices per bond:

Call and Refunding Terms	
Year	Price
1–5	Noncallable
6	109 ($1,090)
7	108 ($1,080)
8	107 ($1,070)
9	106 ($1,060)
10	105 ($1,050)
11	104 ($1,040)
12	103 ($1,030)
13	102 ($1,020)
14	101 ($1,010)
15–19	100 ($1,000)

In the 9th year, the stock jumps suddenly to $27 and the convertible to $1,350.

$$\frac{\text{Face value}}{\text{Conversion price}} = \frac{\text{Price of convertible}}{\text{Price of common stock}}$$

$$\frac{\$1,000}{\$20} = \frac{x}{\$27}$$

$$\$20\,x = \$27,000$$

$$x = \$1,350 \ (135)$$

But the bond is callable at $1,060! If the issuer calls the bond at 106, the investor is out $290.

Parity price for bond	$1,350
Call price	$1,060
Loss to investor	$ 290

What can an investor do when a convertible bond's price is above the call price?

In most cases, corporations give investors ample notice (about 30 days) to take action before a bond is called. Faced with losing money on a convertible bond that is about to be called, investors may:

● *Convert the bond into stock.* Doing so provides the investor with added market value. A $1,000 bond is traded for stock that is worth more.

Example: Refer to the preceding example. After conversion, the investor has, for each bond held, 50 shares of stock trading at $27 a share. The total value of the position is $1,350 (50 shares times $27 a share).

● *Sell the bond.* The investor could probably get close to the parity price.

Example: The holder of the GP convertible can sell for a price at or close to $1,350 and use the proceeds for investment elsewhere.

KEY TERMS

Accrued interest: Interest that accrues to the holder of a bond between interest payment dates.

At par: When a bond's market value is equal to its face (or par) value, it is trading "at par."

Basis point: A unit of measurement of yield to maturity that is equal to .01%.

Bill: A fixed income security with a maturity under one year.

Bond: A debt security, issued by a corporation, that represents a loan agreement between the bondholders and the issuer.

Callable (call feature): A feature of a bond by which the issuer retains the right to retire (that is, repurchase) all or some of the bonds prior to maturity—to "call" them back.

Call protection: A specification in a bond's indenture that "protects" bondholders against the bond's being called, usually for the first five years.

Compound interest: Interest that is left to accumulate with the principal of a loan, so that interest is earning interest.

Conversion: A feature of a bond by which it may be converted into an equivalent number of shares of the issuer's common stock.

Conversion price: The price at which a convertible may be exchanged for the issuer's common stock.

Convertible: A bond that may be converted into the issuer's common stock.

Coupon (nominal) rate: The fixed rate at which a bond pays interest.

Debentures: Unsecured bonds with maturities of as much as 30 or 40 years.

Debt security (instrument): A security that represents a lender-borrower agreement, not a share of ownership (as in the case of stock): bonds, notes, bills, commercial paper, and the like.

Discount: The difference between a bond price that is below its face value and the market value itself. When a bond is trading at a price below its face value, it is said to be trading "at a discount."

Equipment trust certificates: Bonds that are secured by the issuing company's movable equipment, such as railroad cars or planes.

Face (par) value: The denomination of a bond, usually $1,000.

Fixed income securities: Securities that yield an unchanging rate of return, such as bonds. Also used to include generally *all* bonds, even those with floating or adjustable nominal rates.

Floater: A bond with a floating, or adjustable, nominal rate.

Future value: The value of a given amount of money, sometime in the future, either after earning simple or compound interest, or after inflation has eroded its buying power.

Indenture (trust agreement): The statement on the back of a bond certificate that specifies the terms and conditions of the loan.

Interest: The "cost" of borrowing money.

Interest equation: Interest = Principal × Rate × Time

Interest rate: The annual percentage of the amount loaned.

Interest rate risk: The risk that interest rates will rise, creating less of a demand for bonds already held or leading to underutilization of money out on loan.

Intermediate term: In debt securities, a maturity of from one to ten (sometimes up to 20) years. Notes have intermediate maturities.

Inverted (negative) yield curve: A graphic curve that depicts lower yields for longer maturities than those for shorter-term maturities.

Long term: In debt securities, a maturity of 20 or more years. Bonds have long-term maturities.

Maturity: The date on which a bond (or a loan) must be repaid.

Mortgage bonds: Bonds backed by real estate owned by the issuing corporation.

Negative yield curve: *See* Inverted yield curve.

Nominal rate: *See* Coupon rate.

Normal (positive) yield curve: A graphic curve that depicts higher yields on longer-term maturities than those on shorter-term maturities.

Note: A fixed income security with maturities of from one to ten years.

Par value: *See* Face value.

Parity: The price of a given common stock at which conversion of a convertible bond to the stock results in neither a profit nor a loss.

Positive yield curve: *See* Normal yield curve.

Premium: The difference between a bond price that is higher than its face value and the face value. When a bond is trading at a price above par, it is said to be trading "at a premium."

Prevailing interest rates: The general level of interest rates currently available on equivalent debt instruments.

Primary market: The market consisting of issues that are first being offered to the investing public; "primary offerings" or "initial public offerings." *See also* Secondary market.

Principal: (1) The amount of a loan. (2) The face (or par) value of a bond.

Redemption: The repayment by the issuing corporation of the principal to anyone on record as owning the bond on the maturity date.

Refunding: Using the proceeds of the sale of a new issue of bonds to repurchase an older issue.

Retiring: Terminating the lender-borrower arrangement of a bond issue.

Rolling over: The process of frequently reinvesting capital in short-term fixed income investments as they mature.

Secondary market: The market in which securities trade after they are first issued; the exchanges and the over-the-counter market. *See also* Primary market.

Security: A financial instrument, such as a stock or bond, that can be traded in the open market and whose value depends on the management of a business entity.

Secured bonds: Bonds backed by some sort of collateral—the company's plant and equipment, for instance.

Short term: In debt securities, a maturity of one year or less. Bills are short-term debt securities.

Simple interest: Interest only on the original principal, or amount loaned. Interest is paid to the lender and not left to accumulate with the principal.

Sinker: A bond issue with a sinking fund designed to retire a percentage or all of a bond issue before maturity.

Sinking fund: An account into which a corporation deposits a predetermined amount of money periodically so that it will have enough funds to repurchase all or part of a bond issue in the open market.

Spread: The difference between the yields of two fixed income securities, as depicted on the yield curve. The spread is usually expressed in terms of basis points.

Term: The length of time a loan is extended.

Trust agreement: *See* Indenture.

Underutilization: The loss of the opportunity to earn additional interest on capital because it is committed to a loan that yields less than prevailing rates would otherwise command.

Unit of trading: The smallest price increment in bond trading, ⅛-point, which is equal to $1.25, not to $.125.

Unsecured bonds: Bonds backed only by the promise of the issuing corporation. There is no specific security.

Yield curve: A graph is that plots yields against maturities.

Municipal Securities

YOU WILL LEARN TO...

- Compute your taxable equivalent yield.
- Figure the effects of the triple tax exemption on yield.
- Determine the capital gain or loss on a muni for tax purposes.
- Calculate coupon rate, current yield, and yield to maturity on municipal securities.
- Apply the yield curve to serial issues.
- Figure accrued interest when you buy or sell muni.
- Convert a muni bond quote to a dollar amount.
- Evaluate the creditworthiness of a municipal issuer.

INTRODUCTION

States, counties, cities, towns, and various other agencies of local government all need money to operate and to build public facilities. When revenues from taxes do not meet the needs of a municipality, it turns to financing through bond issues. Like a corporation in need of capital, municipalities offer debt securities (municipal bonds and notes) in an initial public offering. The proceeds of these issues are then used to run government or to construct facilities that will generate revenues for the government. After their initial offering, municipal bonds are traded actively in the so-called secondary market (specifically the over-the-counter market).

The key feature of municipal bonds is that their interest payments are usually exempt from federal income tax and sometimes from state and local taxation. Interest rates on munis are therefore generally lower than corporate bonds, because investors retain all or most of the payments.

TYPES OF MUNICIPAL SECURITIES (MUNIS)

What are municipal securities?

Municipal securities (*munis*) are debt instruments issued by states, counties, cities, towns, and other subdivisions of government other than the United States government. They are issued in $1,000 denominations, pay interest semi-annually, and trade in the secondary market (the over-the-counter market in the U.S.). They are quoted like corporate bonds, in percentages of face value.

How many types of municipal securities are there?

Municipal bonds are issued in three forms:

- General obligation bonds (GOs).
- Revenue bonds (Revs).
- Double-barrelled bonds.

   Municipalities also issue notes (short-term debt instruments) of several types:

- Tax anticipation notes (TANs) to provide funds until tax revenues are collected.
- Revenue anticipation notes (RANs) for funds until revenue on a project is in hand.
- Bond anticipation notes (BANs), which supply money until an upcoming bond issue.

Municipal notes are generally not traded or invested in by the individual. This chapter therefore focuses on municipal bonds.

How are general obligation bonds backed?

General obligation bonds are backed by the full taxing power of the issuing authority.

Example: On a State of West Virginia GO bond, the payment of interest and principal is guaranteed by the full faith and credit of the state government. The state can make payments out of the proceeds from income taxes, franchise taxes, corporate taxes, and other sources.

When towns, cities, and counties issue GOs, they can draw on an additional source of revenue—real estate or property taxes, which are generally not paid to the state. This type of tax is of a category known as *ad valorem* ("in proportion to the value").

How are revenue bonds backed?

Revenue bonds are backed by the revenues from the project financed by the muni bond issue.

Example: The investor who purchases a West Virginia Turnpike revenue bond receives interest payments out of the tolls taken along the turnpike, as well as from the commercial rentals of gas station and rest stop sites. If the turnpike does not generate enough revenue to make interest payments or to repay the loan, the State of West Virginia is not obligated to provide the funds.

Note: Some revs are backed by a special tax and are therefore called *special tax bonds*.

Example: Certain bonds issued by the Commonwealth of Puerto Rico are backed by taxes on Puerto Rican rum. Even though the Commonwealth itself is not responsible for payments of interest and principal, the rum is considered popular enough around the world to provide little risk of default.

How are double-barrelled bonds backed?

Double-barrelled munis have features of GOs and revs. Interest and principal are paid first out of revenues from the financed project. If necessary, the payments can also be made out of tax revenues collected by the issuing authority. Because the issuer is ultimately responsible for this type of muni, it is usually classified as a GO.

Example: The Massachusetts Dormitory Authority issued bonds to finance the construction of facilities for students of the state university system. The fees paid by the students are first applied to payment of interest and principal. If the fees are insufficient, the State of Massachusetts is obligated to make up the shortfall.

Are GOs less risky than revs?

Generally, GOs are considered to be of a higher quality than revs. But there are exceptions, and each issue must be considered on its own merits.

Much of the risk in investing in revs has been offset by *municipal bond insurance*, which would make up for shortfalls in revenue. The issuer pays a premium for the insurance, but the bonds are usually classified AAA by the rating services.

BENEFITS OF MUNICIPAL SECURITIES

What do munis offer investors that other debt securities do not?

Tax-exempt municipals provide investors with two benefits:

- Interest payments that are exempt from federal income taxes.
- Flexibility in selecting maturity dates that suit their individual needs.

The Tax-Exempt Feature

How much is the federal tax exemption worth to the investor?

Interest payments that are not subject to federal income taxes mean more after-tax dollars in the investor's pocket. Compared with payment rates from corporate or Treasury securities, municipal bond interest rates can be lower but yield more dollars. For each investor's tax bracket, there is a taxable interest rate that yields the same number of dollars as the tax-exempt (municipal bond) rate. That is called the *equivalent taxable rate*.

$$\text{Equivalent taxable rate} = \frac{\text{Municipal interest rate}}{100\% - \text{Federal tax bracket }(\%)}$$

Example: Barbara Hill is in the 33% federal income tax bracket. She is considering purchasing either a municipal bond with an annual interest rate of 9% or a corporate bond with a 12% rate. Both are of comparable quality, and both maturity dates fit her investment goals. The decision will be based on which yields the greater number of dollars.

$$\text{Equivalent taxable rate} = \frac{\text{Municipal interest rate}}{100\% - \text{Federal tax bracket (\%)}}$$

$$= \frac{.09}{1.00 - .33}$$

$$= \frac{.09}{.67} = .134 \text{ or } 13.4\%$$

Hill decides to buy the muni because, for the corporate bond to yield as many after-tax dollars as the muni, its coupon rate would have to be 13.4%.

Proof: The corporate bond yields $120 in interest a year ($1,000 face value times .12). Of that $120, Hill pays $39.60 in federal income taxes and retains $80.40. The muni yields $90 ($1,000 face value times .09), but Hill retains all of it.

Note: State and local taxes are ignored in both cases. With the exception that some municipals are exempt from state taxation, interest payments on both corporate and muncipal are subject to local taxes.

Are munis of greater value to higher-tax-bracket investors than they are to lower-tax-bracket investors?

Exactly. The higher an investor's tax bracket, the greater the value of the tax-exempt interest payments on a muni. To determine the relative values of various municipal rates to investors in different tax brackets, comparisons are made in terms of the taxable equivalent yield.

$$\text{Equivalent taxable rate} = \frac{\text{Municipal interest rate}}{100\% - \text{Federal tax bracket (\%)}}$$

Example: Barbara Hill, in the 33% tax bracket, and Kevin Culley, in the 15% bracket, are both considering the purchase of a 10% municipal bond. The bond will be worth more in after-tax dollars to Hill than to Culley.

For Hill:

$$\text{Equivalent taxable rate} = \frac{\text{Municipal interest rate}}{100\% - \text{Federal tax bracket (\%)}}$$

$$= \frac{.10}{1.00 - .33}$$

$$= \frac{.10}{.67} = .149 \text{ or } 14.9\%$$

For Culley:

$$\text{Equivalent taxable rate} = \frac{\text{Municipal interest rate}}{100\% - \text{Federal tax bracket (\%)}}$$

$$= \frac{.10}{1.00 - .15}$$

$$= \frac{.10}{.85} = .118 \text{ or } 11.8\%$$

Culley is more likely to find a nonexempt rate of 11.8% or better than Hill is of getting a 14.9% or better nonexempt rate. Therefore the municipal is of greater value to Hill than to Culley.

Is there a rule of thumb in comparing muni and nonexempt rates?

In general, the higher the investor's tax bracket and the higher the municipal rate, the greater the value of the municipal.

Example: In the following table:

The muni rate of:	For the income tax bracket of:			
	15%	*23%*	*28%*	*33%*
	Is equivalent to a taxable yield of:			
7%	8.24%	9.10%	9.72%	10.45%
8%	9.41%	10.39%	11.11%	11.94%
9%	10.59%	11.67%	12.50%	13.43%
10%	11.76%	12.99%	13.89%	14.93%
11%	12.94%	14.29%	15.28%	16.42%
12%	14.12%	15.58%	16.67%	17.91%

Note that, as the muni rate and the investor's tax bracket rises, so does the equivalent taxable yield. An investor in the 33% bracket, for instance, would benefit greatly from a municipal with a 12% yield. On the other hand, someone in the 15% tax bracket considering a 7% muni would not have to look far to find a nonexempt bond with a yield of 8.24% or better.

Isn't a muni with a high interest rate likely to be trading at a premium during times of low prevailing rates?

Yes. A high-yield, tax-exempt bond would probably trade at a slight premium any time. That premium would be greater—bid up by eager buyers—at a time when new issues are coming out with lower rates.

Example: A 12% muni bond trading at a time when prevailing interest rates are, say, 9% or 10% would very likely be trading at a premium. The high-bracket investor who purchases a muni at a premium must factor in the additional purchase price when calculating yield.

Are all municipal bonds exempt from federal income taxes?

No. All munis issued prior to August 7, 1986 are tax-exempt. Of the munis issued after that date, some are and some are not. There are three categories:

- If issued for a public purpose (such as to construct a bridge, a road, or the like), the muni is exempt.
- If issued for a nongovernmental purpose (such as for building dormitories, airports, and the like), interest is considered preferential and must be used in computing the potential tax liability under the alternative minimum tax.
- If issued for a private purpose (a convention center, industrial park, sports arena), the interest is subject to federal income tax.

Note: Investors seeking tax-exempt income should make certain that the munis they buy are indeed exempt.

Are municipal bonds also exempt from local taxation?

Sometimes. Generally, income from munis is exempt from state and local taxes in the state in which the securities are issued. In some states—such as New York, New Jersey, or California—local taxes can be significant. Other states, such as Delaware, New Hampshire, and Texas, impose little or no levies on income. Even some cities, such as New York City, tax income. In addition, interest from bonds issued by territories of the United States and by the Commonwealth of Puerto Rico, the Virgin Islands, and Guam is also exempt from all taxation. Exemption from federal, state, and local taxes, called a *triple tax exemption*, is an added benefit of owning municipal securities.

Example: Residents of New York City are subject to federal, state, and city income taxes. They can avoid all three, however, by purchasing municipal bonds issued within the borders of New York State. The bond does not have to be issued by New York City—it can be from Buffalo, Suffolk county, or elsewhere in the state.

How does the triple tax exemption affect overall yield?

A triple tax exemption enhances yield, more so to high-bracket investors than to those in the lower brackets. In other words, the equivalent taxable yield is raised. For that yield after a triple tax exemption:

$$\text{Equivalent taxable rate} = \frac{\text{Municipal interest rate}}{100\% - \text{Total tax rate (\%)}}$$

Example: Barbara Hill, in the 33% federal income tax bracket, also pays 5% state income taxes. She purchases a 9% muni. Her taxable equivalent yield with just a federal exemption is 13.4%. With the added benefit of saving 5% state tax, that yield becomes:

$$\begin{aligned}
\text{Equivalent taxable rate} &= \frac{\text{Municipal interest rate}}{100\% - \text{Total tax rate (\%)}} \\
&= \frac{.09}{1.00 - (.33 + .05)} \\
&= \frac{.09}{1.00 - .38}
\end{aligned}$$

$$= \frac{.09}{.62} = .145 \text{ or } 14.5\%$$

Are munis exempt from capital gains tax as well?

No. Capital gains on municipal bonds are subject to federal gains taxes, and capital losses may be used to offset gains on other securities. But the calculation of gains and losses on munis depends on the circumstances of the purchase and sale. There are three types of gain and loss computations:

- For bonds purchased at a discount and sold before maturity.
- For bonds purchased at a premium and held to maturity.
- For bonds purchased at a premium and sold before maturity.

When a muni is bought at a discount and sold before maturity, how is gain or loss figured?

For bonds purchased at a discount and resold before maturity, any appreciation in value is subject to federal capital gains taxation, and capital losses can be used to offset capital gains on other securities.

Example: Culley purchases a City of Chicago bond for $920 and one year later sells it for $980. The $60 difference between the purchase and sale price is considered a capital gain and is fully taxable.

On the other hand, if Culley had bought the muni at $840 and sold it a year later for $810, the $30 difference is a capital loss and may be used to offset capital gains elsewhere in his portfolio.

When a muni is held to maturity, how is capital gain or loss figured?

For munis bought at a premium price and held to maturity, the owner is required to amortize the premium over the years remaining to maturity. The reason is that, by law and for tax purposes, the difference between the premium price and the return of principal is not considered a loss. In the absence of such a requirement, clever investors could purchase high-yielding bonds at premium prices, collect the interest payments to maturity, and then use the difference between price and par to avoid capital gains taxes on other securities. So, for tax purposes, the cost of the bond is reduced each year by the following formula:

$$\text{Annual amortization} = \frac{\text{Premium}}{\text{Number of years remaining to maturity}}$$

Example: Investor Culley purchases a muni at 110 ($1,100) with exactly five years left to maturity. The premium is $100 (price of $1,100 less face value $1,000). Culley is required to reduce the premium by $20 each year:

$$\text{Annual amortization} = \frac{\text{Premium}}{\text{Number of years remaining to maturity}}$$

$$= \frac{\$100}{5} = \$20$$

In the year of maturity, Culley has a capital loss of zero.

What is the gain/loss calculation on a muni bought at a premium and sold before maturity?

The premium must be amortized over the *holding period*, that is, over the time that the owner holds the bond. If the bond is sold at less than the purchase price, the remainder of the premium at the time of sale, if any exists, may be considered a capital loss.

$$\text{Annual amortization} = \frac{\text{Premium}}{\text{Number of years remaining to maturity}}$$

$$\text{Capital gain} = \text{Sale price} - \left(\text{Purchase price} - \text{Amortized part of premium}\right)$$

$$\text{Capital loss} = \left(\text{Purchase price} - \text{Amortized part of premium}\right) - \text{Sale price}$$

Example: Culley purchases a muni at 110 ($1,100) with five years to maturity, and sells it three years later at 105 ($1,050). During the holding period he amortizes the premium:

$$\text{Annual amortization} = \frac{\text{Premium}}{\substack{\text{Number of years} \\ \text{remaining to maturity}}}$$

$$= \frac{\$100}{5} = \$20$$

For three years, Culley reduces the cost of the bond by $20, for a total reduction, or amortization, of $60.

$$\substack{\text{Capital} \\ \text{gain}} = \substack{\text{Sale} \\ \text{price}} - \left(\substack{\text{Purchase} \\ \text{price}} - \substack{\text{Amortized} \\ \text{part of} \\ \text{premium}} \right)$$

$$= \$1,050 - (\$1,100 - \$60)$$

$$= \$1,050 - \$1,040 = \$10$$

Culley has a capital gain of $10 for every bond owned.

Example: If Culley sells the bond in three years for $1,150, he would have a capital gain of $110 per bond:

$$\substack{\text{Capital} \\ \text{gain}} = \substack{\text{Sale} \\ \text{price}} - \left(\substack{\text{Purchase} \\ \text{price}} - \substack{\text{Amortized} \\ \text{part of} \\ \text{premium}} \right)$$

$$= \$1,150 - (\$1,100 - \$60)$$

$$= \$1,150 - \$1,040 = \$110$$

How do I know the nominal yield of a municipal bond?

Nominal yield is found in the financial listings next to the name of the bond.

Example: The nominal (or coupon) yield is boldfaced in the following listing:

Tax-Exempt Bonds

Issue	Coupon	Mat	Price	Bid Chg	Yld
Atlanta Rpd Trans Auth	**7.250**	07-01-10	100½	...	7.20

How is the coupon payment on a municipal bond calculated?

Investors who buy municipal bonds are generally looking for a flow of tax-free income in the form of the semiannual interest payments.

$$\text{Annual interest (\$)} = \text{Face value} \times \text{Coupon (nominal) rate (\%)}$$

Example: Refer to the preceding example. Each year for the term of the Atlanta Rapid Transit Authority bond, holders will receive semiannual interest payments at the coupon rate, 7.250%.

$$
\begin{aligned}
\text{Annual interest (\$)} &= \text{Face value} \times \text{Coupon (nominal) rate (\%)} \\
&= \$1,000 \times .0725 = \$72.50 \text{ per year}
\end{aligned}
$$

Since muni bond interest payments are made twice a year, each payment would be $36.25 ($72.50 divided by 2).

At maturity, the bondholders are repaid their $1,000 principal.

Note: The semiannual payments on bonds are a form of simple interest. The interest is not added to principal for compounding.

Do all munis make their semiannual payments at the same times of the year?

No. Payments can be made in any two months of the year. Usually payments are made on the 1st or 15th day of the payment months, but other days are possible. The months in which payments are to be made are generally indicated by their first initials.

J&J	January and July
F&A	February and August
M&S	March and September
A&O	April and October
M&N	May and November
J&D	June and December

How is the "current yield" on a municipal bond calculated?

Current yield is the yield that you get, expressed as a percentage, when you divide the fixed interest payments by the purchase price (not face value). The bondholder receives the fixed interest payment (which is a percentage of the face value), regardless of how much the bond cost. Yet the purchase price is the real amount of the investment, not the face value; and the actual yield should be calculated as a percentage of that investment. Because current yield is based on the fluctuating market value of the bond, it can, and usually does, change often, as the market price of the bond rises or falls in the market.

$$\text{Current yield (\%)} = \frac{\text{Interest (\$)}}{\text{Current price (\$)}}$$

Note that the relationship between current yield and price is *inverse*. That is, as price increases, current yield declines, and vice versa.

Example: A 10% Commonwealth of Massachusetts $1,000 municipal bond is purchased at 103 ($1,030). What is the current yield?

Nominal yield ($) = Face value × Nominal rate (%)

$\qquad\qquad\qquad = \$1,000 \times .10 = \$100$

$\text{Current yield (\%)} = \dfrac{\text{Interest (\$)}}{\text{Current price (\$)}}$

$\qquad\qquad\qquad = \dfrac{\$100}{\$1,030} = .0971 \text{ or } 9.71\%$

For someone who purchased the bond for a price of $1,030, the current yield is 9.71%. For that holder, the current yield will not change because the purchase price will not change.

Note that the current yield is greater than the nominal yield because the investor paid more than face value for the bond, which was trading at a premium. So the fixed return is worth less, percentagewise, to the purchaser.

The current yield on the bond can change over its lifetime. That's why it is called the "current" yield. If the bond drops in market value to 97 ($970), its current yield would change also.

$$\text{Current yield (\%)} = \frac{\text{Interest (\$)}}{\text{Current price (\$)}}$$

$$= \frac{\$100}{\$970} = .1031 \text{ or } 10.31\%$$

Note that, as the price declines, current yield increases. For anyone purchasing this bond at 97 ($970), the current yield is 10.31%. The current yield is higher than the nominal rate because the bond is purchased at a discount. The "savings" in price from the face value is a factor in calculating the current yield.

What is "yield to maturity"?

The computation of *yield to maturity (YTM)*, like current yield, takes the purchase price into account, but it also includes the eventual repayment of principal (face value, $1,000) if the bond is held to maturity.

● If the purchase price is lower than par (that is, discounted), then the bondholder receives more than what was paid, and this extra amount must be considered part of the overall yield.

Example: If a $1,000 face value municipal bond costs $900, the $100 difference between the price and par must be considered additional yield at maturity.

● If the price is higher (that is, at a premium), the bondholder is paid less, and the added cost lessens the yield.

Example: If a $1,000 bond is sold for $1,100, then the additional $100 in price has to be deducted from the yield at maturity.

● With a purchase price at par, yield to maturity is the same as current yield, which in turn is the same as the nominal yield.

Example: If a $1,000 bond sells for $1,000, then nothing needs to be added or deducted from the yield at maturity.

And, since the purchase price (the basis of the current yield formula) equals par value, the current yield is the same as the nominal yield.

Yield to maturity is a better assessment of return than current yield because it considers all the factors affecting yield—interest rate, market price, and time to maturity.

What's the easiest way to find a muni's yield to maturity?

For municipal bonds, the yield to maturity is part of the financial listing. For about 30 of the largest muni issues, you can look up YTM in the newspaper. Professional muni investors also have access to the *Blue List*, sometimes known as the *Blue Book*, which contains information on most muni issues. For each issue, this list contains face value, issuer, nominal rate, yield to maturity, and the dealers who "make markets" in the issue.

Example: In the following quotation, "Yld" means "yield to maturity."

Tax-Exempt Bonds

Issue	Coupon	Mat	Price	Bid Chg	Yld
Atlanta Rpd Trans Auth	7.250	07-01-10	100½	...	**7.20**

How is a municipal bond's yield to maturity calculated?

For munis that are not listed in the financial news, the investor may use the yield to maturity rule of thumb formula. The calculation for YTM entails two steps:

● Spread out, or *prorate*, the premium or discount over the years remaining to maturity.

$$\text{Prorated premium/discount} = \frac{\text{Difference between face value and price}}{\text{Years remaining to maturity}}$$

- Apply the YTM formula.

$$\text{Yield to maturity} = \frac{\text{Nominal rate} + \begin{pmatrix} + \text{ Prorated discount (\$) or} \\ - \text{ Prorated premium (\$)} \end{pmatrix}}{(\text{Price} + \text{Face value})/2}$$

Note: This formula is called the *rule of thumb* because it is not as exact as the true formula, which involves the use of calculus and a computer. (That is why the yield to maturity in the financial listings is never the same as calculated by the rule of thumb method.) This method, however, serves the purpose for the individual investor, particularly if it is expressed in terms of days to maturity.

Example: A Commonwealth of Massachusetts $1,000 municipal bond is purchased at 103 ($1,030), pays 10% nominal interest ($100), and has exactly 15 years remaining to maturity. What is the yield to maturity?

- *Prorate the premium.*

$$\begin{aligned} \text{Prorated premium/discount} &= \frac{\text{Difference between face value and price}}{\text{Years remaining to maturity}} \\ &= \frac{\$1,030 - \$1,000}{15 \text{ years}} \\ &= \frac{\$30}{15 \text{ years}} = \$2 \text{ per year} \end{aligned}$$

The bond is worth an additional $2 per year in yield.

- *Apply the YTM formula:*

$$\begin{aligned} \text{Yield to maturity} &= \frac{\text{Nominal rate} + \begin{pmatrix} + \text{ Prorated discount (\$) or} \\ - \text{ Prorated premium (\$)} \end{pmatrix}}{(\text{Price} + \text{Face value})/2} \\ &= \frac{\$100 - \$2}{(\$1,030 + \$1,000)/2} \end{aligned}$$

$$= \frac{\$98}{\$2,030/2} = \frac{\$98}{\$1,015} = .0996 \text{ or } 9.96\%$$

If held to maturity, this bond's yield to maturity will be
9.96%. The bondholder, having bought the bond at a
premium, receives a yield that is less than the nominal rate
(10%).

Can yield to maturity change like current yield?

Yes. Yield to maturity changes from moment to moment in
the marketplace, as a bond's price goes up or down. For
two different investors who purchased the same bond at
different times, the yields to maturity are probably going to
be different for two reasons: The purchase prices may be
different, and the times remaining to maturity will certainly
be different.

• Yield increases as price decreases, and vice versa.
• Yield on a discounted bond increases as the time to
  maturity decreases.
• Yield on a bond selling at a premium decreases as the
  time to maturity decreases.

Example: Refer to the preceding example. The 10%,
$1,000 municipal bond is purchased at a different price, 95
($950), and with exactly 7 years remaining to maturity.
What is the yield to maturity?

• *Prorate the discount:*

$$\frac{\text{Prorate}}{\text{premium/discount}} = \frac{\text{Difference between face value and price}}{\text{Years remaining to maturity}}$$

$$= \frac{\$1,000 - \$950}{7 \text{ years}}$$

$$= \frac{\$50}{7 \text{ years}} = \$7.14 \text{ per year}$$

The bond is worth an additional $7.14 per year in yield.

• *Apply the YTM formula.*

$$\text{Yield to maturity} = \frac{\text{Nominal rate} + \left(\begin{array}{l}+ \text{ Prorated discount (\$) or} \\ - \text{ Prorated premium (\$)}\end{array}\right)}{(\text{Price} + \text{Face value})/2}$$

$$= \frac{\$100 + \$7.14}{(\$950 + \$1,000)/2}$$

$$= \frac{\$107.14}{\$1,950/2} = \frac{\$107.14}{\$975.00} = .1099 \text{ or } 10.99\%$$

If held to maturity, this bond's yield to maturity will be 10.99%. The bondholder, having bought the bond at a discount, enjoys a yield that is greater than the nominal rate (10%). The YTM is higher than it was for the investor who bought the bond at $1,030 8 years earlier. In this case, both the lower (discount) price and the shorter time to maturity increased the yield. (If the bond had been bought at a premium, the shorter time to maturity would have lessened yield.)

What if the bond is not bought with an exact number of years remaining to maturity?

In the real world, bonds are usually *not* bought exactly on the date of their issuance. In these cases, the prorating and YTM formulas are restated using months, weeks, or—as is usually the case—days remaining to maturity.

$$\text{Prorated premium/discount} = \frac{\text{Difference between face value and price}}{\text{Days remaining to maturity}}$$

$$\text{Yield to maturity} = \frac{\text{Nominal rate}/365 + \left(\begin{array}{l}+ \text{ Prorated discount (\$) or} \\ - \text{ Prorated premium (\$)}\end{array}\right)}{(\text{Price} + \text{Face value})/(2 \times 365 \text{ days})}$$

Note: This formula is called the *rule of thumb* because it is not as exact as the true formula, which involves the use of calculus and a computer. (That is why the yield to maturity in the financial listings is never the same as calculated by the rule of thumb method.) This method, however, serves the purpose for the individual investor, particularly if it is expressed in terms of days to maturity.

Example: The same 10%, $1,000 municipal bond is purchased at 95 ($950). It is purchased so that the buyer becomes the owner of record on December 15 of 19X1 and maturity is on April 5 of 19X5. What is the yield to maturity? The first step is to determine the number of days to maturity:

19X1	
December	17 (the 15th is counted)
19X2	365
19X3	365
19X4	365
19X5	365
January	31
February	28
March	31
April	5
Total days to maturity	1,572

● *Prorate the discount.*

$$\text{Prorate premium/discount} = \frac{\text{Difference between face value and price}}{\text{Days remaining to maturity}}$$

$$= \frac{\$1,000 - \$950}{1,572 \text{ days}}$$

$$= \frac{\$50}{1,572 \text{ days}} = \$.0318066 \text{ per day}$$

● *Apply the YTM formula.*

$$\text{Yield to maturity} = \frac{\dfrac{\text{Nominal rate}}{365} + \left(\begin{array}{l}+ \text{ Prorated discount (\$) or} \\ - \text{ Prorated premium (\$)}\end{array}\right)}{(\text{Price} + \text{Face value})/(2 \times 365 \text{ days})}$$

$$= \frac{(\$100/365 \text{ days}) + \$.0318066}{(\$950 + \$1,000)/(2 \times 365)}$$

$$= \frac{\$.27397 + \$.0318066}{\$1,950/(730 \text{ days})} = \frac{\$.305777}{\$.267123} = \begin{array}{l} .1144 \\ \text{or} \\ 11.44\% \end{array}$$

If held to maturity, this bond's yield to maturity will be 11.44%. The bondholder, having bought the bond at a discount, enjoys a yield that is greater than the nominal rate (10%).

Note: This formula is called the *rule of thumb* because it is not as exact as the true formula, which involves the use of calculus and a computer. (That is why the yield to maturity in the financial listings is never the same as calculated by the rule of thumb method.) This method, however, serves the purpose for the individual investor, particularly if it is expressed in terms of days to maturity.

Flexible Maturities

Why are muni maturities more "flexible" than maturities on other fixed income instruments?

A municipal issue usually contains at least some bonds whose maturities are staggered over a number of years. In any single issue, therefore, an investor is likely to find a maturity date that suits a need in the overall investment program. This type of offering is called a *serial issue*. It is distinguished from the *term* portion of the issue, in which all of the bonds mature at the same time.

Example: In 1987, the Commonwealth of Massachusetts raised $200,000,000 by issuing general obligation bonds. Of that amount, $179,375,000 is in the form of serial bonds, listed on the prospectus as follows:

Amounts, Maturities, Rates, and Yields or Prices

Amount	Due	Rate	Yield or Price
$11,035,000	1988	5%	NR
$11,030,000	1989	5%	4.50%
$11,025,000	1990	5%	100
$11,015,000	1991	5.25%	100
. . .			
$10,660,000	1999	7%	100
$10,655,000	2000	7%	7.05%
$10,565,000	2001	7.10%	7.15%
$10,560,000	2002	7.20%	7.25%
$ 9,440,000	2003	7.25%	7.30%
$ 8,530,000	2004	7.25%	7.35%

$20,625, 7.25% Term Bonds due July 1, 2007 @ 97½

Given the serial and term parts of the issue, the investor has a selection of maturities that run for 19 years.

In a serial issue, why do the yields to maturity and coupon yields rise as the maturities get longer?

Each maturity date in a serial issue carries a different price and yield to maturity, both of which are associated with the time to maturity.

- The coupon rates rise because the money is being borrowed for successively longer terms and the principal is longer at risk of being underutilized if prevailing rates rise in the future. Bond purchasers therefore demand higher rates in return for the greater risk. If the rates were plotted on a graph against maturities, the result would be a "normal" yield curve.

- The yields to maturity rise because the short-term bonds sell at a premium (decreasing YTM), the intermediate-term bonds are offered at par (making the nominal rate the same as YTM), and the long-term bonds carry discounts from face value (which enhance yield).

Example: In the offering by the Commonwealth of Massachusetts:

Amounts, Maturities, Rates, and Yields or Prices

	Amount	Due	Rate	Yield or Price
Short	$11,035,000	1988	5%	NR
term	$11,030,000	1989	5%	4.50%
Inter-	$11,025,000	1990	5%	100
mediate	$11,015,000	1991	5.25%	100
term				
		. . .		
	$10,660,000	1999	7%	100
Long	$10,655,000	2000	7%	7.05%
term	$10,565,000	2001	7.10%	7.15%
	$10,560,000	2002	7.20%	7.25%
	$ 9,440,000	2003	7.25%	7.30%
	$ 8,530,000	2004	7.25%	7.35%

Longest $20,625, 7.25% term bonds due July 1, 2007 @ 97½ term

- One of the *short-term* loans due in 1988 (one year after the offering) carry no price. These were "NR"—not reoffered, possibly because the syndicate handling the offering must have already had orders for them. The other short-maturity 1989 bonds carry a 5% coupon rate, but the yield to maturity (price) is only 4.50%. Buyers of these bonds are paying a premium (which decreases YTM) for the short-term rate.

- The *intermediate* bonds maturing from 1990 to 1999 are all offered at par (100, or $1,000), making the coupon rate the same as the yield to maturity. In these cases, stating the price as "100" is the same as saying that the yield to maturity is the same as the coupon rate. The same bonds could be quoted as follows:

Amount	Due	Rate	Yield or Price
		. . .	
$11,025,000	1990	5%	5%
$11,015,000	1991	5.25%	5.25%
		. . .	
$10,660,000	1999	7%	7%
		. . .	

- The *long-term* bonds, from 2000 to 2004, are all offered at successively greater discounts, with correspondingly greater yields to maturity.

- The *longest-term* bonds (those that go to the full "term") have the highest nominal rates.

How can serial and term bonds be compared on an equal basis?

For term bonds (the longest-term bonds in the issue), prices are expressed as percentages of face value. To compare the two portions of the issue, convert the price of the term bonds to a yield to maturity.

$$\text{Prorated premium/discount} = \frac{\text{Difference between face value and price}}{\text{Years remaining to maturity}}$$

$$\text{Yield to maturity} = \frac{\text{Nominal rate} + \left(\begin{array}{l}+ \text{ Prorated discount (\$) or} \\ - \text{ Prorated premium (\$)}\end{array}\right)}{(\text{Price} + \text{Face value})/2}$$

Example: Refer to the preceding example. The 7.25%, 2007 term bonds are being offered at 97½ ($975). There are 20 years to maturity (1987 to 2007), and the bond pays $72.50 annually ($1,000 times .0725).

● *Prorate the discount.*

$$\begin{aligned} \text{Prorated premium/discount} &= \frac{\text{Difference between face value and price}}{\text{Years remaining to maturity}} \\ &= \frac{\$1,000 \text{ face value} - \$975}{20} \\ &= \frac{\$25}{20} = \$1.25 \text{ per year} \end{aligned}$$

The prorated discount is $1.25 per year.

● *Apply the YTM formula.*

$$\begin{aligned} \text{Yield to maturity} &= \frac{\text{Nominal rate} + \left(\begin{array}{l}+ \text{ Prorated discount (\$) or} \\ - \text{ Prorated premium (\$)}\end{array}\right)}{(\text{Price} + \text{Face value})/2} \\ &= \frac{\$72.50 + \$1.25}{(\$975 + \$1,000)/2} \\ &= \frac{\$73.75}{\$1,975/2} \\ &= \frac{\$73.75}{\$987.50} = .747 \text{ or } 7.47\% \end{aligned}$$

The YTM for the term portion of the issue is 7.47%. This can be compared with the YTMs of the various maturities of the serial bonds.

Note: This formula is called the *rule of thumb* because it is not as exact as the true formula, which involves the use of calculus and a computer. (That is why the yield to maturity in the financial listings is never the same as calculated by the rule of thumb method.) This method, however, serves the purpose for the individual investor, particularly if it is expressed in terms of days to maturity.

Why is it so important to have varying maturity dates in a portfolio?

An effectively hedged portfolio of municipal securities is diversified in many ways. It has a balance of GO bonds and revs (with their related degrees of risk and reward), geographically distributed issues (from various states, territories, and so on), and various ratings (again with related risk/reward ratios). Still another way to diversify a portfolio is mixing maturities, thereby mixing rates of return. As interest rates rise and fall over the years, each municipal bond carries a nominal rate that reflects the rates prevailing when it was issued. A lack of diversified maturities exposes the portfolio holder to the risk of underperformance.

Example: An investor purchases a portfolio of municipal securities, all of which mature in 20 years and carry a nominal yield of 7.5%. Five years after the purchase, prevailing interest rates have risen to the extent that current muni issues are paying 9%. The portfolio holder suffers in two ways. First, the 7.5% munis have undoubtedly declined in the market to a price that reflects a yield of maturity of 9%. Selling the bonds would have to take place at a loss. Second, the investor has no liquidity. If some of the securities were higher-yielding, they could be liquidated at a profit and the proceeds used to purchase 9% bonds.

ACCRUED INTEREST

Do munis make semiannual interest payments?

Yes, just as corporate and Treasury bonds do: January and June (J&J), February and August (F&A), and so on.

Is accrued interest calculated for munis as it is for other bonds?

The formula is the same, but municipals count each month as 30 days and a year as 360 days. The accrual, or seller's holding, period extends from the day after the last accrual period ends to the day before the settlement date of the trade. In most cases, munis are traded "regular way," which means that the trade settles 5 business days (7 calendar days, barring holidays) after the trade.

Accrued interest = Principal × Rate × Time

Example: On September 12, Investor Hill purchases a $1,000 8% M&N State of Arizona GO bond at 101½ ($1,015). The bond pays $40 interest twice a year on May 1 and November 1. Because Hill buys the bond between interest payment dates, interest has accrued to the seller for the months of May through August and part of September. Hill has to pay the seller the interest accrued for that period and then collect the next full interest payment in November.

First, the number of days in the seller's holding period has to be added up:

May	30 days
June	30 days
July	30 days
August	30 days
September	18 days
Total	138 days

There are 18 days in September because the trade took place on the 12th and settlement will take place on the 19th (5 business days and 7 calendar days later). But the settlement date is not considered part of the accrual period.

Now the formula can be applied:

$$\text{Accrued interest} = \text{Principal} \times \text{Rate} \times \text{Time}$$

$$= \$1,000 \times .08 \times \frac{138 \text{ days}}{360 \text{ days}}$$

$$= \$80 \times \frac{138 \text{ days}}{360 \text{ days}} = \$30.67$$

Hill owes the seller $30.67 in accrued interest. Her total payment to the seller is $1,045.67 (the price of $1,015 plus $30.67 in accrued interest). On November 1, Hill will receive the full semiannual interest payment of $40. The $9.33 difference between what she paid the seller ($30.67) and the interest payment ($40) represents the part of the interest period during which she owned the bond.

MUNICIPAL BOND QUOTATIONS

Are munis quoted like other bonds?

During the initial offering, muni prices are quoted in terms of yield to maturity. In the secondary market, many issues (usually the revenue term issues) are quoted on a *dollar price* basis, that is, as a percentage of face value.

Dollar price = Price (%) × Face value

Example: Municipal bonds issued by the Atlanta Rapid Transit Authority pay a nominal rate of 7.250%, mature on July 1, 2010, and are trading at 101½. The yield to maturity based on the price is 7.20%.

TAX-EXEMPT BONDS

Issue	Coupon	Mat	Price	Bid Chg	Yld
Atlanta Rpd Trans Auth	7.250	07-01-10	100½	...	7.20

The dollar price of 101½ is equal to a percentage—101½%—of the face value.

Dollar price = Price (%) × Face value
= 1.015 × $1,000 = $1,015

Note: The yield in the rightmost column is a yield to maturity calculated to the day, usually automatically by means of a sophisticated formula.

MUNICIPAL SECURITIES FUNDS

*Do municipal bond funds work like other types of
mutual trusts?*

Like any investment company, municipal bond funds pool
the capital of many individuals to take positions in munis.
Initial investments can be as low as $1,000, and subsequent
investments can be as little as $50. Through such funds,
individual investors can enjoy safety of principal, diversification, and the benefits of professional money management.

The typical muni bond fund is not, however, a mutual
fund, which is an incorporated business. More often, the
fund takes the form of a *unit investment trust*, which invests
in a portfolio of municipal securities. The sponsor of the
trust determines the size of the portfolio and then purchases
the securities, placing them into an accumulation account.
Once the trust has reached the intended size, the sponsor
offers investors the opportunity to share in the trust by
buying *units* of participation. Unit holders are paid a pro-
portional share of the income from the munis and a return of
principal as the bonds mature. A popular type of trust
invests in municipals issued exclusively within one state.

As for repayment of principal, trusts have two options.
One is to distribute principal repayments among unit holders. When the last of the bonds have matured, the trust
ceases to exist. The other is to use the principal of maturing
issues to purchase new ones, thereby keeping the trust in
existence.

In the latter case, unit holders wishing to leave the trust
would have to sell their units to other investors at the
current market value, which might be more or less than the
original purchase price.

Do muni funds involve a sales charge?

Many muni funds that are incorporated as mutual funds
exact a sales charge, or *load*. This is the fee for purchasing
shares.

Example: An individual purchases $1,000 worth of shares
in a muni trust, which is averaging a 9% return. The load is

2%. The first year's yield is immediately reduced to 7% (9% average return less 2% load).

Do muni funds involve other charges?

Municipal bond funds that are organized as corporations, not as trusts, have their portfolios managed. (In trusts, the portfolio is not managed.) These funds may charge *management fees*, which erode return on investment and must be weighed against the benefits of performance, diversification, and liquidity.

Example: Investor Stein holds $10,000 worth of units in a muni fund yielding 9%, for a dollar return of $900. The fund charges a management fee of .5% of Stein's holding in the fund. That fee amounts to $50 a year (.005 times $10,000), reducing the dollar return to $850.

What benefits does a muni fund provide that other funds do not?

In addition to professional management, diversified portfolio, and liquidity, which all mutual funds have to offer, muni funds provide investors with interest income that is exempt from federal income taxes and that may be exempt from state and local taxes. The taxable equivalent yield rates of such tax-free income can be difficult to attain outside of such funds.

Example: Investor Stein, a resident of New York State, purchases units in a fund that invests exclusively in municipal bonds issued within the borders of New York State, yielding 9.32% annually. She is in the 33% federal tax bracket and the 5% state tax bracket. Her return from the fund is exempt from federal income taxes *and* from New York State taxes.

$$\text{Equivalent taxable rate} = \frac{\text{Municipal interest rate}}{100\% - \text{Federal and State tax brackets (\%)}}$$

$$= \frac{.0932}{1.00 - (.33 + .05)}$$

$$= \frac{.0932}{1.00 - .38}$$

$$= \frac{.0932}{.62} = .1503 \text{ or } 15.03\%$$

ANALYZING MUNICIPAL SECURITIES

Can the individual investor do anything to analyze the investment-worthiness of munis?

The major services analyze and research muni issues before assigning ratings. The individual investor, however, can perform, or at least be aware of, some of the analytical methods employed by the services.

How does an investor determine the capability of a municipal issuer to make interest payments and ultimately repay the loan?

There are several computations to make such a determination:

For general obligation bonds:

● The ratio of debt service to the municipality's total budget.
● The percentage of debt to the value of taxable property.

For revenue bonds:

● Revenues required to service the debt.

How is the ratio of debt service to total budget calculated?

The municipality's debt service obligation (which includes both interest payments and the repayment of principal) is divided by its overall budget.

$$\text{Debt service (\%)} = \frac{\text{Interest payments} + \text{Principal repayments}}{\text{Total budget}}$$

According to the so-called *25% guideline*, in any given year, the issuer's debt service percentage should not exceed 25% of its total budget. A percentage under this level is considered a positive sign. Anything over it is regarded as negative in that tax revenues may fall short, resulting in the need for special taxes and assessment—or even in new debt to service the old.

Example: In one year, Climax County, Arkansas has $10,000,000 of bonds maturing. In addition, it has to service all its outstanding debt with $6,500,000 worth of interest payments. The county's debt service for the year is $16,500,000: the total of the maturing issue ($10,000,000) and interest payments ($6,500,000). The total county budget for the year is $82,000,000, including every obligation—salaries, improvements, social programs, road work, and so on.

$$\text{Debt service (\%)} = \frac{\text{Interest payments} + \text{Principal repayments}}{\text{Total budget}}$$

$$= \frac{\$6,500,000 + \$10,000,000}{\$82,000,000}$$

$$= \frac{\$16,500,000}{\$82,000,000} = \begin{matrix} .2012 \text{ or} \\ 20.12\% \end{matrix}$$

Climax County is well within the 25% guideline.

Example: Refer to the previous example. If Climax County's budget is $52,000,000:

$$\text{Debt service (\%)} = \frac{\text{Interest payments} + \text{Principal repayments}}{\text{Total budget}}$$

$$= \frac{\$6,500,000 + \$10,000,000}{\$52,000,000}$$

$$= \frac{\$16,500,000}{\$52,000,000} = \begin{matrix} .3173 \text{ or} \\ 31.73\% \end{matrix}$$

This percentage of debt service puts the county's ability to pay in doubt.

How is the percentage of debt to the value of taxable property computed?

The amount of taxable property within a municipality is a good measure of its financial capability. If the amount of debt incurred by that community is divided by the total value of taxable property, the resulting percentage is an effective way to evaluate the quality of the debt.

$$\text{Debt (\%)} = \frac{\text{Outstanding debt}}{\text{Value of taxable property}}$$

A conservative standard is that the average amount of incurred debt should not exceed 10% of the value of taxable property.

Example: The city of Leadville, Illinois, has outstanding debt of $16,450,000 and an assessed value of property within the city of $194,320,000.

$$\text{Debt (\%)} = \frac{\text{Outstanding debt}}{\text{Value of taxable property}}$$
$$= \frac{\$16,450,000}{\$194,320,000} = .8465 \text{ or } 8.47\%$$

Leadville's percentage of debt is within the 10% guideline.

Note: The information for these calculations can be found in the official statement, which is available when larger issues are offered.

How can an investor determine whether a financed project will generate enough money to cover the debt service on a revenue bond?

This is a multistep process, which involves both computation and common sense. Questions must be asked, such as:

● What is the cost of construction?
● How long will construction take?
● Have cost overruns been factored in?
● Does the amount of the issue cover start-up expenses?
● Once the facility is constructed, what will the operating costs be?
● What is the probability that the facility will be used as much as is needed to generate the revenues required to pay all expenses, interest, and principal? A rule of thumb

is that the financed facility's revenues should equal 120% of all expenses, to allow for unexpected increases in expenses.

Minimum revenues = 1.2 × Expenses

Example: The Tri-County Bridge Authority, a municipal authority of the State of Maine, intends to construct a bridge over the Roaring Red River. It will issue bonds to finance construction, and all revenues from the facility will go toward paying expenses, interest, and ultimately principal.

● *What is the cost of construction?* An engineering survey estimates $50,000,000.

● *How long will construction take?* The same survey estimates three years, so that the bonds maturing within the first three years ($4,500,000 worth of principal) will have to be repaid before revenues are being earned. In addition, some $15,000,000 in interest payments will also have to be made in those three years.

● *Have cost overruns been factored in?* To allow for errors in the engineer's study, $15,500,000 (roughly 30% of total cost) is added to the construction estimate.

● *Does the amount of the issue cover start-up expenses?* So far, the facility is going to cost:

Construction	$50,000,000
Repayment of principal	$ 4,500,000
Interest payments during construction	$15,000,000
Overruns	$15,500,000
Total	$85,000,000

If the issue is for less than this figure, the probability of even completing construction is lessened.

● *Once the facility is constructed, what will the operating costs be?* Once the bridge is open, the so-called *flow of funds* can begin, paying for operation and maintenance, debt service, a reserve maintenance ("emergency") fund, and a replacement fund. All these items are estimated to total $5,000,000 a year.

● *What is the probability that the facility will be used as much as is needed to generate the revenues required to pay all expenses, interest, and principal?* According to the rule of thumb for expenses, the facility needs to generate 120% of its total expenses.

$$\text{Minimum revenues} = 1.2 \times \text{Expenses}$$
$$= 1.2 \times \$5,000,000 = \$6,000,000$$

The bridge has to furnish $6,000,000 in revenues every year. How will that be done? If the engineering survey projects 1,500,000 trips across the bridge in a year, the tolls clearly can be no less than $4 ($6,000,000 minimum revenue divided by 1,500,000 trips). If this is considerably more than "the traffic will bear," the facility may not be able to pay its debt service.

KEY TERMS

Bond anticipation notes (BANs): Short-term debt securities issued by municipalities to supply money until the revenues of an upcoming bond issue are available.

Capital gain: The appreciation in market value of a bond or other security over a year or more.

Capital loss: The loss of market value of a bond or other security over a year or more.

Dollar price basis: The form in which municipal securities are quoted in the secondary market; that is, prices are quoted as percentages of face value.

Double-barrelled bonds: Municipal bonds with features of GOs and revs. Interest and principal are paid first out of revenues from the financed project. If necessary, the payments can also be made out of tax revenues collected by the issuing authority.

Equivalent taxable rate: For each investor's tax bracket, the interest rate on a taxable debt security that yields the same number of dollars as the tax-exempt (municipal bond) rate.

Flow of funds: The generation of revenues from a project financed by a municipal bond issue, once it is up and running.

General obligation bonds (GOs): Municipal bonds that are backed by the full taxing power of the issuing authority.

Holding period: The period during which an investor owns, or holds, a bond.

Load: The sales charge an investor pays when buying shares of some mutual funds.

Municipal bond insurance: Insurance on municipal securities that guarantees payment of interest and principal.

Municipal securities (munis): Debt instruments issued by states, counties, cities, towns, and other subdivisions of government other than the United States government.

Percentage of debt to the value of taxable property: The percentage of debt in a municipality's budget, compared to the amount of taxable property within its jurisdiction.

Ratio of debt service: The ratio between a municipality's debt service obligation (which includes both interest payments and the repayment of principal) and its overall budget.

Revenue anticipation notes (RANs): Short-term debt securities issued by municipalities until revenue on a project is in hand.

Revenue bonds (revs): Municipal bonds that are backed by the revenues from the project financed by the bond issue.

Revs: *See* Revenue bonds.

Serial issue: In a municipal bond issue, the bonds with staggered maturities and varying yields.

Special tax bonds: Municipal bonds that are backed by the proceeds of a special tax.

Tax anticipation notes (TANs): Short-term debt securities issued by municipalities to provide funds until tax revenues are collected.

Term bonds: The portion of a municipal bond issue in which all of the bonds mature at the same time.

Triple tax exemption: With regard to municipal bond interest payments, exemption from federal, state, and local taxes.

25% guideline: A guideline that states, in any given year, the issuer's debt service percentage should not exceed 25% of its total budget.

Unit investment trust: A fund organized as a trust, not as a corporation, that pools investors' capital in a portfolio of securities. Unit trusts are not professionally managed, as are mutual funds (open end investment companies).

Unit of participation: A share in a municipal bond unit trust fund.

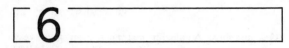

6

U.S. Treasury and Government Agency Securities

YOU WILL LEARN...

- How Treasury bills, notes, and bonds are issued and priced.
- What the financial quotations for these and other securities mean in dollar values.
- How accrued interest is computed on federal securities.
- How discounted instruments, including zero coupon bonds, are priced and traded

INTRODUCTION

The federal government is the biggest issuer of debt instruments in the world. The Treasury Department issues bills, notes, and bonds continually, while government agencies issue their own bonds to fund their operations. All these securities are purchased and traded by a circle of 40 or so major brokerage houses and banks, called *primary dealers*, who are authorized to deal directly with the Treasury.

TREASURY SECURITIES

What are Treasury securities?

Treasury securities are debt instruments issued by the United States Treasury, whose payment of interest and principal are guaranteed by the federal government. Because of their low risk, they are in high demand among individual, institutional, and governmental investors, both with the United States and abroad. The dollar amount of outstanding Treasury securities far outweighs the total issued by all U.S. corporations.

Treasury instruments are many and varied, their maturities ranging from a few months to many years. The federal government issues numerous different types of securities in order to attract investment capital from as many types of investors as possible. Sometimes the Treasury issues one type of instrument for the sole purpose of paying off (that is, *refunding*) a former issue whose maturity date has arrived.

How many types of Treasury securities are there?

The U.S. Treasury issues three types of ''negotiable'' debt securities: Treasury bills, Treasury notes, and Treasury bonds (or T bills, T notes, and T bonds). These instruments are *negotiable* in that they may be traded in the open market. Not included in this category are U.S. savings bonds, which are also issued by the Treasury but which may not be traded freely.

U.S. Treasury Bills

How are Treasury (or T) bills issued?

Treasury bills do not have a fixed rate of interest and do not make semiannual payments, like corporate bonds. Instead, they are issued, in $10,000 denominations, on a *discount* basis. That is, the Treasury (the issuer) sells the bill at a discount from its face value, with the discount equal to the fixed interest paid by the bill. Then, at maturity, the Treasury pays the owner the full face value. T bills have three maturities: 13 weeks (3 months), 26 weeks (6 months), and 52 weeks (1 year). For a 52-week bill, the price is simple to calculate:

$$\text{Price} = \text{Face value} - \text{Discount (\%)} \times \text{Face value}$$

Example: An investor buys a $1,000, 52-week Treasury bill at an 8% discount. What price does the investor pay?

$$\begin{aligned} \text{Price} &= \text{Face value} - \text{Discount (\%)} \times \text{Face value} \\ &= \$1,000 - .08 \, (\$1,000) \\ &= \$1,000 - \$80.00 = \$920 \end{aligned}$$

The investor pays $920 for the T bill. At maturity, the Treasury pays the investor $1,000.

Are all T bill prices computed in the same way?

Basically yes, but the computation for the 13- and 26-week bills is a little more complicated than for the year bill. The difference is that the *annual* discount rate has to be reduced to reflect the shorter term to maturity. For 13-week (or 3-month) bills, which represent a quarter of a year, the discount rate is divided by 4. For 26-week (6-month) bills, the rate is halved.

Given an annualized discount rate, the price of a T bill rises as its maturity decreases.

$$\begin{array}{l}\text{13-week}\\\text{price}\end{array} = \text{Face value} - \frac{\text{Discount (\%)} \times \text{Face value}}{4}$$

$$\begin{array}{l}\text{26-week}\\\text{price}\end{array} = \text{Face value} - \frac{\text{Discount (\%)} \times \text{Face value}}{2}$$

Example: If the 8%, $1,000 T bill in the previous example had a 3-month (13-week) maturity:

$$\begin{aligned}\begin{array}{l}\text{13-week}\\\text{price}\end{array} &= \text{Face value} - \frac{\text{Discount (\%)} \times \text{Face value}}{4}\\[2mm]
&= \$1,000 - \frac{.08\,(\$1,000)}{4}\\[2mm]
&= \$1,000 - \frac{\$80}{4}\\[2mm]
&= \$1,000 - \$20 = \$980\end{aligned}$$

Example: If the same bill had a maturity of 6 months (26 weeks):

$$\begin{aligned}\begin{array}{l}\text{26-week}\\\text{price}\end{array} &= \text{Face value} - \frac{\text{Discount (\%)} \times \text{Face value}}{2}\\[2mm]
&= \$1,000 - \frac{.08\,(\$1,000)}{2}\end{aligned}$$

$$= \$1,000 - \frac{\$80}{2}$$

$$= \$1,000 - \$40 = \$960$$

Note that the highest price is paid for the 13-week bill ($980), the lowest for the 52-week bill ($920). But all three types of T bills have an annualized discount of 8%.

How is the discount determined on a T bill?

Treasury bill discounts are determined by means of bidding in an *auction* conducted by the Federal Reserve System. In these auctions, investors and traders bid for portions of the issue.

- 13-week and 26-week bills are auctioned on the first business day of each week (usually Monday) at about 4:30 P.M. Eastern Standard Time, at the local District Bank of the Federal Reserve.

- The 52-week bills are auctioned separately on a monthly basis.

In these auctions, as in any auction, bidders attempt to "top" all other bidders, yet submit the lowest price possible. The prices bid depend on many factors—such as prevailing interest rates, the yield curve, and so on. In a T bill auction, however, the bidders are major banks (such as Citibank, Chase Manhattan, Harris Trust) and large brokerage firms (like Merrill Lynch, Goldman Sachs, Salomon Bros.), who are called *primary dealers*. These companies qualify as authorized bidders by demonstrating to the Federal Reserve that they do a great enough volume of business to be able to handle major purchases of Treasury securities and that their capital reserves are substantial enough to guarantee stability. Once a firm qualifies as a primary dealer, it is permitted to install a direct phone line to the Federal Reserve, which enables it to deal one-on-one with the (Federal Reserve) "System."

Example: In the weekly auction of 13-week bills, a brokerage firm bids an annualized discount of 10.40% for $5,000,000 worth of bills. A commercial bank bids 10.41% for the same amount. Here are the prices each would pay *per $1,000 bill*:

Brokerage firm:

$$\text{13-week price} = \text{Face value} - \frac{\text{Discount (\%)} \times \text{Face value}}{4}$$

$$= \$1,000 - \frac{.1040 \, (\$1,000)}{4}$$

$$= \$1,000 - \frac{\$104}{4}$$

$$= \$1,000 - \$26 = \$974$$

Bank:

$$\text{13-week price} = \text{Face value} - \frac{\text{Discount (\%)} \times \text{Face value}}{4}$$

$$= \$1,000 - \frac{.1041 \, (\$1,000)}{4}$$

$$= \$1,000 - \frac{\$104.10}{4}$$

$$= \$1,000 - \$26.025 = \$973.975$$

In what quantities may T bills be purchased?

The minimum purchase is $10,000. Beyond that, purchases must be in increments of $5,000. Since most of the participants in the T bill market are institutional, the quantities bought and sold are high, usually in multiples of $1,000,000.

Example: In the preceding example, the difference of less than three cents translates into $125 between the two bids ($.025 per $1,000 times 5,000).

With the bidding range for T bills so narrow, why does the Treasury bother with an auction (as opposed to a regular offering)?

The small bidding range seems inconsequential until you realize that the amount of a typical weekly issue is often in excess of $15,000,000,000! Small differences in bids can mean big savings in interest for the Treasury.

Example: Refer to the preceding example. On a $10-billion issue of 13-week bills, a hundredth of a percentage point between a bid of 10.40% and another of 10.41% means the federal government pays $250,000 less in debt service over the 13-weeks to maturity ($.025 per $1,000 times 10,000,000).

The impact on 26- and 52-week bills is even greater. (The following examples are slightly oversimplified because they use the same bid for instruments with longer maturities, which in practice usually calls for lower discounts. Nevertheless, the point is that small differences in the bids make for great differences in the federal government's debt service):

If the T bill matures in 26 weeks:

Brokerage firm:

$$\text{26-week price} = \text{Face value} - \frac{\text{Discount (\%)} \times \text{Face value}}{2}$$

$$= \$1,000 - \frac{.1040 \, (\$1,000)}{2}$$

$$= \$1,000 - \frac{\$104}{2}$$

$$= \$1,000 - \$52 = \$948$$

Bank:

$$\text{26-week price} = \text{Face value} - \frac{\text{Discount (\%)} \times \text{Face value}}{2}$$

$$= \$1,000 - \frac{.1041 \, (\$1,000)}{2}$$

$$= \$1,000 - \frac{\$104.10}{2}$$

$$= \$1,000 - \$52.05 = \$947.95$$

The difference of five cents ($948 less $947.95) means a savings in interest for the government of $500,000.

If it were a 52-week bill:

Brokerage firm:

Price = Face value − Discount (%) × Face value
     = $1,000 − .1040 ($1,000)
     = $1,000 − $104 = $896

Bank:

Price = Face value − Discount (%) × Face value
     = $1,000 − .1041 ($1,000)
     = $1,000 − $104.10 = $895.90

The difference of ten cents ($896.00 less $895.90) saves the government $1,000,000 in debt service over the course of the year.

Can individual investors participate in the auction and purchase T bills?

Even though most of the auction participants are institutional—pension funds, insurance companies, brokerage firms, banks, and the like—individual investors may submit bids and purchase T bills through the nearest Federal Reserve Bank. The bid, called a *tender*, must be received by the nearest District Federal Reserve Bank by 1:30 Eastern Standard Time on the day of the auction. The prospective buyer specifies the minimum discount that he or she will accept. During the auction, the Treasury attempts to sell the bills to bidders offering the lowest discounts. (Remember that a lower discount means a higher price—more dollars—for the Treasury.) If all the bills are distributed among bidders at lower discounts than the one on the tender, the investor will not be able to purchase any bills. In practice, since the institutional bidding at a T bill auction is usually for many times the amount of securities being offered, the issue is easily distributed at discounts well below any offered by private investors.

Example: Jane Smith, an individual investor, submits a tender for a 3-month bill with a minimum acceptable discount of 8.10%. The bidding proceeds during the auction, at which none of the discounts bid is higher than 8.08%. This represents a price of $979.75.

$$\text{13-week price} = \text{Face value} - \frac{\text{Discount (\%)} \times \text{Face value}}{4}$$

$$= \$1,000 - \frac{.0810\ (\$1,000)}{4}$$

$$= \$1,000 - \frac{\$81}{4}$$

$$= \$1,000 - \$20.25 = \$979.75$$

At the auction, the highest discount bid is 8.08%, which represents a price of $979.80.

$$\text{13-week price} = \text{Face value} - \frac{\text{Discount (\%)} \times \text{Face value}}{4}$$

$$= \$1,000 - \frac{.0808\ (\$1,000)}{4}$$

$$= \$1,000 - \frac{\$80.80}{4}$$

$$= \$1,000 - \$20.20 = \$979.80$$

The Treasury distributes the weekly issue among the bidders at the auction; Jane is not able to purchase any T bills this week.

Is there any way that an individual investor can guarantee a T bill purchase?

Yes. The investor can submit what is called a *noncompetitive bid*, which does not specify a minimum discount. All noncompetitive bids are accepted by the Treasury and assigned a rate of discount equal to the average rate of accepted competitive bids.

Example: In Figure 6–1, the 13-week (3-month) bills were awarded competitively at discounts ranging from 8.05% to 8.08%. The quotations on the issue are broken down into average, highest, and lowest prices, with the discount (or discounted) rate and coupon yield for each category.

Figure 6-1

	(000 omitted in dollar figures)	
	3-Mo. Bills	6-Mo. bills
Average Price	**97.960**	**96.067**
Discounted Rate	8.07%	7.78%
Coupon Yield	8.35%	8.21%
High Price	**97.965**	**96.097**
Discounted Rate	8.05%	7.72%
Coupon Yield	8.33%	8.15%
Low Price	**97.958**	**96.057**
Discounted Rate	8.08%	7.80%
Coupon Yield	8.36%	8.23%
Accepted at low price	30%	52%
Total applied for.............	$24,793,560	$19,418,405
Accepted	$ 6,418,090	$ 6,418,405
N.Y. applied for.............	$21,819,145	$17,249,615
N.Y. accepted	$ 5,495,305	$ 5,444,015
Noncompetitive	$ 1,146,735	$ 813,995

Jane will be able to purchase T bills at an average price of 97.960, or $979.60. Her purchase will be among the noncompetitive bid purchases of $1,146,735 listed at the bottom of the quotations.

Note: In this auction, the Treasury received competitive bids on 13-week (3-month) bills for $24,793,500,000, but it accepted bids for only $6,418,090,000.

What is the "coupon yield" of a T bill?

The *coupon yield* on a T bill is a calculated yield. Corporate or municipal bonds carry a prescribed rate of interest, at which seminannual payments are made. Treasury bills, as discounted instruments, do not have a "coupon" or "nominal" rate and do not make interest payments at fixed rate. Instead, because T bills are issued at discounts, their yields depend on what a purchaser pays, not on a fixed percentage of the face value. As a result, a T bill's yield may be, and often is, different from its rate of discount.

$$\text{Coupon yield} = \frac{(\text{Face value} - \text{Price}) \times 365}{\text{Price} \times \text{Days to maturity}}$$

In this formula:

Face value = $1,000 (unless otherwise specified)

Price = what the purchaser paid

365 = days in the year (leap years are ignored)

Days to maturity = 91 days for 13-week (3-month) bills

182 days for 26-week (6-month) bills

365 days for 52-week (1 year) bills

In general, for a T bill bought at the same discount rate, as the maturity increases:

● The price decreases (see preceding example).
● Yield increases.

Example: A purchaser of a 3-month T bill at an 8% discount pays $980. To calculate the yield:

$$\text{Coupon yield} = \frac{(\text{Face value} - \text{Price}) \times 365}{\text{Price} \times \text{Days to maturity}}$$

$$= \frac{(\$1,000 - \$980) \times 365}{\$980 \times 91}$$

$$= \frac{\$20 \times 365}{\$980 \times 91} = \frac{\$7,300}{\$89,180} = .0819 = 8.19\%$$

For a 6-month, 8% bill, purchased at $960:

$$\text{Coupon yield} = \frac{(\text{Face value} - \text{Price}) \times 365}{\text{Price} \times \text{Days to maturity}}$$

$$= \frac{(\$1,000 - \$960) \times 365}{\$980 \times 182}$$

$$= \frac{\$40 \times 365}{\$960 \times 182} = \frac{\$14,600}{\$174,720} = .0836 = 8.36\%$$

For the year bill, purchased at $920:

$$
\begin{aligned}
\text{Coupon yield} &= \frac{(\text{Face value} - \text{Price}) \times 365}{\text{Price} \times \text{Days to maturity}} \\[6pt]
&= \frac{(\$1{,}000 - \$920) \times 365}{\$920 \times 365} \\[6pt]
&= \frac{\$80 \times 365}{\$920 \times 365} = \frac{\$29{,}200}{\$335{,}800} = .0870 = 8.70\%
\end{aligned}
$$

Note: This method for computing a T bill yield is adequate for comparison against other types of T bills. However, the yield resulting from this formula is *not* suitable for comparison with annual yields of other debt instruments with fixed annual rates of interest. The reason is that the holder of a T bill does not receive a semiannual payment of interest and therefore does not have the opportunity to reinvest the payment, thereby earning "interest on interest." In general, an 8% discounted Treasury year bill will not offer as great a yield as an 8% debt instrument whose holder reinvests interest payments.

Is the T bill yield the "coupon yield" listed in the quotations in the financial news?

Yes. You can "check out" the listings by applying the formulas for price and coupon yield in this section.

Example: In the T bill auction listings in Figure 6–1 (part of which is reproduced here), you will find that the price, discount rate, and coupon yield all "compute" according to the formulas in this section. Let's look at the 26-week (6-month) bills:

	3-Mo. Bills	6-Mo. bills
Average Price................	97.960	96.067
Discounted Rate.............	8.07%	7.78%
Coupon Yield................	8.35%	8.21%

$$\text{26-week price} = \text{Face value} - \frac{\text{Discount (\%)} \times \text{Face value}}{2}$$

$$= \$1{,}000 - \frac{.0778\,(\$1{,}000)}{2}$$

$$= \$1{,}000 - \frac{\$77.80}{2}$$

$$= \$1{,}000 - \$38.90 = \$961.10$$

$$\text{Coupon yield} = \frac{(\text{Face value} - \text{Price}) \times 365}{\text{Price} \times \text{Days to maturity}}$$

$$= \frac{(\$1{,}000 - \$960.67) \times 365}{\$960.67 \times 182}$$

$$= \frac{\$39.33 \times 365}{\$960.67 \times 182} = \frac{\$14{,}355.45}{\$174{,}841.94}$$

$$= .0821 = 8.21\%$$

The Secondary Market for T Bills

Can T bills be bought and sold after they are auctioned?

Yes. Treasury bills are traded constantly on the *over-the-counter* market in the United States and elsewhere in the world. This global market is known as the *secondary market* (the auction is the *primary market*). In fact, T bill trading—averaging over $10 billion per trading session—accounts for more than half the volume of trading in all Treasury securities (bills, notes, and bonds), which is the largest single market in the world. While an order for $5 million worth of corporate or municipal bonds would be considered sizable, the same order for T bills would be no more than average.

How are Treasury bills traded in the secondary market?

T bills trade in the secondary market in the same way as in the auction: on a discounted basis. Quotations in the financial news for T bills reflect discounts from face value. Both bid and asked prices are expressed in terms of the discount rate.

- The *bid price* is the price that buyers are willing to pay to buy the bill.
- The *asked price* is the price that sellers are willing to accept to sell the bill.

Quotations in the financial news list bills by their maturity dates, followed by their "bid" price, their "asked" price, and the yield associated with the asked price. See Figure 6–2. Normally in a securities transaction, the bid is lower than the asked. Yet in Figure 6–2 the bid is higher than the asked because both are expressed in terms of discount. Remember: As the discount increases, the price goes down.

Figure 6–2

Treasury Bills

Maturity	Bid	Asked	Yield
	Discount		
	. . .		
Oct 1989*	8.09	8.03	8.35
Oct 2689	8.11	8.07	8.41
Nov 0289	8.07	8.01	8.36
	. . .		

*"Oct 1989" means "October 19, 1989."

Example: In Figure 6–2, compute the bid and asked prices, and verify the (coupon) yield for the Oct 1989 13-week T bill.

Bid price:

$$\text{Price} = \text{Face value} - \frac{\text{Discount (\%)} \times \text{Face value}}{4}$$

$$= \$1{,}000 - \frac{.0809 \, (\$1{,}000)}{4}$$

$$= \$1{,}000 - \frac{\$80.90}{4}$$

$$= \$1{,}000 - \$20.23 = \$979.77$$

Asked price:

$$\text{Price} = \text{Face value} - \frac{\text{Discount (\%)} \times \text{Face value}}{4}$$

$$= \$1,000 - \frac{.0803\,(\$1,000)}{4}$$

$$= \$1,000 - \frac{\$80.30}{4}$$

$$= \$1,000 - \$20.08 = \$979.92$$

Thus the bid, $979.77, is lower than the asked, $979.92.

How is the yield in the last column of the listing computed?

The yield in the listings is the yield to maturity, computed not by the rule of thumb YTM formula, but rather by a computer-executed formula that involves calculus. In the real world of trading, this yield is calculated by sophisticated computer systems.

TREASURY NOTES

The Primary Market

How do Treasury (or T) notes differ from T bills?

Both T notes and bills are:

- Treasury-issued debt instruments,
- with a face value of $1,000,
- that carry the unconditional promise of the federal government to pay, and
- that are issued in an auction.

Notes differ from bills in that:

- Their maturities are longer, ranging from two to ten years.

- Auctions are held less frequently than bill auctions. Subject to change when conditions demand, the two-year notes are usually auctioned on a monthly basis, while the three-, four-, five-, seven-, and ten-year notes are issued quarterly. As in the T bill auction, noncompetitive bids are accepted for T note issues.

How are T note bids expressed?

Bids for Treasury notes are normally expressed as percentages of face value, carried out to two decimal places. Sometimes, however, a bid may be submitted in the form of a minimum acceptable bid, which is also expressed as a percentage carried to two decimal places.

What is the dollar value of a bid expressed as a percentage of face value?

To convert the percentage-of-face-value bid into a dollar amount, convert it to decimal form and multiply it by the face value.

Price = Bid (in decimal form) × Face value

Example: A bid of 99.10 for a T note is actually an offer to pay 99.10% of the $1,000 face value. Convert the bid of 99.10(%) to a decimal—.9910—and then use the formula:

Price = Bid (in decimal form) × Face value
     = .9910 × $1,000
     = $991.00

The Secondary Market

How are T notes traded after being issued?

Unlike Treasury bills, which trade at a discount from their face value, notes trade at a percentage of their face value (carried out to two decimal places). Because the volume of trading in notes is so high and the competitive factors so strong, the difference between what prospective buyers are willing to pay and what would-be sellers are willing to accept is very slight. The unit of trading is therefore very small, only $\frac{1}{32}$ of 1%; that is, successive trades may take place in increments of $\frac{1}{32}$ of 1%. (Compare this unit with the $\frac{1}{8}$ of 1% used in corporate and municipal bond trading.)

If the unit of trading for T notes is ¹/₃₂ of 1%, then what do the "decimal" places in the quotation stand for?

Ordinarily, digits after the decimal place stand for tenths, hundredths, thousandths, and so on. In a Treasury note quotation, the two numbers after the decimal stand for so many 32nds.

Example: In a quotation of 103.08, the ".08" stands for "⁸/₃₂," not "⁸/₁₀₀."

How are quotations using 32nds converted to dollar amounts?

To convert a T note quotation to a dollar value, two steps are necessary:

1. Consider the numbers before the percentage and multiply it by the face value.
2. Translate the numbers after the decimal point to dollars and add the value in step 1.

$$\text{Price} = \begin{matrix} \text{Numbers} \\ \text{before} \\ \text{decimal (as} \\ \text{percentage)} \end{matrix} \times \begin{matrix} \text{Face} \\ \text{value} \end{matrix} + \frac{\begin{matrix} \text{Numbers} \\ \text{after} \\ \text{decimal} \end{matrix}}{32} \times \$10$$

Note that the 32nd part of the quotation is multiplied by $10. Ordinarily, the second digit after the decimal signifies hundredths, and one hundredth of a face value of $1,000 is $10. That is,

$$.01 \times \$1,000 = \$10$$

But in a T note quotation, the two places to the right of the decimal do not represent tens and hundreds, but rather 32nds. Tens and hundreds are not small enough units of trading for T notes. So each $10 of face value is segmented, for trading purposes, into 32 parts. The numbers to the right of the decimal reflect so many 32nds of $10.

Note: Each 32nd equals $.3125 ($10 divided by 32).

Example: A T note quotation (bid or asked) is 101.12. The face value is $1,000. What is the price of the note?

$$\text{Price} = \begin{array}{c}\text{Numbers}\\ \text{before}\\ \text{decimal (as}\\ \text{percentage)}\end{array} \times \begin{array}{c}\text{Face}\\ \text{value}\end{array} + \dfrac{\begin{array}{c}\text{Numbers}\\ \text{after}\\ \text{decimal}\end{array}}{32} \times \$10$$

$$= .101 \times \$1{,}000 + \frac{12}{32} \times \$10$$

$$= \$1{,}010 + \frac{3}{8} \times \$10$$

$$= \$1{,}010 + \$3.75 = \$1{,}013.75$$

The price related to the T note bid is $1,013.75.

Note: T note prices can be converted quickly in three steps:

1. Change the predecimal numbers to dollars by adding a zero.
2. Multiplying the postdecimal numbers by $.3125.
3. Adding the amounts of steps 1 and 2.

Example: Convert a bid of 101.12.

1. 101	=	$1,010.00
2. 12 × $.3125	=	$ 3.75
3. Price	=	$1,013.75

How are Treasury notes listed in the financial news?

T notes are listed, intermingled with Treasury bonds (bills are separate), in order of their maturities, with the nearest maturities first. Notes are denoted by two letter symbols:
n indicates "note."
p means "note; nonresident aliens exempt from withholding taxes."
(A third letter designation, *c*, is for a Treasury note "stripped" of its principal, an instrument covered later in this chapter.)
All other quotations are bonds (*b*).

Each listing includes:

- Coupon rate.
- Maturity.
- Current *bid price*, or the price buyers are willing to pay.
- Current *asked price*, or the price sellers are willing to accept; sometimes also known as the *offering price*.
- The change in the bid price from the last trading session.
- Yield based on the current asked (or offering) price.

Example:

Gov't. Bonds & Notes

Rate	Maturity	Bid	Asked	Bid Chg.	Yld.
7.37	June 89p	99.30	100.01	...	3.48
9.62	June 89p	99.30	100.01	−.01	5.59
14.50	Jul 89n	100.06	100.09	...	8.28
13.00	Nov 90n	105.20	105.24	−.04	8.49
12.37	Apr 91n	106.11	106.15	−.01	8.41

Are the bid and asked prices converted to dollar amounts in the same way that bids are in the primary market?

Yes. The numbers before the decimal represent a percentage of face value, while the numbers to the right of the decimal are actually 32nds.

Example: In the following listing, convert the bid and asked prices to dollar values.

Rate	Maturity	Bid	Asked	Bid Chg.	Yld.
		...			
13.00	Nov 90n	**105.20**	**105.24**	−.04	8.49

Bid price: 105.20

$$\text{Price} = \begin{array}{c}\text{Numbers} \\ \text{before} \\ \text{decimal (as} \\ \text{percentage)}\end{array} \times \begin{array}{c}\text{Face} \\ \text{value}\end{array} + \frac{\begin{array}{c}\text{Numbers} \\ \text{after} \\ \text{decimal}\end{array}}{32} \times \$10$$

$$= .105 \times \$1,000 + \frac{.20}{32} \times \$10$$

$$= \$1,050 + \$6.25 = \$1,056.25$$

The bid is $1,056.24.

Asked price: 105.24

$$\text{Price} = \begin{array}{c}\text{Numbers} \\ \text{before} \\ \text{decimal (as} \\ \text{percentage)}\end{array} \times \begin{array}{c}\text{Face} \\ \text{value}\end{array} + \frac{\begin{array}{c}\text{Numbers} \\ \text{after} \\ \text{decimal}\end{array}}{32} \times \$10$$

$$= .105 \times \$1,000 + \frac{.24}{32} \times \$10$$

$$= \$1,050 + \$7.50 = \$1,057.50$$

The asked price is $1,057.50.

What does the change in bid say about the prior trading day's bid?

The change in the bid represents the difference between the bids at the close of the current day's trading and at the prior day's trading. The change gives you the information you need to compute the prior closing bid.

$$\begin{array}{c}\textbf{Prior closing} \\ \textbf{bid}\end{array} = \textbf{Current closing bid} \pm \textbf{Change in bid}$$

- If it is preceded by a plus sign, then the previous day's closing bid was lower. To get the prior close, deduct the change from the current day's bid.
- If today's bid has a minus sign, then the previous day's closing bid was higher. Add the change to today's bid.

By inference, you also know roughly where the prior day's asked price was, by adding the spread of the prior day's close.

Example: In the following listing, calculate the prior day's bid.

Rate	Maturity	Bid	Asked	Bid Chg.	Yld.
		• • •			
13.00	Nov 90n	**105.20**	105.24	−.04	8.49

Since the change is a negative number, it has to be added to the current bid.

Prior closing bid = Current closing bid ± Change in bid
$$= 105.20 + .04 = 105.24$$

The prior closing bid was 105.24. By implication, the *rough* closing asked price was probably about 4/32nds higher. Why? The current difference between bid and asked prices is 4/32nds (105.20 bid versus 105.24 asked).

What is the dollar value of the change in the bid, as it appears in the financial listings?

The change in bid may be translated to a dollar value by multiplying it by \$.3125 (the value of each 32nd).

Change in bid (\$) = Change in bid (32nds) × \$.3125

Example: In the following listing, the change in bid is −.04.

Rate	Maturity	Bid	Asked	Bid Chg.	Yld.
		• • •			
13.00	Nov 90n	105.20	105.24	**−.04**	8.49

Change in bid (\$) = Change in bid (32nds) × \$.3125
$$= 4 × \$.3125 = \$1.25$$

The closing bid changed by $1.25 from one trading session to the next.

How is the yield in the financial listings calculated?

The yield on T notes, as listed in the financial news, is the yield to maturity, but it is computed by means of a sophisticated formula that involves calculus. In the real world it is done only by computers. It is not calculated by means of the rule of thumb YTM formula.

What does it mean when a T note trades "at a premium," "at par," or "at a discount"?

The market value of a T note can be higher than, the same as, or lower than its face (or *par*) value.

- When the price is *higher* than par, the note is said to be trading at a *premium*.
- When the price is *equal* to par, the note is trading *at par*.
- When the price is *below* par, the note is trading at a *discount*.

Note: A "discounted" price in secondary market trading is not to be confused with the "discounted" price in the primary market. When first issued, a T note is deliberately discounted in order to attract buyers. When the note is trading, however, its price rises or falls (above or below par) in reaction to market influences—supply and demand, prevailing interest rates, and so on.

Example: In the following listing, notes trading at a premium, at a discount, and at par are noted:

Gov't. Bonds & Notes

	Rate	Maturity	Bid	Asked	Bid Chg.	Yld.
Discount	7.37	June 89p	99.30	100.01	...	3.48
Discount	9.62	June 89p	99.30	100.01	−.01	5.59
Par	14.50	Jul 89n	100.06	100.09	...	8.28
Premium	13.00	Nov 90n	105.20	105.24	−.04	8.49
Premium	12.37	Apr 91n	106.11	106.15	−.01	8.41

How do premium, par, and discount prices affect yield?

● Premium prices lower current yield and yield to maturity.

● Par prices make current yield and yield to maturity the same as the coupon yield.

● Discount prices raise current yield and yield to maturity.

Do Treasury notes make interest payments even though they are sold on a discounted basis?

Yes. T notes make semiannual payments that are equal to one-half their *coupon rate* (the fixed rate of interest for that note) times the face value. The payment is "one-half" because the coupon rate is an annual figure and must be halved for each semiannual payment.

$$\text{Semiannual interest payment} = \frac{\text{Face value} \times \text{Coupon rate}}{2}$$

Example: A November 90 note, with a $1,000 face value, pays 13% interest. To calculate its semiannual interest payment:

$$\text{Semiannual interest payment} = \frac{\text{Face value} \times \text{Coupon rate}}{2}$$

$$= \frac{\$1,000 \times .1300}{2}$$

$$= \frac{\$130}{2} = \$65$$

This note pays $65 twice a year.

Is accrued interest for T notes calculated in the same way as for other debt instruments?

Basically yes, but the difference is that T note accrued interest calculations use actual calendar days, not an artificial 30-day month or 365-day year. The computation is a derivation of the interest formula:

$$\textbf{Interest} = \textbf{Principal} \times \textbf{Rate} \times \textbf{Time}$$

Time is a fraction, in which the numerator consists of the actual calendar days from the day of the transaction (when the T note changes hands) to, and including, the day before settlement. The denominator is 365 (the actual days in the year).

Example: Sam Jones sells a 9%, $1,000 T note to Mary Smith on Monday, October 5, at a price of 99. Interest payments are made on February 1 and August 1 (''F1 and A1''). Settlement for Treasury securities transactions is the next business day; on October 6, Jones (the seller) is to deliver the note, and Smith (the buyer) is to make payment, each through his or her brokerage firm.

In addition to payment of the purchase price, Smith has to pay Jones the interest that the note accrued from the last interest payment date to the day before settlement. (She will then take the next full interest payment.) The principal is the face (or par) value of the note, $1,000, and the rate is 9%. But what is the time? Time is expressed in terms of calendar days:

August	31 days
September	30 days
October	5 days
Total	66 days

August is considered to have 31 days because the interest payment on the first of that month covered the period through the end of July. Five days in October are included because interest accrues up to and including the day before settlement. In the case of Treasuries, the business day before settlement is also the trade date.

$$\text{Interest} = \text{Principal} \times \text{Rate} \times \text{Time}$$
$$= \$1,000 \times .09 \times \frac{66}{365}$$
$$= \$1,000 \times .09 \times .1808 = \$16.27$$

Smith pays Jones the purchase price of $990 (99) plus the accrued interest of $16.27, for a total of $1,006.27. On February 1 of the next year, the next interest payment date, Smith will receive $45 (the semiannual interest payment; see the preceding section for this calculation).

TREASURY BONDS

Primary Market

How do Treasury bonds compare with other Treasury securities?

Treasury (or T) bonds are most like T notes, which are both very different from T bills. Like the notes, Treasury bonds:

- Are available in minimum denominations of $1,000.
- Make semiannual interest payments.
- Come to market by means of an auction (in which noncompetitive bids are accepted).
- Are traded in the secondary market by primary dealers.
- Can trade at a premium, a discount, or par.
- Trade in variations of 32nds.
- Are quoted in fundamentally the same way as notes.

Bonds differ from notes in their maturities. Bonds are issued with maturities of 20 to 30 years. The 30-year instrument acts as a measurement of market movement because, with its decades-long duration, its price reacts more dramatically to economic conditions. Also, since bonds are not issued at a discount, their yields (current, yield to maturity) are calculated just like those of corporate bonds.

Can a T bond quotation be read in the same way as a T note quote?

For the most part, yes. T bond and T note quotations are intermingled, listed in chronological order by their maturities. T note maturities are followed by an *n* or a *p* (see section on T notes in this chapter). T bond maturities are not followed by any letter symbol, except sometimes *k*, which means that nonresident alien bondholders will not have withholding taxes taken out of their interest payments.

The yield in the leftmost column is the coupon (or nominal) rate.

In the bid and asked prices, the digits to the left of the decimal can be converted to a percentage of the face value, and the digits to the right of the decimal are 32nds.

$$\text{Price} = \frac{\text{Numbers}}{\text{before}} \times \frac{\text{Face}}{\text{value}} + \frac{\text{Numbers after decimal}}{32} \times \$10$$

The bid change (the difference between the current closing bid and that of the last trading session) is expressed in the same way as for T notes.

Change in bid (\$) = Change in bid (in 32nds) × \$.3125

The yield in the rightmost column is calculated on the basis of the asked price in the listing, not on face value. It will therefore be different from the coupon rate.

Example:

Rate	Maturity	Bid	Asked	Bid Chg.	Yld.
7.50	May 16k	92.04	92.08	+.10	8.21

The "Rate" in the leftmost column is the nominal yield. The "Yield" in the rightmost column is yield to maturity, calculated on the basis of the asked price.

How is the nominal (or coupon) yield computed on a T bond?

The *nominal* (or *coupon*) yield is the percentage of the face value that the bond pays. This type of yield is "fixed" throughout the life of the bond. It is not affected by the market price of the bond or by any other factors.

Nominal yield (\$) = Face value × Nominal rate (%)

Example: A T bond has a 12% nominal rate and a face (par) value of \$1,000.

Nominal yield (\$) = Face value × Nominal rate (%)
= \$1,000 × .12 = \$120

This bond pays \$120 in interest every year, regardless of

market price or any other factors affecting the value the bond.

How do I know the nominal yield of a bond?

Nominal yield is found in the leftmost column of the financial listings.

Rate	Maturity	Bid	Asked	Bid Chg.	Yld.
7.50	May 16k	92.04	92.08	+.10	8.21

How is the "current yield" on a T bond calculated?

Current yield is the yield that you get, expressed as a percentage, when you divide the annual fixed interest payment by the purchase price (not face value). The bondholder receives the fixed interest payment (which is a percentage of the face value), regardless of how much the bond cost. Yet the purchase price is the real amount of the investment, not the face value; and the actual yield should be calculated as a percentage of that investment. Because current yield is based on the fluctuating market value of the bond, it can, and usually does, change often, as the market price of the bond rises or falls in the market.

$$\text{Current yield } (\%) = \frac{\text{Interest (\$)}}{\text{Current price}}$$

Note that the relationship between current yield and price is *inverse*. That is, as price increases, current yield declines, and vice versa.

Current yield is not reflected in the financial listings.

Example: A $1,000 T bond, purchased for 99 ($990), pays annual interest of 8%. What is the current yield?

$$\text{Nominal yield (\$)} = \text{Face value} \times \text{Nominal rate (\%)}$$
$$= \$1,000 \times .08 = \$80$$

$$\text{Current yield (\%)} = \frac{\text{Interest (\$)}}{\text{Current price (\$)}}$$
$$= \frac{\$80}{\$990} = 8.08\%$$

For someone who purchases the bond for a price of $990, the current yield is 8.08%. For that holder, the current yield does not change because the purchase price does not change.

But the current yield on the bond can change over its lifetime. If the bond drops in market value to $970, its current yield would change also.

$$\text{Current yield (\%)} = \frac{\text{Interest (\$)}}{\text{Current price (\$)}}$$
$$= \frac{\$80}{\$970} = 8.25\%$$

Note that, as the price declines, current yield increases. For anyone purchasing this bond at 97 ($970), the current yield is 8.25%.

Does the price of a T bond affect its yield to maturity?

Yes. The computation of *yield to maturity* (*YTM*), like current yield, takes the purchase price into account, but it also includes the eventual repayment of principal if the bond is held to maturity. At some point in the future, the issuer is going to repay the principal (face value, $1,000).

● If the purchase price is lower than par (that is, discounted), then the bondholder receives more than what was paid, and this extra amount must be considered part of the overall yield.

Example: If a $1,000 face value T bond costs $900, the $100 difference between the price and par must be considered additional yield at maturity.

● If the price is higher (that is, at a premium), the bondholder is paid less, and the loss lessens the yield.

Example: If a $1,000 bond is sold for $1,100, then the additional $100 in price has to be deducted from the yield at maturity.

● With a purchase price at par, yield to maturity is the same as current yield, which in turn is the same as the nominal yield.

Example: If a $1,000 bond sells for $1,000, then nothing needs to be added or deducted from the the yield at maturity. And, since the purchase price (the basis of the current yield formula) equals par value, the current yield is the same as the nominal yield.

Yield to maturity is a better assessment of return than current yield because it considers all the factors affecting yield—interest rate, market price, and time to maturity.

The yield to maturity is found in the financial listings in the rightmost column.

Is a T bond's yield to maturity calculation the same as for other types of bonds?

Yes. The calculation for YTM entails two steps:

- Spread out, or *prorate*, the premium or discount over the years remaining to maturity.
- Apply the YTM formula.

$$\text{Prorated premium/discount} = \frac{\text{Difference between face value and price}}{\text{Years remaining to maturity}}$$

$$\text{Yield to maturity} = \frac{\text{Nominal rate} + \begin{pmatrix} + \text{ Prorated discount (\$) or} \\ - \text{ Prorated premium (\$)} \end{pmatrix}}{(\text{Price} + \text{Face value})/2}$$

Example: A $1,000 T bond is purchased at 92 ($920), pays 12% nominal interest ($120), and has exactly 8 years remaining to maturity. What is the yield to maturity?

- *Prorate the discount:*

$$\begin{aligned} \text{Prorate premium/discount} &= \frac{\text{Difference between face value and price}}{\text{Years remaining to maturity}} \\ &= \frac{\$1,000 - \$920}{8 \text{ years}} \\ &= \frac{\$80}{8 \text{ years}} = \$10 \text{ per year} \end{aligned}$$

The bond is worth an additional $10 per year in yield.

● *Apply the YTM formula:*

$$\text{Yield to maturity} = \frac{\text{Nominal rate} + \left(\begin{array}{l} + \text{ Prorated discount (\$) or} \\ - \text{ Prorated premium (\$)} \end{array}\right)}{(\text{Price} + \text{Face value})/2}$$

$$= \frac{\$120 + \$10}{(\$920 + \$1,000)/2}$$

$$= \frac{\$130}{\$1,920/2} = \frac{\$130}{\$960} = 13.54\%$$

If held to maturity, this bond's yield to maturity will be 13.54%. The bondholder, having bought the bond at a discount, enjoys a yield that is greater than the nominal rate (12%).

How do I know the yield to maturity of a T bond?

Yield to maturity is listed in the rightmost column of the T bond quotations in the financial news.

Example: In the following quotation, the rightmost column displays the yield to maturity.

Rate	Maturity	Bid	Asked	Bid Chg.	Yld.
7.50	May 16k	92.04	92.08	+.10	**8.21**

Does yield to maturity change like current yield?

Yes. Yield to maturity changes from moment to moment in the marketplace, as a bond's price goes up or down. For two different investors who purchase the same bond at different times, the yields to maturity are probably going to be different for two reasons: The purchase prices may be different, and the times remaining to maturity will certainly be different.

● Yield increases as price decreases, and vice versa.
● Yield on a discounted bond increases as the time to maturity decreases.

● Yield on a bond selling at a premium decreases as the time to maturity decreases.

Example: Refer to the preceding example. The 12%, $1,000 T bond is purchased at a different price, 95 ($950), and with only 7 years remaining to maturity (exactly). What is the yield to maturity?

● *Prorate the discount.*

$$\begin{matrix} \text{Prorate} \\ \text{premium/discount} \end{matrix} = \frac{\begin{matrix} \text{Difference between} \\ \text{face value and price} \end{matrix}}{\text{Years remaining to maturity}}$$

$$= \frac{\$1,000 - \$950}{7 \text{ years}}$$

$$= \frac{\$50}{7 \text{ years}} = \$7.14 \text{ per year}$$

The bond is worth an additional $7.14 per year in yield.

● *Apply the YTM formula:*

$$\begin{matrix} \text{Yield to} \\ \text{maturity} \end{matrix} = \frac{\begin{matrix} \text{Nominal} \\ \text{rate} \end{matrix} + \begin{pmatrix} + \text{ Prorated discount (\$) or} \\ - \text{ Prorated premium (\$)} \end{pmatrix}}{(\text{Price} + \text{Face value})/2}$$

$$= \frac{\$120 + \$7.14}{(\$950 + \$1,000)/2}$$

$$= \frac{\$127.14}{\$1,950/2} = \frac{\$127.14}{\$975.00} = 13.04\%$$

If held to maturity, this bond's yield to maturity will be 13.04%. The bondholder, having bought the bond at a discount, enjoys a yield that is greater than the nominal rate (12%). But the YTM is lower than it was for the investor who bought the bond at $920 one year earlier. In this case:

● The higher price lessens the yield.
● The short time to maturity increases the yield (because the bond is discounted).

What if the bond is not bought with an exact number of years remaining to maturity?

In the real world, bonds are usually *not* bought exactly on the date of their issuance. In these cases, the prorating and YTM formulas are restated using months, weeks, or—as is usually the case—days remaining to maturity.

$$\text{Prorate premium/discount} = \frac{\text{Difference between face value and price}}{\text{Days remaining to maturity}}$$

$$\text{Yield to maturity} = \frac{\dfrac{\text{Nominal rate}}{365} + \left(\begin{array}{l}+\text{ Prorated discount (\$) or}\\ -\text{ Prorated premium (\$)}\end{array}\right)}{(\text{Price} + \text{Face value})/(2 \times 365 \text{ days})}$$

Example: A 12%, $1,000 T bond is purchased at 95 ($950). It is purchased on May 1 of 19X1, and maturity is on February 15 of 19X6. What is the yield to maturity? The first step is to determine the number of days to maturity:

19X1	
May-December	245
19X2	365
19X3	365
19X4	365
19X5	365
19X6	
January	31
February	15
Total days to maturity	1,751

● *Prorate the discount.*

$$\begin{aligned}\text{Prorated premium/discount} &= \frac{\text{Difference between face value and price}}{\text{Days remaining to maturity}}\\[2mm] &= \frac{\$1,000 - \$950}{1,751 \text{ days}}\\[2mm] &= \frac{\$50}{1,751 \text{ days}} = \$.02855 \text{ per day}\end{aligned}$$

● *Apply the YTM formula:*

$$
\text{Yield to maturity} = \frac{\dfrac{\text{Nominal rate}/365} + \left(\begin{array}{l} + \text{ Prorated discount (\$) or} \\ - \text{ Prorated premium (\$)} \end{array}\right)}{(\text{Price} + \text{Face value})/(2 \times 365 \text{ days})}
$$

$$
= \frac{(\$120/365 \text{ days}) + \$.02855}{(\$950 + \$1,000)/(2 \times 365)}
$$

$$
= \frac{\$.32876 + \$.02855}{\$1,950/(730 \text{ days})} = \frac{\$.35731}{\$2.67123} = 13.38\%
$$

If held to maturity, this bond's yield to maturity will be 13.38%. The bondholder, having bought the bond at a discount, enjoys a yield that is greater than the nominal rate (12%).

Note: This formula is called the *rule of thumb* because it is not as exact as the true formula, which involves the use of calculus and a computer. (That is why the yield to maturity in the financial listings is never the same as calculated by the rule of thumb method.) This method, however, serves the purpose for the individual investor, particularly if it is expressed in terms of days to maturity.

Are the bid and asked prices of T bonds quoted in the same way as they are for T notes?

Yes, they are quoted in 32nds. But there is a difference: T bond quotations can sometimes be calibrated in 64ths.

$$
\text{Price} = \begin{array}{c} \text{Numbers} \\ \text{before} \\ \text{decimal (as} \\ \text{percentage)} \end{array} \times \begin{array}{c} \text{Face} \\ \text{value} \end{array} + \frac{\begin{array}{c} \text{Numbers} \\ \text{after} \\ \text{decimal} \end{array}}{32} \times \$10
$$

Example: What are the dollar values of the bid price and asked price in the following quotation?

Rate	Maturity	Bid	Asked	Bid Chg.	Yld.
7.50	May 16k	92.04	92.08	+.10	8.21

Bid price:

$$\text{Price} = \begin{array}{c}\text{Numbers}\\ \text{before}\\ \text{decimal (as}\\ \text{percentage)}\end{array} \times \begin{array}{c}\text{Face}\\ \text{value}\end{array} = \frac{\begin{array}{c}\text{Numbers}\\ \text{after}\\ \text{decimal}\end{array}}{32} \times \$10$$

$$= .92 \times \$1,000 + \frac{4}{32} \times \$10$$

$$= \$920 + \$1.25 = \$921.25$$

Buyers are bidding $921.25 for this T bond.

Asked price:

$$\text{Price} = \begin{array}{c}\text{Numbers}\\ \text{before}\\ \text{decimal (as}\\ \text{percentage)}\end{array} \times \begin{array}{c}\text{Face}\\ \text{value}\end{array} + \frac{\begin{array}{c}\text{Numbers}\\ \text{after}\\ \text{decimal}\end{array}}{32} \times \$10$$

$$= .92 \times \$1,000 + \frac{8}{32} \times \$10$$

$$= \$920 + \$2.50 = \$922.50$$

Sellers are asking $922.50.

How is a price quoted in 64ths converted to a dollar figure?

There are two ways to adjust a Treasury security's price for a 64th:

1. Convert the 32nds to 64ths and use the price formula in 64ths.

$$\text{Price} = \begin{array}{c}\textbf{Numbers}\\ \textbf{before}\\ \textbf{decimal (as}\\ \textbf{percentage)}\end{array} \times \begin{array}{c}\textbf{Face}\\ \textbf{value}\end{array} + \frac{\begin{array}{c}\textbf{Numbers}\\ \textbf{after}\\ \textbf{decimal}\end{array}}{64} \times \textbf{\$10}$$

2. Add or deduct the dollar value of a 64th to whatever price you get from the price formula.

Method 1—Converting 32nds to 64ths: (1) Double the number of 32nds. (2) Add or deduct 1 to the numerator. (3) Use the fraction in 64ths in the price formula.

Example: A Treasury's bid price is quoted as 101.25a. What is the dollar value of the bid price? The letter "a" indicates an additional 64th in the price.

1. *Double the number of 32nds:*

   Number of 64ths = 2 × 32nds = 2 × 25 = 50

2. *Add 1 to the result* (because the quote is followed by an *a*).

$$50 + 1 = 51$$

(You deduct 1 if a *d* follows the quote.)

3. *Use the price formula with a fraction in 64ths:*

$$\text{Price} = \frac{\text{Numbers before decimal (as percentage)}}{} \times \text{Face value} + \frac{\text{Numbers after decimal}}{64} \times \$10$$

$$= 1.01 \times \$1,000 + \frac{51}{64} \times \$10$$

$$= \$1,010 + \$7.9688 = \$1,017.97$$

Method 2—Adding the Dollar Value of a 64th to the Price: (1) Calculate the price in the normal manner.

$$\text{Price} = \frac{\text{Numbers before decimal (as percentage)}}{} \times \text{Face value} + \frac{\text{Numbers after decimal}}{32} = \$10$$

(2) Add or deduct the dollar value of a 64th, which is $.1563 (half the dollar value of a 32nd, $.3125).

Example: Calculate the dollar value of 105.12d.

1. *Calculate the price in 32nds:*

$$\text{Price} = \begin{array}{c}\text{Numbers}\\\text{before}\\\text{decimal (as}\\\text{percentage)}\end{array} \times \begin{array}{c}\text{Face}\\\text{value}\end{array} + \frac{\begin{array}{c}\text{Numbers}\\\text{after}\\\text{decimal}\end{array}}{32} \times \$10$$

$$= 1.05 \times \$1,000 + \frac{12}{32} \times \$10$$

$$= \$1,050 + \$3.75 = \$1,053.75$$

2. *Deduct the value of the 64th:*

$$\text{Price} = \text{Price in 32nds} - \text{64th (\$)}$$
$$= \$1,053.75 - .1563 = \$1,053.59$$

Is the bid change in a T bond quote calculated in the same way as for T notes?

Yes. The same formula applies.

Change in bid (\$) = Change in bid (32nds) × \$.3125

Example: In the following quotation, calculate the dollar value of the bid change and the prior trading session's closing bid. Also estimate the prior session's asking price.

Rate	Maturity	Bid	Asked	Bid Chg.	Yld.
7.50	May 16k	92.04	92.08	+.10	8.21

Bid change:

$$\text{Change in bid (\$)} = \text{Change in bid (in 32nds)} \times \$.3125$$
$$= 10 \times \$.3125 = \$3.125$$

The bid change is \$3.125 per bond. Since this is a positive number, yesterday's closing bid was lower—\$918.125, to be exact (today's close of \$921.25 less the change in bid of \$3.125). By inference, yesterday's closing asked price was *probably about* $919.375 (today's asked price of $922.50 less the change in bid of $3.125).

Can Treasury bonds be callable?

Yes. Like some corporate and municipal bonds, T bonds can be *callable*; that is, the issuer (the Treasury) retains the right to retire the bonds prior to maturity—to call them back. The so-called *call feature* always works to the benefit of the issuer because the bond will be called only when it is in the issuer's best interest to do so. Consequently, the call feature must be clearly stated at the time of issuance.

Note: The Treasury has not issued callable bonds for a number of years. Many outstanding callable issues, however, are still traded.

What are the terms of the call feature on a T bond?

While corporate and municipal call features can become rather complicated, T bond call features are quite simple. Callable Treasury bonds become callable at par value (or face value, $1,000) beginning 5 years from their maturity date.

In the financial listings, callable bonds have two maturity dates, one the normal maturity year and one the year in which the call feature becomes operable.

Example: In the following quotation, the normal maturity is November of the year 2011. The call feature becomes operable in November of 2006.

Rate	Maturity	Bid	Asked	Bid Chg.	Yld.
14.00	Nov 06-11	150.27	151.01	+.15	8.37

Under what circumstances would a T bond be called?

Once a T bond becomes callable, the Treasury determines whether it would lower its debt service expense to *refund* the issue, that is, issue new bonds at a lower rate of interest and use the proceeds to call in the existing bonds. Generally, if the prevailing interest rates are lower than the coupon (or nominal) rate on the existing debt, the Treasury will call the bond and issue new debt at a lower interest rate.

Example: The November '11 T bonds, with a coupon rate of 14%, become callable in 2006. If at that time the Treasury determines that it can issue new bonds that pay a rate lower than 14%, it will most likely call the November '11 14% bonds and issue new debt at the lower rate.

If prevailing rates are higher than 14%, the Treasury will likely not call the bonds. Note that the yield in the right-hand column, 8.37%, is based on the purchase price, not face value. Buyers are willing to pay 150 ($1,500) for a $1,000 bond with a 14% coupon rate. In other words, buyers are happy to get a return of 8% to 9%. If this or a similar condition exists in November of 2006, the Treasury will undoubtedly call the 14% bonds—and auction off a new issue of, say, 8.5% bonds.

What good does the yield to maturity do if a T bond can be called prior to maturity?

Not much good. That is why you must calculate the *yield to call*. This is basically the same calculation as the yield to maturity but the remaining life of the bond is assumed to end in the year that it becomes eligible for call.

$$\text{Prorated premium/discount} = \frac{\text{Difference between face value and price}}{\text{Years remaining to call}}$$

$$\text{Yield to call} = \frac{\text{Nominal rate} + \begin{pmatrix} + \text{ Prorated discount (\$) or} \\ - \text{ Prorated premium (\$)} \end{pmatrix}}{(\text{Price } + \text{ Face value})/2}$$

Don't forget:

- Shortening the life of a bond purchased at a discount increases the yield.
- Shortening the life of a bond bought at a premium decreases the yield.

Therefore, a call enhances the yield on a discounted bond and worsens the yield on a premium-priced bond.

Example: An investor purchases a callable 14%, $1,000 T bond at 106 ($1,060). The bond matures in exactly 10 years.

Yield to maturity:

$$\text{Prorated premium/discount} = \frac{\text{Difference between face value and price}}{\text{Years remaining to maturity}}$$

$$= \frac{\$1,060 - \$1,000}{10}$$

$$= \frac{\$60}{\$10} = \$6 \text{ per year}$$

$$\text{Yield to maturity} = \frac{\text{Nominal rate} + \left(\begin{array}{l} + \text{ Prorated discount (\$) or} \\ - \text{ Prorated premium (\$)} \end{array}\right)}{(\text{Price} + \text{Face value})/2}$$

$$= \frac{\$140 - \$6}{(\$1,060 + \$1,000)/2}$$

$$= \frac{\$134}{\$2,060/2} = \frac{\$134}{\$1,030} = 13.01\%$$

Yield to maturity is 13.01%.

Yield to call: It is assumed that the Treasury will call the bond, and that the life of the bond shrinks from 10 years to 5.

$$\text{Prorated premium/discount} = \frac{\text{Difference between face value and price}}{\text{Years remaining to call}}$$

$$= \frac{\$1,060 \text{ (price)} - \$1,000 \text{ (face value)}}{5}$$

$$= \frac{\$60}{\$5} = \$12 \text{ per year}$$

$$\text{Yield to call} = \frac{\text{Nominal rate} + \left(\begin{array}{l} + \text{ Prorated discount (\$) or} \\ - \text{ Prorated premium (\$)} \end{array}\right)}{(\text{Price} + \text{Face value})/2}$$

$$= \frac{\$140 - \$12}{(\$1,060 + \$1,000)/2}$$

$$= \frac{\$128}{\$2,060/2} = \frac{\$128}{\$1,030} = 12.43\%$$

Since this bond is selling at a premium, the yield to call is lower than the yield to maturity.

What are "flower bonds"?

Some years ago, the Treasury issued bonds that carried an advantage in the payment of estate taxes. The bonds were purchased at a discount from face value, but they could be used at face value in the payment of estate taxes. Hence the name, "flower bonds."

Example: An investor could buy a flower bond at 88 ($880) and hold it until death. At that time, the bond could be submitted as payment of estate taxes at the full face value of $1,000.

Flower bonds carried much lower interest rates than other T bonds issued at the time. For example, a November 98 flower bond has a nominal rate of only 4.22%, while other Treasury bonds maturing in the same year average 8.25%. The investor gives up interest payments for the estate tax advantage, while the Treasury gives up tax revenues for a reduced debt service.

Although no flower bonds have been issued since 1971, and none are in the offing, they are still outstanding and will be for years to come.

What are STRIPs?

STRIPs are Treasury bonds that have been "stripped" of their coupon rate; they pay no interest over their lives. They are purchased at a deep discount and redeemed at maturity at full face value. *Stripped Treasuries* are a variety of debt securities known as *zero coupon bonds*, which may also be issued by corporations and municipalities.

Example: A STRIP with a face value of $1,000 matures in 15 years. It is purchased at $280, pays no interest during its term, but pays the full par value of $1,000 to the holder at maturity.

Why would an investor buy STRIPs?

"STRIPs" are useful to anyone with a need for a lump sum of money in the distant future, such as for college tuition, purchasing a home, or retirement.

Example: An investor with $28,000 has a 3-year-old daughter. He buys 100 15-year zero coupon bonds at 28, or $28,000 (100 bonds times $28). In 15 years, when the daughter is ready for college, he receives $100,000 in face value.

How is the return on zero coupon bonds taxed?

The tax aspect of zeros is a drawback. The holder of a zero coupon bond must accrete the discount each year and, in effect, pay federal taxes on money that is not received. (Interest on Treasury securities is exempt from state and local taxes.) Because of this tax drawback, zero coupon bonds are most attractive to investors who are tax-exempt. A pension fund manager, for instance, could take a position in zeros, in anticipation of the need to pay retired employees in the distant future.

How do zero coupon bonds show up in the financial listings?

Zeros are listed separately, under the heading of "Stripped Treasuries," but otherwise in the same format as other T bonds.

a denotes "stripped interest."

b means "Treasury bond, stripped principal."

c means "Treasury note, stripped principal."

Example: In the following quotation:

Rate	Maturity	Bid	Asked	Bid Chg.	Yld.
.00	Nov 11a	16.22	17.01	+.03	8.04

- Rate is ".00" because the interest is stripped (*a*).
- Maturity is in November of 2011, at which time the holder receives $1,000.
- The bid and asked prices are calculated on the basis of 32nds, like any other T bonds.

Bid price:

$$\text{Price} = \begin{array}{c}\text{Numbers}\\ \text{before}\\ \text{decimal (as}\\ \text{percentage)}\end{array} \times \begin{array}{c}\text{Face}\\ \text{value}\end{array} + \frac{\begin{array}{c}\text{Numbers}\\ \text{after}\\ \text{decimal}\end{array}}{32} \times \$10$$

$$= .16 \times \$1{,}000 + \frac{22}{32} \times \$10$$

$$= \$160 + \$6.875 = \$166.88$$

Asked price:

$$\text{Price} = \begin{array}{c}\text{Numbers}\\ \text{before}\\ \text{decimal (as}\\ \text{percentage)}\end{array} \times \begin{array}{c}\text{Face}\\ \text{value}\end{array} + \frac{\begin{array}{c}\text{Numbers}\\ \text{after}\\ \text{decimal}\end{array}}{32} \times \$10$$

$$= .17 \times \$1{,}000 + \frac{1}{32} \times \$10$$

$$= \$170 + \$.3125 = \$170.31$$

● The bid change is computed in the same way as T bonds.

$$\text{Change in bid (\$)} = \text{Change in bid (32nds)} \times \$.3125$$
$$= 3 \times \$.3125 = \$.9375$$

● The yield stated in the rightmost column is calculated by prorating the discount (the difference between the current price and face value) over the remaining time to maturity. It is calculated by computer according to a sophisticated formula.

Can individual investors purchase Treasury securities?

Yes, but they should understand the nature of the Treasury securities market. The minimum purchase for notes and bonds is only $1,000 ($10,000 for bills). But the individual placing a minimum purchase would be a nuisance in a market dominated by large institutions and very wealthy individuals, where a small order is measured in the hundreds of thousands of dollars. Brokerage firms are often reluctant to handle small individual orders and, as compensation, may attach additional handling charges. These charges, although they may not seem like much compared to the size of the order, detract from the profitability of the transaction.

Example: An individual investor places an order to buy an 8%, $5,000 Treasury note at its face value. The brokerage firm handling the order charges a $100 commission, which reduces the first year's yield by 2%.

$$\text{Nominal yield (\$)} = \text{Face value} \times \text{Nominal yield (\%)}$$
$$= \$5,000 \times .08 = \$400$$

But the $100 commission must be deducted, making the first year's yield, for a total of $300, which reduces the yield to 6%.

$$\text{Yield} = \frac{\text{Return}}{\text{Investment}} = \frac{\$300}{\$5,000} = .06 \text{ or } 6\%$$

Are there other ways for an individual to invest in Treasuries?

There are two other ways for individuals to invest in Treasury securities:

- By purchasing shares in a government securities mutual fund.
- By investing in U.S. Treasury savings bonds.

GOVERNMENT SECURITIES MUTUAL FUND SHARES

What are the benefits of purchasing government securities mutual fund shares?

Government securities mutual funds pool the investment capital of many individuals to take positions in Treasuries and in government agency securities, which are rated only slightly lower than Treasuries. (See the next section in this chapter for more on government agency securities.) Initial investments can be as low as $500, and subsequent investments can be as little as $50. Through such funds, individual investors can enjoy safety of principal, diversification, and the benefits of professional money management.

Do these funds have any drawbacks?

Some funds exact a sales charge, or *load*, which is the fee for purchasing shares in the fund; it goes to the broker who handles your order for the shares, not to the fund's investment manager. The load for a government securities fund averages 2%, which compares favorably with loads of 8.5% for stock funds but which erodes the yield on the shares.

Example: An individual purchases $1,000 worth of shares in a government securities fund, which is averaging a 9% return. The load is 2%. The first year's yield is immediately reduced to 7% (9% average return less 2% load).

TREASURY SAVINGS BONDS

How do savings bonds differ from T bills, notes, and bonds?

Savings bonds differ from Treasury securities in two ways:

● Their denominations are much lower, all under $500.

● They are non-negotiable; that is, they are not traded in any securities market.

They are perfectly geared for the small investor.

What are Series EE savings bonds?

Series EE savings bonds are Treasury bonds issued at a 50% discount from their face value. The purchaser pays the discounted price and at maturity is repaid the full face value at maturity in 12 years. No interest payments are made during the life of the bond. Although no interest is paid, it is accrued in the form of the discount between purchase price and face value. The interest does not accrue, however, in even increments from year to year. Rather, it accumulates in small amounts in the early years, in larger amounts as maturity nears.

Federal law prohibits anyone from purchasing more than $15,000 worth of Series EE bonds in one year. But the $15,000 cap refers to the purchase price, not the face value.

Example: An investor may buy a $100 Series EE bond at $50. In 5 years, the investor is repaid $100.

How is interest on Series EE bonds taxed?

The owner has an option. The prorated amount of interest can be declared and taxes paid each year (as is the case with zero coupon bonds). Or taxes can be paid in a lump sum when the bond is redeemed at maturity.

What if the Series EE bond is returned before its maturity date?

After a holding period specified on the back of the bond certificate, the Series EE bond may be redeemed for the purchase price plus interest earned to the redemption date. The interest rate is 85% of the average yield on 5-year Treasury securities for the holding period. The interest is calculated by the Treasury at the time of redemption. A *rough approximation* of the amount of interest can be calculated by means of a variation on the interest formula:

$$\text{Interest (\$)} = \text{Price} \times \begin{array}{c} .85 \text{ (5-year} \\ \text{Treasury} \\ \text{average)} \end{array} \times \dfrac{\begin{array}{c}\text{Holding} \\ \text{period} \\ \text{(days)}\end{array}}{365 \text{ days}}$$

Example: The investor who bought a $100 bond at the discounted price of $50 holds the bond for a little over 2 years (750 calendar days) and then turns it in (prior to maturity). During the 2-year-plus holding period, 5-year Treasuries averaged 10%.

$$\text{Interest (\$)} = \text{Price} \times \begin{array}{c} .85 \text{ (5-year} \\ \text{Treasury} \\ \text{average)} \end{array} \times \dfrac{\begin{array}{c}\text{Holding} \\ \text{period} \\ \text{(days)}\end{array}}{365 \text{ days}}$$

$$= \$50 \times .85 \, (.10) \times \dfrac{750 \text{ days}}{365 \text{ days}}$$

$$= \$50 \times .085 \times 2.055 = \$6.31 \text{ per bond}$$

What are Series HH bonds?

Series HH bonds are Treasury-issued bonds that are received in exchange for Series E or Series EE bonds. They are exchanged at their face value and pay interest semiannually. The rate of interest, stated on the bond certificate, is fixed to maturity, which is 10 years. The bonds may be redeemed at face value at any time before maturity, at which time face value is repaid to the holder.

Federal law imposes a cap of $20,000 on Series HH bonds for any individual. That cap applies to face value, not to purchase price.

Example: A $1,000 Series HH bond is purchased for $1,000. The stated rate of interest is 8%. Annual interest is $80 ($1,000 times .08). The holder of the bond receives two checks a year, each for $40.

How are Series HH bonds interest taxed?

Annual interest is taxed as ordinary income and is included on the individual's tax return as such. The return of principal at maturity is not taxed because it is a return of capital.

U.S. GOVERNMENT AGENCY SECURITIES

What are U.S. government agency securities?

These securities are issued not by the Treasury, but rather by two types of agencies (see Figure 6–3):

- *Federal agencies*, which are government corporations.
- *Government-sponsored agencies*, which were once owned by the federal government but which are now owned by the public or by organizations they are designated to serve.

Both types of agencies need capital to serve the purpose for which they were created—provide loans for construction, farming, mortgages, and so on. They raise the capital by issuing debt instruments whose rating is only slightly lower than that of Treasuries.

How are agency securities issued?

These securities are issued not by auction, but rather through a selling group, which consists of primary dealers who have demonstrated their ability to distribute such issues. Each agency acts through its fiscal agent, who functions something like a corporate treasurer. The interest

Figure 6–3.

List of government agencies

Agriculture—The following agencies issue securities under the umbrella organization of the Federal Farm Credit System:

Banks for Cooperatives (COOP)

Federal Intermediate Credit Banks (FICB)

Federal Land Banks (FLB)

Home Financing:

Federal National Mortgage Association (FNMA, or Fannie Mae)

Government National Mortgage Association (GNMA, or Ginnie Mae)

Federal Home Loan Banks (FHLB)

Federal Home Loan Mortgage Corporation (FHLM, or Freddie Mac)

rates are determined in much the same manner as they are for corporate or municipal primary offerings.

How do agency securities trade in the secondary market?

After issuance, these securities are traded and quoted very much like Treasury notes and bonds. (The market participants are also the same—large institutions and very wealthy individuals.) There are some differences in the listings:

● Each agency's issues are grouped in the listings.

Example:

FNMA Issues				
Rate	Mat	Bid	Asked	Yld
8.00	7-89	99-30	100-01	6.88
10.05	8-89	100-02	100-05	8.41
		. . .		

● A bid change is not shown.

● A hyphen (not a decimal) separates the 32nds from the rest of the price.

Example: The asked price of 101-01 in the preceding listing means 101$\frac{1}{32}$.

● The trading unit can be as small as a 64th. A lower-case *a* indicates that you must *add* a 64th to the price as quoted in 32nds. A *d* means you must *deduct* a 64th. (More detail is provided later in this section.)

● A lower-case *b* indicates that the yield is the yield to call, not to maturity.

Example: In the following agency quotation:

Rate	Maturity	Bid	Asked	Yield
11.90	10-97	118-24	119-02	8.63

● The fixed rate of interest, the nominal yield, is 11.90%.

● The bond matures in October of 1997.

● The bid and asked prices are calculated just as they are for T bonds.

Bid price:

$$\text{Price} = \begin{array}{c}\text{Numbers} \\ \text{before} \\ \text{decimal (as} \\ \text{percentage)}\end{array} \times \begin{array}{c}\text{Face} \\ \text{value}\end{array} + \frac{\begin{array}{c}\text{Numbers} \\ \text{after} \\ \text{decimal}\end{array}}{32} \times \$10$$

$$= 1.18 \times \$1,000 + \frac{24}{32} \times \$10$$

$$= \$1,180 + \$7.50 = \$1,187.50$$

Asked price:

$$\text{Price} = \begin{array}{c}\text{Numbers} \\ \text{before} \\ \text{decimal (as} \\ \text{percentage)}\end{array} \times \begin{array}{c}\text{Face} \\ \text{value}\end{array} + \frac{\begin{array}{c}\text{Numbers} \\ \text{after} \\ \text{decimal}\end{array}}{32} \times \$10$$

$$= 1.19 \times \$1,000 + \frac{2}{32} \times \$10$$

$$= \$1,190 + \$.6250 = \$1,190.63$$

- The yield in the rightmost column is the yield to maturity based on the purchase price and the remaining time to maturity. It is calculated not by the rule of thumb method, but rather by a more sophisticated method.

When a 64th has to be added to or deducted from an agency security price, how is that done?

There are two ways to adjust an agency security's price for a 64th:

1. Convert the 32nds to 64ths and use the price formula in 64ths.

$$\text{Price} = \begin{matrix}\text{Numbers} \\ \text{before} \\ \text{decimal (as} \\ \text{percentage)}\end{matrix} \times \begin{matrix}\text{Face} \\ \text{value}\end{matrix} + \dfrac{\begin{matrix}\text{Numbers} \\ \text{after} \\ \text{decimal}\end{matrix}}{64} \times \$10$$

2. Add or deduct the dollar value of a 64th to whatever price you get from the price formula.

Method 1—Converting 32nds to 64ths: (1) Double the number of 32nds. (2) Add or deduct 1 to the numerator. (3) Use the fraction in 64ths in the price formula.

Example: An agency security's bid price is quoted as 101-25a. What is the dollar value of the bid price?

1. *Double the number of 32nds:*

   Number of 64ths = 2 × 32nds = 2 × 25 = 50

2. *Add 1 to the result* (because the quote is followed by an *a*).

$$50 + 1 = 51$$

(You deduct 1 if a *d* follows the quote.)

3. *Use the price formula with a fraction in 64ths:*

$$\text{Price} = \begin{array}{c}\text{Numbers}\\\text{before}\\\text{decimal (as}\\\text{percentage)}\end{array} \times \begin{array}{c}\text{Face}\\\text{value}\end{array} + \frac{\begin{array}{c}\text{Numbers}\\\text{after}\\\text{decimal}\end{array}}{64} \times \$10$$

$$= 1.01 \times \$1{,}000 + \frac{51}{64} \times \$10$$

$$= \$1{,}010 + \$7.9688 = \$1{,}017.97$$

Method 2—Adding the Dollar Value of a 64th to the Price: (1) Calculate the price in the normal manner.

$$\text{Price} = \begin{array}{c}\textbf{Numbers}\\\textbf{before}\\\textbf{decimal (as}\\\textbf{percentage)}\end{array} \times \begin{array}{c}\textbf{Face}\\\textbf{value}\end{array} + \frac{\begin{array}{c}\textbf{Numbers}\\\textbf{after}\\\textbf{decimal}\end{array}}{32} \times \$10$$

(2) Add or deduct the dollar value of a 64th, which is $.1563 (half the dollar value of a 32nd, $.3125).

Example: Calculate the dollar value of 105-12d.

1. *Calculate price in 32nds:*

$$\text{Price} = \begin{array}{c}\text{Numbers}\\\text{before}\\\text{decimal (as}\\\text{percentage)}\end{array} \times \begin{array}{c}\text{Face}\\\text{value}\end{array} + \frac{\begin{array}{c}\text{Numbers}\\\text{after}\\\text{decimal}\end{array}}{32} \times \$10$$

$$= 1.05 \times \$1{,}000 + \frac{12}{32} \times \$10$$

$$= \$1{,}050 + \$3.75 = \$1{,}053.75$$

2. *Deduct the value of the 64th:*

$$\text{Price} = \text{Price in 32nds} - \text{64th (\$)}$$
$$= \$1{,}053.75 - .1563 = \$1{,}053.59$$

KEY TERMS

Asked: The price sellers are willing to accept in the open market.

Auction: The bidding system by which the U.S. Treasury brings its debt securities to market and in which primary dealers bid for portions of new issues.

Bid: The price buyers are willing to pay for a security in the open market.

Callable: A feature of T bonds that permits the Treasury to "call" in the securities (that is, repay the face value to holders) any time within a 5-year period prior to maturity.

Discount: When the price of a debt security is lower than face value, the difference between face value and price. *See also* premium.

Federal agency: An agency that is a part of the organization of the U.S. government.

Flower bonds: Treasury bonds that may be used to pay estate taxes upon the death of the owner.

Government-sponsored agency: An agency that is backed by the U.S. government but that is privately owned.

Negotiable: A feature of Treasury bills, notes, and bonds that means that these instruments may be freely traded in the securities markets.

Premium: When the price of a debt security is higher than face value, the difference between face value and the price.

Primary dealer: A major brokerage firm or bank that is authorized to bid on new issues of Treasury securities and trade them in the secondary market.

Prorating: Spreading out an amount over a time period, such as prorating the discount or premium on a debt instrument to maturity.

Refunding: The repayment of principal on a maturing debt issue with the proceeds of a new debt issue.

Savings bonds: Bonds issued by the Treasury in low denominations, that may not be traded as securities.

Series EE: A Treasury savings bond that is issued at 50% of its face value and that pays full face value at maturity.

Series HH: A Treasury savings bond that is issued at face value in exchange for Series EE bonds, and that makes semiannual interest payments.

Spread: The difference between the bid and asked prices.

STRIPs: Treasury bonds that have been stripped of their coupon rates. They are bought at deep discount, make no interest payments, and pay the face value at maturity. They are a form of zero coupon bond.

Tender: An offer to buy.

Treasury bills: Short-term Treasury debt instruments issued and traded on a discount basis, in a minimum denomination of $10,000 and in multiples of $5,000, with maturities of 13 weeks (90 days), 26 weeks (180 days), and 52 weeks (1 year).

Treasury bonds: Long-term Treasury debt instruments issued and traded with a stated coupon rate, paying interest semiannually. Minimum denominations are $1,000, and maturities range from 20 to 30 years.

Treasury notes: Intermediate-term Treasury debt instruments with maturities of from two to ten years that make semiannual interest payments. They are quoted and traded as a percentage of face value.

Zero coupon bond: A bond (such as a Treasury bond) that trades at a deep discount and that pays no semiannual interest; hence the name "zero coupon."

7

Securities Calculations

YOU WILL LEARN:

- How commissions are computed and how they affect return.
- The mechanics of a short sale.
- The leverage that buying on margin gives investors.
- How interest on loans in margin accounts can affect return.
- The effects of meeting margin calls with cash versus securities.

INTRODUCTION

Investing in securities incurs many expenses, all of which affect profitability and return. Yet many investors are unaware of the effects of these expenses on their returns. When the broker executes an order, a fee is charged. When the broker extends a loan in a margin account, interest is charged. This chapter enables investors to calculate, anticipate, and minimize the effects of these and other expenses.

ROUND AND ODD LOTS

What are "round lots"?

Round lots are fixed units of trading for a given type of security.

Example: On the New York Stock Exchange (and on most exchanges), stocks are traded in multiples, or round lots, of 100 shares, and bonds are traded in multiples of $1,000 face value (principal amount).

What are "odd lots"?

Odd lots are units that are not multiples of a round lot.

Example: A purchase of 75 shares of a stock on the New York Stock Exhange is an odd lot transaction. So would a sale of $2,500 face amount in a corporate bond.

SHORT SALES

What does it mean "to sell short"?

In a *short sale*, an investor sells a stock that he or she does not own or one that he or she owns but does not wish to deliver to the buyer. Given a short sale instruction from an investor, the broker:

- Executes the order in the appropriate market.
- Processes the trade in the investor's margin account.
- Borrows the stock, either from another of its margin account customers or another broker.
- Delivers the stock to the purchasing broker and takes payment.
- Charges the investor interest on the amount by which the short market value of the borrowed stock exceeds the investor's overall credit balance. If a margin account has an overall debit balance, interest is charged on the debit balance plus the short market value. (Margin requirements on short sales are covered later in this chapter.)

The investor now has a *short position*.

Example: Investor Jane Smith tells her broker to sell 100 shares of Hitech short at $100. Her broker executes the order, borrows 100 shares from another broker (the lending broker) that are being held in street name, delivers them to the purchasing broker, and takes payment.

What requirements must an investor meet to enter into a short sale?

To be eligible to engage in a short sale, an investor must:

- Be able to borrow the security to be sold (which the broker normally is able to do).
- Make sure the order is marked "short."
- Be aware that, for securities traded on a national securities exchange, the short sale can be executed only on an *uptick* or *plus tick* (at a price that is higher than that of the previous trade) or on a *zero plus tick* (at a price equal to the preceding price, which was an uptick).

Example: Investor Jane Smith enters an order to sell "short." When the order hits the trading floor of the exchange, the trades take place at the following prices:

20	19⅝	19½	19⅝	19⅝

Smith's short sale can be executed on the trade at the second 19⅝, which is an uptick, or plus tick, from 19½. The first 19⅝ was a *downtick* from 20. It could also be executed on the third 19⅝, which is a zero plus tick; the preceding price is the same (19⅝), but it is an uptick from 19½.

Why do investors sell short?

Investors sell short to practice an old maxim in reverse. Instead of buying low and selling high, they sell high and *then* buy low. In other words, investors sell short when they expect a security's value to decline. They then buy the security at the lower price, give back the borrowed stock, and make a profit. The return is the difference between the short sale price and the price at which the investor buys the stock.

$$\text{Return (\$)} = \begin{pmatrix} \text{Short} \\ \text{sale} \\ \text{price (\$)} \end{pmatrix} - \begin{pmatrix} \text{Purchase} \\ \text{price (\$)} \end{pmatrix} \times \begin{pmatrix} \text{Number of} \\ \text{shares} \\ \text{held} \end{pmatrix}$$

Example: Smith's short position in the prior example remains in effect for exactly 3 months, during which time Hitech declines in price to $85. She buys 100 shares of Hitech at $85 and uses the stock to *cover* her short position; Smith's broker, the borrowing broker, then gives the 100 shares back to the lending broker.

$$\text{Return (\$)} = \begin{array}{c}\text{Short}\\\text{sale}\\\text{price (\$)}\end{array} - \begin{array}{c}\text{Purchase}\\\text{price (\$)}\end{array} \times \begin{array}{c}\text{Number of}\\\text{shares}\\\text{held}\end{array}$$

$$= [\$100 - \$85] \times 100 \text{ shares}$$

$$= \$15 \times 100 \text{ shares} = \$1,500$$

Smith's total return is $1,500.

Note: Smith's broker could have also borrowed the Hitech stock from one its own margin customers, subject to certain regulatory conditions.

When is it not a good idea to sell short?

Selling short can lead to big losses when prices move upward. Theoretically, there is no limit to how much an investor can lose. Short sales should not be entered into when there is any possibility that prices will rise quickly and dramatically.

Example: If after Smith sells Hitech short at $100, prices rise to $125 over exactly 3 months, Smith has lost a considerable percentage of her investment. At that point, she purchases 100 shares of Hitech for $12,500 and closes her short position.

$$\text{Return (\$)} = \begin{array}{c}\text{Short}\\\text{sale}\\\text{price (\$)}\end{array} - \begin{array}{c}\text{Purchase}\\\text{price (\$)}\end{array} \times \begin{array}{c}\text{Number of}\\\text{shares}\\\text{held}\end{array}$$

$$= [\$100 - \$125] \times 100 \text{ shares}$$

$$= -\$25 \times 100 \text{ shares} = -\$2,500$$

Smith has lost $2,500.

COMMISSIONS

What are commissions?

Commissions are the fees charged by brokerage houses for executing orders on behalf of investor/clients. Prior to May of 1975, commissions were fixed by NYSE rule. Since then, they have been deregulated and are fully negotiable. As a result, *discount* brokerage houses have sprung up. These firms specialize in handling orders at reduced commission rates. *Full-service houses* charge higher rates of commission but offer their clients more services, particularly in the area of market research and analysis. Volume rates can also be negotiated with brokerage firms by investors who deal in large purchases.

How are commissions figured?

Commissions are figured in basically two ways:

- As a percentage of the transaction price.
- As a flat dollar amount determined by the number of shares exchanged in the transaction.

How is a percentage commission figured?

The percentage is applied directly to the transaction price of the order.

$$\textbf{Commission (\$)} = \textbf{Transaction price} \times \begin{array}{c}\textbf{Commission}\\\textbf{rate (\%)}\end{array}$$

Example: Investor Robert Jones purchases 200 shares of Hitech at $95 a share. The transaction price is $19,000 (200 shares times $95 per share). Jones's brokerage house, a full-service firm, charges a commission rate of 2.5%.

$$\text{Commission (\$)} = \text{Transaction price} \times \begin{array}{c}\text{Commission}\\\text{rate (\%)}\end{array}$$
$$= \$19,000 \times .025 = \$475$$

Jones pays a commission of $475.

How is a commission figured if it is a flat dollar amount?

A flat dollar commission is applied directly to the number of shares of stock (or bonds) in the transaction.

$$\textbf{Commission (\$)} = \begin{array}{c}\textbf{Number of}\\\textbf{shares/bonds}\end{array} \times \begin{array}{c}\textbf{\$ per}\\\textbf{share/bond}\end{array}$$

Example: Jones's broker charges $.75 per share as a commission. The purchase of 200 shares of Hitech would then entail a commission of:

$$\text{Commission (\$)} = \text{Number of shares/bonds} \times \frac{\text{\$ per}}{\text{share/bond}}$$

$$= 200 \text{ shares} \times \$.75 \text{ per share} = \$150$$

The commission for the transaction is a flat $150.

How do commissions affect return on investment?

Because they are an expense to the investor, commissions detract from the return on investment and must be included in calculating total return.

$$\textbf{Return on investment (ROI)} = \frac{\begin{array}{c}\textbf{Return (\$)} - \\ \textbf{Commission (\$)}\end{array}}{\textbf{Investment (\$)}}$$

In either case, commission is the total of the opening and closing transaction.

Example: Jones purchases 1,000 shares of Hitech at $95 (the opening transaction) and sells them later for $120 (the closing transaction). His investment is $95,000 (1,000 shares times $95 per share). His per-share profit, or return, is $25 ($120 sale price less $95 purchase price), for a total return of $25,000.

If the broker charges a 2.5% commission rate on the purchase and the sale, the ROI is computed as follows:

Opening transaction:

$$\text{Commission (\$)} = \text{Transaction price} \times \frac{\text{Commission}}{\text{rate (\%)}}$$

$$= \$95,000 \times .025 = \$2,375$$

Closing transaction:

$$\text{Commission (\$)} = \text{Transaction price} \times \frac{\text{Commission}}{\text{rate (\%)}}$$

$$= \$120,000 \times .025 = \$3,000$$

Total commissions paid are $5,375 ($2,375 plus $3,000).

$$\text{Return on investment (ROI)} = \frac{\text{Return (\$)} - \text{Commission (\$)}}{\text{Investment (\$)}}$$

$$= \frac{\$25,000 - \$5,375}{\$95,000}$$

$$= \frac{\$19,625}{\$95,000} = .2066 \text{ or } 20.66\%$$

Without commissions deducted from the return, the ROI would be:

$$\text{Return on investment (ROI)} = \frac{\text{Return (\$)}}{\text{Investment (\$)}}$$

$$= \frac{\$25,000}{\$95,000} = .2632 \text{ or } 26.32\%$$

Note: The same formula for return can be employed if the broker charges a flat dollar amount per share. Only the commission is figured differently.

MARGIN TRANSACTIONS

How does a margin transaction work?

On the day that an investor purchases stocks or bonds on margin, the investor's brokerage firm arranges to pay the selling firm for the securities and to take delivery. At this point, the brokerage firm, acting on behalf of the investor, has purchased the securities in the investor's margin account. The investor owes the firm the full purchase price; that is, the investor's *debit balance* with the firm is equal to the entire purchase price of the purchased securities.

The investor's firm then:

- Keeps the purchased securities in its own name (in *street name*) as collateral for the loan.
- Requires the investor to deposit a percentage of the purchase cost—the *initial margin* amount required under Regulation T issued by the Federal Reserve Board.
- Extends a loan to the investor equal to the remaining debit balance after the required deposit has been made.

Example: Investor Jane Smith purchases 100 shares of Hitech stock, on margin, at $100 per share for a total purchase cost of $10,000. Smith's broker executes the order and is now obliged to take delivery and pay the selling brokerage firm on the *settlement date* in 5 business days. At this point, Smith has a *long position* in Hitech (that is, she owns the stock). Her account looks like this:

Long market value	$10,000
Debit balance	$10,000
Equity	0

Her debit balance—what she owes the firm—is equal to the purchase cost—or market value—of the securities purchased.

Smith's broker then issues a Regulation T call, which is due within 7 business days following the day of the purchase (the *trade date*), requiring her to deposit 50% of the purchase cost ($5,000). The broker extends a loan of $5,000, which represents the *maximum loan value* (the complement of the Reg T requirement).

Within 7 business days of the transaction, Smith deposits the $5,000 with her broker. Her account is now:

Long market value	$10,000
Debit value	$ 5,000
Equity	$ 5,000

On settlement day, Smith's broker makes payment in full to the selling broker, takes delivery of the stock and keeps it in street name, and starts to charge interest on the loan extended to Smith.

Notes: (1) Since 1974, the initial margin requirement has been 50%, according to Regulation T ("Reg T") of the Federal Reserve Board. That requirement is not likely to change in the near future. In some cases, brokerage firms may require a *house rate*, which is more than 50%; they are allowed the higher rates because the Reg T requirement is a minimum. In this chapter, 50% is used throughout. Whatever the percentage, however, the calculations remain the same.

(2) While it is common for investors to borrow less than the maximum loan value, all the examples in this chapter assume that the investor chooses to borrow the maximum amount.

How does a cash account differ from a margin account?

Investors may also trade securities in a *cash account*, in which all purchases are paid for in full—investors may not borrow money from the broker. The cash account is the "normal" account for an individual investor, particularly new investors.

If the cash account is so commonly used, why trade on a margin basis?

Investors trade on margin basically for two purposes: to gain greater leverage or to sell short.

Leverage

How does a margin transaction give investors leverage?

Buying on margin gives the individual investor *leverage*, that is, the ability to increase the rate of return by decreasing the dollar amount of the investment. With any given amount of investment capital, an investor can purchase more shares of stock or more bonds. The following formula shows that by decreasing the amount of investment, return on the investment is increased.

$$\text{Return on investment (ROI)} = \frac{\text{Return (\$)}}{\text{Investment (\$)}}$$

Example: Investor Smith purchases 100 shares of Hitech common stock at $100 in a cash account. She deposits $10,000 with her broker and either tells the broker to hold the certificates or takes delivery herself. Hitech stock rises to $110 a share. For her 100 shares, she has a total return of $1,000 (100 shares times $10 increase in value). Smith's return on investment (ROI) is:

$$\text{Return on investment (ROI)} = \frac{\text{Return (\$)}}{\text{Investment (\$)}}$$

$$= \frac{\$1,000}{\$10,000} = .10 \text{ or } 10\%$$

Smith could have increased her rate of return by buying on margin. Suppose, using the same $10,000, she had purchased 200 shares of Hitech at $100 on margin. The purchase price (market value) would be $20,000 (200 shares at $100). She would deposit the same amount of money for half of the purchase price and take a loan from the broker for the balance. Her account would look like this:

Long market value	$20,000
Debit value	$10,000
Equity	$10,000

Now when Hitech's price moves up to $110, the market value increases by $2,000 (200 shares times a $10 increase in value). Yet, because she has only invested $10,000, her rate of return is much higher:

$$\text{Return on investment (ROI)} = \frac{\text{Return (\$)}}{\text{Investment (\$)}}$$

$$= \frac{\$2,000}{\$10,000} = .20 \text{ or } 20\%$$

If the leverage is so great, why not always purchase on margin?

Margin purchases have to be selective for several reasons:

- Any profit is affected by interest charges (in addition to commissions that are charged on any order execution by a brokerage firm).

- Leverage works two ways. Stock exchange requirements also oblige brokers to demand maintenance margin from investors if the market value of the securities falls. That means the investor may have to pour more investment capital into a stock or bond that is losing value.

- Not all securities can be purchased on margin.

Interest Rates

When do interest rates hamper the profitability of a margin transaction?

If the securities have to be held for a long time before they appreciate, interest charges can significantly decrease the return on investment. Sometimes they can even lead to losses.

Example: Smith purchases 200 shares of Hitech at $100 on margin (as in the previous example). She pays the broker 8% annualized interest on the loan of $10,000. If Hitech common takes exactly one year to rise in price to $110, Smith will have carried a loan of $10,000 at a cost of $800 (8% of $10,000), thereby reducing her ROI to $1,200.

$$\text{Return on investment (ROI)} = \frac{\text{Return (\$)}}{\text{Investment (\$)}}$$

$$= \frac{\$1,200}{\$10,000} = .12 \text{ or } 12\%$$

Note: Interest charges are not included in the margin calculations in this chapter. Suffice it to say that a margin transaction should therefore be as short-term as possible, one in which the price moves fast enough to overcome interest expenses. Commissions are also excluded from the margin examples in this chapter.

Marginable Equity Securities

Which equity securities can be purchased on margin?

Investors can buy, on margin, any security:

- Listed on a national securities exchange.
- On the Federal Reserve's *over-the-counter margin list*.
- Traded on the National Association of Securities Dealers Automatic Quotation (NASDAQ) National Market System (NMS).

These are called *marginable securities*. Other types of equity securities are not marginable.

May a broker refuse to extend credit on a marginable security?

Yes. Some securities are so low-priced that margining them simply makes no sense. Even if the broker extends the loan, the maintenance requirements may be higher than usual. Also, some marginable securities have what is known as a *thin market*; that is, they are not traded much and would therefore be difficult to liquidate at a favorable price, if at all. Finally, securities that are subject to rapid and dramatic price changes are not good candidates for being margined. They could easily become drastically undermargined before the broker and investor can react.

THE MARGIN EQUATION

When the market price of a security held in a margin account changes, does that change affect the account?

Changes in market price change the relationships of equity, debit balance, and credit balance constantly. The reason is that the margin account must always remain in balance, since its components are based on the accounting equation. A variation of the accounting equation is called the *margin equation*.

Accounting equation:

$$\text{Assets} = \text{Liabilities} + \text{Equity}$$

Or:

$$\textbf{Equity} = \textbf{Assets} - \textbf{Liabilities}$$

Margin equation:

$$\text{Equity} = \text{Assets} - \text{Liabilities}$$

Or:

$$\text{Equity} = \begin{array}{l} \text{Assets: Long market value} \\ + \text{ Credit balance} \\ - \text{ Liabilities: Short market value} \\ + \text{ Debit balance} \end{array}$$

Or:

$$\text{Equity} = (\text{LMV} + \text{Cr}) - (\text{SMV} + \text{Dr})$$

- *Long market value* is the market value of securities that have been purchased on margin.
- *Short market value* is the market value of securities that have been sold short and that are owed to the broker.
- *Credit balance* is the money that is held in a margin account for an investor.
- *Debit balance* is the money an investor owes to the broker, such as the loan on the purchase of securities.

The usual format for margin calculations is:

Long/short market value	$000
Credit/debit balance	$000
Equity	$000

MARGIN REQUIREMENTS ON THE INITIAL TRANSACTION

Long Positions—Buying Securities

What is an investor obliged to do when taking a margined long position?

To take a margined long position, an investor is obliged to deposit enough cash to satisfy the initial Regulation T requirement (currently 50% of the purchase cost).

Example: Smith purchases 100 shares of Hitech at $100 on margin, for a purchase cost of $10,000. She deposits 50% of the purchase price ($5,000, her equity), and the broker extends a loan of $5,000 (debit balance). The account looks like this:

Long market value	$10,000
Debit balance	$ 5,000
Equity	$ 5,000

Note: The Federal Reserve makes an exception for Regulation T calls of $500 or less. Such calls may be waived by the broker depending on the circumstances of the margin account.

What effect do rising stock prices have in a margin account with only long positions?

Increased market value in a margin account with only long positions creates additional equity.

Example: Refer to Smith's account in the previous example. If Hitech rises in value to $140 per share, the long market value increases (and so does the equity in Smith's account):

Long market value	$14,000
Debit balance	$ 5,000
Equity	$ 9,000

Smith now has equity of $9,000. The broker does not share in this profit; the firm merely finances the purchase and charges interest on the debit balance. Correspondingly, the broker does not participate in any losses due to declines in long market values.

Note: In an actual account, the debit balance would have increased since the purchase date, due to interest charges on the loan of $5,000. For purposes of simplicity, interest charges will not be included in these calculations.

Can an investor make use of additional equity in a margin account?

Yes, as long as all regulatory requirements are satisfied. Any additional equity is considered—and called—*Regulation T excess equity*, and the investor may make use of it. Withdrawal of the Reg T excess equity is one option. Investors should remember, however, that withdrawing funds results in an increase in their debit balance, with related increases in interest charges. Long security positions may also be withdrawn provided certain conditions are met.

Example: Refer to Smith's account in the previous example, after the rise in Hitech's market value:

Long market value	$14,000
Debit balance	$ 5,000
Equity	$ 9,000

The Reg T requirement is $7,000 (50% of the long market value of $14,000). Since her equity is actually $9,000, she has $2,000 in Reg T excess equity. Smith may withdraw up to $2,000 from the account, which would then be:

Long market value	$14,000
Debit balance	$ 7,000
Equity	$ 7,000

When she takes out the $2,000 in equity, her debit balance increases by the amount of the withdrawal. (The margin "equation" must always remain in balance.) The broker automatically extends her margin—that is, extends the loan—an additional $2,000 for a total of $7,000, which Regulation T permits the broker to do.

What else can an investor do with Regulation T excess equity?

Regulation T excess equity may be used for even greater leverage. The additional equity may be applied toward the purchase of more securities on margin without incurring a Regulation T call. The maximum amount of securities that can be purchased without incurring a Regulation T call is termed *buying power*.

$$\text{Buying power} = \frac{\text{Reg T excess equity}}{\text{Regulation T requirement}}$$

Example: With $2,000 of Reg T excess equity in her account and a Reg T requirement of 50%, Smith can purchase up to $4,000 worth of securities without incurring a Regulation T call.

$$\begin{aligned} \text{Buying power} &= \frac{\text{Reg T excess equity}}{\text{Regulation T requirement}} \\ &= \frac{\$2,000}{.50} = \$4,000 \end{aligned}$$

If she chooses to purchase $4,000 worth of additional securities, the broker applies the Reg T excess equity of $2,000 toward the purchase and extends her loan an additional $4,000.

Before the purchase:

Long market value	$14,000
Debit balance	$ 5,000
Equity	$ 9,000

After the purchase:

Long market value	$18,000
Debit balance	$ 9,000
Equity	$ 9,000

Why does the broker extend the loan by $4,000 and not $2,000 (half of the purchase price of the additional securities)? Smith's $2,000 of Reg T excess equity is applied toward the newly purchased securities valued at $4,000, thereby satisfying the initial Regulation T requirement (50% of $4,000).

If an investor's margin account exactly meets the Reg T requirement, can additional securities by bought?

Certainly. With Regulation T requirements satisfied, any further purchases are handled the same way. The investor deposits part of the purchase price (within 7 business days of the trade date), and the broker extends a loan for the rest.

Example: With Regulation T requirements met exactly, Smith buys $5,000 worth of securities on margin. She responds to the Reg T call by depositing $2,500 with the broker, who then extends her margin loan by $2,500.

Before the purchase:

Long market value	$18,000 (+ $5,000 in market value)
Debit balance	$ 9,000 (+ $2,500 in loan)
Equity	$ 9,000 (+ $2,500 deposited equity)

After the purchase:

Long market value	$23,000
Debit balance	$11,500
Equity	$11,500

Is cash the only way to meet a Regulation T call?

No. Marginable securities may also be used. Their current market value is added to the account, both as market value and as equity. However, since they increase the long market value, they also increase the Reg T requirement when calculating Regulation T excess equity. The resulting debit balance is also higher compared to when funds are deposited to satisfy a Reg T call.

Example: Smith purchases the $5,000 in additional securities (as in the previous example) and then responds to the Reg T call by depositing still another $5,000 worth of marginable securities. She thereby increases the long market value and equity in her margin account by $5,000. The broker is obliged to increase the loan (or debit balance) by the full amount of the purchase cost.

Before the purchase:

Long market value	$18,000 (+ $5,000 for the purchased securities and $5,000 for the deposited securities)
Debit balance	$ 9,000 (+ $5,000 in loan)
Equity	$ 9,000 (+ $5,000 deposited equity)

After the purchase:

Long market value	$28,000
Debit balance	$14,000
Equity	$14,000

Smith's debit balance and interest charges are higher because she used marginable securities to meet the Reg T call.

What happens in a margin account when stock prices decline?

In a margin account with only long positions, a decline in market value decreases equity. The debit balance is unaffected because it is a loan and does not vary with market value. If the drop in market value wipes out any Regulation T excess equity, the account is then said to be *restricted*—that is, margined at less than 50%, the initial Reg T requirement. Any additional purchases will require the deposit of cash or marginable securities to meet the Reg T call.

Example: Refer to the previous example. Smith's $28,000 securities become worth only $24,000, decreasing the equity in her account.
    Before the decline:

Long market value	$28,000
Debit balance	$14,000
Equity	$14,000

   After the decline:

Long market value	$24,000
Debit balance	$14,000
Equity	$10,000

Smith's account is restricted. If she wishes to purchase any additional securities, she will have to meet a Reg T call.
    Smith puts in an order for $10,000 in securities. The order is executed, and she gets a Reg T call for $5,000. She responds by depositing $5,000 with the broker.
    Before the purchase:

Long market value	$24,000 (+ $10,000 in market value)
Debit balance	$14,000 (+ $5,000 in margin)
Equity	$10,000 (+ $5,000 in deposited equity)

   After the purchase:

Long market value	$34,000
Debit balance	$19,000
Equity	$15,000

The purchase of $10,000 worth of securities is now proper-ly margined.

Why can an account remain restricted? Shouldn't the broker issue a Reg T call to meet requirements?

An account can be restricted because Regulation T is an *initial requirement*, applicable only to the original purchase commitment. What happens in a margin account in relation to calls for additional margin after the purchase is not covered by Reg T. Subsequent changes in market prices are covered, however, by exchange and "house" maintenance requirements (explained later in this chapter).

Example: Refer to the previous example. After Smith buys the $10,000 in securities, she needs only to meet the Reg T requirement on that purchase. The rest of the account is no longer affected by the regulation. Her equity is less than 50% of the long market value ($17,000).

Long market value	$34,000
Debit balance	$19,000
Equity	$15,000

Long Positions—Selling Securities

How is a margin account affected by a sale of long security positions?

A long sale is a liquidating transaction. According to Reg-ulation T, when any type of margin position is liquidated, the current Regulation T margin that was required on the liquidated position is released and is available for with-drawal or credit to the Special Memorandum Account (SMA). The amount released is calculated by multiplying the sales proceeds by the current initial Reg T requirement, which we assume to be 50% for purposes of illustration.

Funds released = Sales proceeds × Reg T requirement

Also, a margin account may have Regulation T excess equity after a liquidating transaction, such as a long sale. To account for this, the maximum amount available for withdrawal from a margin account at the close of a business day is the amount released on the long sale or the amount of Reg T excess equity, whichever is greater.

Withdrawable amount	=	Greater of: 50% of long sales proceeds, or Regulation T excess equity

The sale of securities also decreases the debit balance, because the broker delivers the securities held as collateral, which, in effect, repays all or part of the loan. Equity remains the same providing the market prices of the remaining securities held in the account are unchanged.

Example: Refer to the previous example. Smith places an order with her broker to sell $8,000 worth of securities. The broker executes the order, delivers the securities held as collateral, and takes payment of $8,000. The sales proceeds are then used to decrease the amount of the loan.
  Before the sale:

Long market value	$34,000 (−$8,000)
Debit balance	$19,000 (−$8,000)
Equity	$15,000

  After the sale:

Long market value	$26,000
(Reg T requirement = $13,000)	
Debit balance	$11,000
Equity	$15,000

What amount of funds can be withdrawn as the result of the long sale of securities?

	Greater of:
Withdrawable amount =	50% of long sales proceeds, or Regulation T excess equity

The funds available for withdrawal from Smith's account consist of the $4,000 (.50 times $8,000 sales proceeds) released on the sale. This amount is used because it exceeds the Regulation T excess equity of $2,000 ($15,000 equity

less $13,000 Regulation T requirement) in the account after
the sale.

The withdrawal will increase the debit balance (and
interest charges to the investor).

Example: Refer to the previous example. If Smith withdraws the funds released on the sale ($4,000), her debit
balance increases by the same amount.

Before the withdrawal:

Long market value	$26,000
Debit balance	$11,000 (+ $4,000)
Equity	$15,000 (− $4,000)

After the withdrawal:

Long market value	$26,000
Debit balance	$15,000
Equity	$11,000

*How is a purchase and sale in the same account
handled?*

When an investor purchases one security and sells another
in the same day (so that the trade dates coincide), the two
transactions are known as a *same day substitution*, and they
are handled as such. The proceeds of the sale are used to
reduce the debit balance, while the cost of the purchase
increases the debit balance. In effect, if the purchase cost
exceeds the sales proceeds, the debit balance is increased
by the net difference. If the sales proceeds exceed the
purchase cost, the debit balance is reduced by the net
difference.

Example: Refer to the previous example. Smith sells 100
shares of Hitech at $40 ($4,000 in sales proceeds) and, on
the same day, buys 100 shares of Big Business at $60
($6,000 purchase cost).

Before any activity:

Long market value	$26,000
Debit balance	$15,000
Equity	$11,000

After the purchase:

Long market value	$32,000
Debit balance	$21,000
Equity	$11,000

After the sale:

Long market value	$28,000
Debit balance	$17,000
Equity	$11,000

Smith will get a Reg T call for $1,000, or 50% of $2,000, the net difference between the purchase cost ($6,000) and the sales proceeds ($4,000).

Can a substitution release funds for withdrawal?

Yes, if the sales proceeds are greater than the purchase cost, the amount available for withdrawal is the greater of 50% of the net sale proceeds or the Reg T excess equity.

Greater of:
Withdrawable amount = Net sales proceeds × .50, or
Reg T excess equity

Example: Smith sells 100 shares of Big Business at $60 ($6,000 in sales proceeds) and, on the same day, buys 100 shares of Hitech at $40 ($4,000 purchase cost).

Before any activity:

Long market value	$26,000
Debit balance	$15,000
Equity	$11,000

After the purchase:

Long market value	$30,000
Debit balance	$19,000
Equity	$11,000

After the sale:

Long market value	$24,000
(Reg T requirement = $12,000)	
Debit balance	$13,000
Equity	$11,000

What amount of funds may be withdrawn as the result of the purchase ($4,000) and sale ($6,000) with net proceeds of $2,000?

$$\text{Withdrawable amount} = \begin{array}{l} \text{Greater of:} \\ \text{Net sales proceeds} \times .50, \text{ or} \\ \text{Reg T excess equity} \end{array}$$

$$= \$2,000 \times .50 = \$1,000, \text{ or}$$
$$= \text{Reg T excess equity} = 0$$

Reg T excess equity is zero because the equity of $11,000 is less than the initial Reg T requirement of $12,000 on the long security position. Smith may withdraw up to $1,000, which is the amount released on the sale.

If Smith withdraws the equity, the account is:

Long market value	$24,000
Debit balance	$14,000
Equity	$10,000

The debit balance is increased; so the equity is reduced.

Short Sales Margin Requirements

Is the short portion of a margin account separate and distinct from the long portion of a margin account?

Not really. A short sale is a margin transaction and, as such, is another type of security commitment that investors may make in their margin account. (Short sales are prohibited in cash accounts.) All long and short margin transactions are processed in the same margin account for an investor. All long and short positions and money balances are calculated together for margin purposes in the one margin account.

Note: For purposes of explanation, the long portion of a margin account will be identified as "the long account" and the short portion as "the short account." In fact, they are parts of the same account.

Are the initial requirements the same for short sale as for a purchase?

Yes. A short sale is a margin transaction, and Regulation T requires the deposit of 50% of the sales proceeds.

Example: Investor Robert Jones sells $15,000 worth of Big Business common stock short. The sale is executed, and he gets a Reg T call from the broker for $7,500 (the 50% requirement). He has no other positions in his account.

Long Account	Short Account	
-0-	Short market value	$15,000
	Credit balance	$15,000
	Reg T call	$ 7,500

What is the status of the account after the Reg T call is met?

Deposits made in response to Reg T calls are put into the margin account, creating equity there.

Example: When Jones sends in his check for $7,500, his account is:

Long Account		Short Account	
Long market value	-0-	Short market value	$15,000
Credit balance	$7,500	Credit balance	$15,000
Equity	$7,500		

How do rising prices affect a short account?

Rising prices mean that the broker who is lending the securities has been pledged less money than the securities are currently worth in the market. The broker therefore has to *mark the account to the market*. That is, the broker takes the increase in price from the short seller and gives them to the lending broker. The long and short balances are then adjusted accordingly.

Example: Big Business common rises in value, so that the securities in Jones's short sale are now worth $17,000. At that point, the account looks like this:

Long Account		Short Account	
Long market value	-0-	Short market value	$17,000
Credit balance	$7,500	Credit balance	$15,000
Equity	$7,500		

The difference between what the lending broker has been pledged ($15,000) and the current market value ($17,000) is $2,000. The broker takes $2,000 from Jones's margin account and pledges it to the lending broker. The long and short account balances are adjusted accordingly. Thus the account is "marked to the market."

Long Account		Short Account	
Long market value	-0-	Short market value	$17,000
Credit balance	$5,500	Credit balance	$17,000
Equity	$5,500		

What effect do declining prices have on a short account?

Declining prices are exactly what the short seller is expecting. When prices drop, the money pledged to the lending broker is greater than what the securities are worth. The short seller could "buy in" (that is, cover) the securities and pocket the difference. The borrowed securities would then be returned to the lending broker, who would return the funds and/or securities to the borrowing broker. Assuming the short seller does not close the position, the borrowing broker does a *reverse mark to the market*. Funds are returned by the lending broker, so that the funds on deposit with the lending broker are equal to the current market value of the borrowed securities. The long and short balances are adjusted to reflect the change in short market value.

Example: Big Business common drops in price, bringing Jones's shares down to $14,000.

Long Account		Short Account	
Long market value	-0-	Short market value	$14,000
Credit balance	$5,500	Credit balance	$14,000
Equity	$5,500		

The difference between the short sale prices ($17,000) and the current market value ($14,000) is $3,000. Assuming Jones does not close the short position, $3,000 is transferred from the short account to the long account. This is a "reverse mark to the market."

Long Account		Short Account	
Long market value	-0-	Short market value	$14,000
Credit balance	$8,500	Credit balance	$14,000
Equity	$8,500		

Equity has been increased by the decline in price.

How is Reg T excess equity computed in a short account?

In a short account, Regulation T excess equity is calculated in the same way as in a long position. Any amount over 50% of the short market value is considered excess.

$$\text{Regulation T excess equity} = \text{Equity} - \text{Reg T requirement}$$

Example: Refer to the previous example. Jones needs $7,000 in equity to meet initial requirements, and he has $8,500 in equity in his margin account.

$$\text{Regulation T excess equity} = \text{Equity} - \text{Reg T requirement}$$
$$= \$8,500 - \$7,000 = \$1,500$$

Jones has $1,500 in Reg T excess equity.

How is a short position "closed"?

At any time (preferably when prices have dropped), the short seller can purchase ("buy in") the securities and return them to the lender, thereby terminating the obligation to deliver.

How does closing a short position affect an investor's margin account?

The buy-in (or covering) of a short position is a liquidating (or closing) transaction. According to Reg T, when any type of margin position is liquidated, the current initial Reg T margin that was required on the liquidated position is released and is available for withdrawal, or for crediting to the Special Memorandum Account (SMA). The amount released on the buy-in is calculated by multiplying the purchase cost by the current initial Reg T requirement (assumed to be 50% for purposes of illustration).

Withdrawable amount = Purchase cost × .50

Also, a margin account may have Regulation T excess equity after a liquidating transaction, such as a buy-in. To account for this possibility, the formula used to determine the maximum permissible withdrawal at the close of a business day is the greater of the amount released by the buy-in or the Reg T excess equity.

Greater of:
Withdrawable amount = Buy-in cost × .50, or
Reg T excess equity

Example: Jones closes his short position when the Big Business stock involved in the sale goes to $14,000.

Long Account		Short Account	
Long market value	-0-	Short market value	$14,000
Credit balance	$8,500	Credit balance	$14,000
Equity	$8,500		

After the buy-in the status of Jones's account is:

Long Account		*Short Account*	
Long market value	-0-	Short market value	-0-
Credit balance	$8,500	Credit balance	-0-
Equity	$8,500		

$$\text{Regulation T excess equity} = \text{Equity} - \text{Reg T requirement}$$

$$= \$8,500 - 0 = \$8,500$$

What amount of funds is available for withdrawal?

$$\text{Withdrawable amount} = \begin{array}{l} \text{Greater of:} \\ \text{Buy-in cost} \times .50, \text{ or} \\ \text{Reg T excess equity} \end{array}$$

$$= \$14,000 \times .50 = \$7,000, \text{ or}$$

$$= \text{Reg T excess equity} = \$8,500$$

The Reg T excess equity ($8,500) is the maximum amount available for withdrawal or crediting to the SMA.

MAINTENANCE MARGIN

Long Positions

Does Regulation T apply to the reduction in equity due to security price changes after the initial transaction?

No, Regulation T applies only to initial margin requirements. Thereafter, all exchanges and the National Association of Securities Dealers have a minimum *maintenance* requirement of 25% of the current market value of the long margined security positions.

$$\text{Minimum maintenance requirement} = \text{Long market value} \times .25$$

$$\text{Maintenance call} = \text{Minimum maintenance requirement} - \text{Equity}$$

Note: In addition, brokerage firms themselves often apply their own higher maintenance requirements.

Example: Jane Smith's long margin account is as follows:

Long market value	$24,400
Debit balance	$14,400
Equity	$10,000

The market value declines to $20,000, decreasing equity:

Long market value	$20,000
Debit balance	$14,400
Equity	$ 5,600

Does this account meet the minimum maintenance requirement?

$$\text{Minimum maintenance requirement} = \text{Long market value} \times .25$$

$$= \$20,000 \times .25 = \$5,000$$

It does. The equity, at $5,600, exceeds the maintenance requirement by $600. The $600 is called the *maintenance excess*, the amount by which equity exceeds the maintenance requirement.

Note: Equity in excess of minimum maintenance requirements may not be withdrawn or converted to buying power.

The market value declines further to $18,000.

Long market value	$18,000
Debit balance	$14,400
Equity	$ 3,600

$$\text{Minimum maintenance requirement} = \text{Long market value} \times .25$$

$$= \$18,000 \times .25 = \$4,500$$

$$\text{Maintenance call} = \text{Minimum maintenance requirement} - \text{Equity}$$

$$= \$4,500 - \$3,600 = \$900$$

With equity at $3,600, this account is undermargined for maintenance purposes. The broker will notify the investor—that is, issue a *maintenance margin call*. The investor will have to respond to the call by depositing enough funds to bring equity up to at least $4,500. When the investor sends in the $900 difference between the equity ($3,600) and the minimum maintenance requirement ($4,500), the account is properly margined.

Long market value	$18,000
Debit balance	$13,500 ($14,400 − $900)
Equity	$ 4,500 ($3,600 + $900)

Notes: In the "real world" of securities, the broker would likely request more than $900, that is, apply the higher *house maintenance* requirement. Investors should inquire about higher house maintenance requirements when opening a margin account.

Is cash the only way to meet a maintenance margin call?

There are four ways to meet a maintenance call:

- Depositing cash (as in the previous example).
- Liquidating securities in the account.
- Depositing marginable securities.
- Appreciation in market value in the case of long market positions.
- Depreciation in market value in the case of short market positions.

How can an investor meet a maintenance call by liquidating securities?

The investor must liquidate four times the amount of the margin call. The reason is that only 25 cents out of every dollar of sales proceeds may be released to meet the call. Hence:

$$\text{Securities needed to meet maintenance call} = \text{Maintenance call (\$)} \times 4$$

Example: Refer to the previous example. Smith can meet the maintenance call for $900 by liquidating four times the amount of the call:

Securities needed to meet maintenance call $= $ Maintenance call (\$) $\times$ 4

$$= \quad \$900 \times 4 = \$3,600$$

Before liquidating:

Long market value	$18,000
Debit balance	$14,400
Equity	$ 3,600

After liquidating:

Long market value	$14,400 ($18,000 − $3,600)
Debit balance	$10,800 (75% of $14,400)
Equity	$ 3,600 (25% of $14,400)

The account is again properly margined for maintenance purposes.

How is a maintenance margin call met by depositing marginable securities?

To meet a margin call in this way, the investor has to deposit securities worth ⁴⁄₃ the amount of the call. A dollar-for-dollar reduction of the call amount is not possible because, as soon as the securities are deposited, they become subject to the 25% maintenance requirement. While the securities increase equity dollar for dollar, they also raise the maintenance margin required by 25% of their value.

Note: The fraction ⁴⁄₃ is the reciprocal of ¾, which is the amount that the broker is allowed to lend the investor for maintenance purposes.

Marginable securities needed to meet a maintenance call $=$ Maintenance call $\times \dfrac{4}{3}$

Example: Refer to the previous example. Smith can meet her $900 margin call by depositing $1,200 worth of marginable securities.

$$\begin{array}{l}\text{Marginable securities} \\ \quad\text{needed to meet a} \\ \quad\text{maintenance call}\end{array} = \text{Maintenance call} \times \frac{4}{3}$$

$$= \$900 \times \frac{4}{3} = \$1,200$$

Before depositing the securities:

Long market value	$18,000
Debit balance	$14,400
Equity	$ 3,600

After depositing the securities:

Long market value	$19,200 ($18,000 + $1,200)
Debit balance	$14,400 (75% of $19,200)
Equity	$ 4,800 (25% of $19,200)

The account is again properly margined for maintenance purposes.

How can an investor meet a margin call through appreciation in market value?

Technically, the investor cannot. This last and least likely way of meeting the call depends on the securities' price activity, over which the investor has no control. To eliminate the need for the call, the securities in the account have to rise to $\frac{4}{3}$ the amount of the call. (Again, the rise in market value increases equity but also increases the maintenance requirement.)

$$\begin{array}{l}\textbf{Rise in market value} \\ \quad\textbf{needed to meet a} \\ \quad\textbf{maintenance call}\end{array} = \textbf{Maintenance call} \times \frac{4}{3}$$

Note: Meeting a call in this way is highly improbable since the price move must take place before the investor is obliged to meet the call—a matter of days. Even when market appreciation does offset the need for the call, the broker may still require the investor to make a deposit or liquidate, depending on the circumstances of the account and the market.

Example: Refer to the preceding example. Smith is about to deposit cash to meet the $900 margin call when the market value of the margined securities rises to $19,200.

$$\begin{aligned} \text{Rise in market value needed to meet a maintenance call} &= \text{Maintenance call} \times \frac{4}{3} \\ &= \$900 \times \frac{4}{3} = \$1,200 \end{aligned}$$

Before depositing the cash:

Long market value	$18,000
Debit balance	$14,400
Equity	$ 3,600

After the securities rise in value:

Long market value	$19,200 ($18,000 + $1,200)
Debit balance	$14,400 (75% of $19,200)
Equity	$ 4,800 (25% of $19,200)

The maintenance margin call may be waived. The account is again properly margined for maintenance purposes.

SPECIAL MEMORANDUM ACCOUNT (SMA)

What is a special memorandum account (SMA)?

The SMA is an account whose purpose is to preserve the investor's buying power. The account is opened automatically whenever an investor first engages in a margin transaction. Any time equity is deposited in a margin account for any reason other than to meet a Reg T call, or any time Regulation T excess equity accumulates in an account due to market appreciation, a "memorandum" of it is recorded in the SMA. The equity itself, however, remains in the margin account.

How is the equity "memorandum" recorded in the special memorandum account?

As soon as Reg T excess equity accumulates in a margin account, the excess is recorded in the SMA.

Example: John Walker opens a margin account and purchases $10,000 worth of securities. He deposits $5,000 (to meet the 50% Reg T call) and the broker extends a loan of $5,000. The account looks like this:

Long market value	$10,000	SMA
Debit balance	$ 5,000	-0-
Equity	$ 5,000	

The securities appreciate in value to $12,000:

Long market value	$12,000	SMA
Debit balance	$ 5,000	$1,000 Cr
Equity	$ 7,000	

The account now has Reg T excess equity of $1,000: $7,000 equity less the Reg T requirement of $6,000 (50% of $12,000). That excess equity can be withdrawn or converted to buying power. To preserve the equity, the broker makes a memorandum of it in the SMA. No offsetting debit is made in the margin account, because the equity is not actually transferred.

What happens if the market value of the securities declines after the SMA notation is made?

The equity recorded in the SMA may still be withdrawn or converted to buying power, provided the withdrawal does not create a maintenance call.

Example: The long market value declines to $9,000, and

Walker chooses to withdraw $1,000. The margin account and SMA are both debited by the amount of the withdrawal:

Before the withdrawal:

Long market value	$9,000	SMA
Debit balance	$5,000	$1,000 Cr
Equity	$4,000	

After the withdrawal:

Long market value	$9,000	SMA
Debit balance	$6,000	$1,000 Cr
Equity	$3,000	$1,000 Dr
Balance		-0-

The account is restricted (that is, margined below the 50% Regulation T requirement), but it is still properly margined in that the equity ($3,000) is well above the minimum maintenance level of 25% ($3,000 divided by $9,000 is 33.3%).

Can investors use the SMA balance to purchase securities even if the long market value has gone down?

Yes. Even if an account is restricted, the balance noted in the SMA can be used to make purchases. Noting excess equity, funds released on liquidating transactions, and other credits in the SMA preserves an investor's buying power.

Example: Refer to the preceding example. After the long market value drops to $9,000, investor Walker buys $2,000 worth of additional securities on margin. The $1,000 balance in the SMA is debited, bringing the SMA balance to zero:

Before the purchase:

Long market value	$9,000	SMA
Debit balance	$5,000	$1,000 Cr
Equity	$4,000	

After the purchase:

		SMA
Long market value	$11,000	
Debit balance	$ 7,000	$1,000 Cr
Equity	$ 4,000	$1,000 Dr
Balance		-0-

If the balance had not been noted in the SMA, any previous Reg T excess, released funds on liquidating transactions, etc., would have been lost as market value declined.

If equity is deposited in a margin account to meet a maintenance call, is it noted in the SMA?

Yes, but with a qualification. Any time equity is deposited for any reason other than to meet a Reg T call, it may be noted in the SMA. However, if an account also has a Reg T call, the equity deposited is first applied to meet the Reg T call; any additional deposit may be noted in the SMA.

Example: Refer to the previous example. The market value declines to $8,000, reducing equity to $1,000. Since the 25% minimum maintenance amount is $2,000 ($8,000 times .25), this account is undermargined. A maintenance call goes out for $1,000. When the money is deposited, it is also recorded in the SMA.

Before the call:

		SMA
Long market value	$8,000	
Debit balance	$7,000	
Equity	$1,000	
Balance		-0-

After depositing the $1,000:

		SMA
Long market value	$8,000	
Debit balance	$6,000	$1,000 Cr
Equity	$2,000	

Note: Although the $1,000 equity is recorded in the SMA, it may not be withdrawn since doing so would bring the account below the minimum maintenance level and create a maintenance call.

If an investor uses marginable securities to meet a call, is the Regulation T loan value recorded in the SMA?

Yes. The Regulation T loan value (50%) on the deposited securities is noted in the SMA after all Reg T calls, if any, are met. The Reg T loan value percentage (50%) is the complement of the initial Regulation T requirement percentage (50%).

Note: If, for example, the Reg T requirement is changed to 60%, then the Reg T loan value percentage would become the complement, 40%.

$$\text{Marginable securities needed to meet a maintenance call} = \text{Maintenance call} \times \frac{4}{3}$$

Example: Refer to previous example. If Walker chooses to meet the $1,000 maintenance call with marginable securities, he would have to deposit $1,334 worth of them (⁴⁄₃ the amount of the call).

Before the call:

Long market value	$8,000	SMA
Debit balance	$7,000	
Equity	$1,000	
Balance		-0-

After depositing the securities:

Long market value	$9,334	SMA
Debit balance	$7,000	$667 Cr
Equity	$2,334	

$$\text{Marginable securities needed to meet a maintenance call} = \text{Maintenance call} \times \frac{4}{3}$$

$$= \$1,100 \times \frac{4}{3} = \$1,334$$

Once the securities are deposited, the SMA is increased by $667, the loan value (50%) on $1,334 worth of margin stock.

MIXED ACCOUNTS

What is a mixed account?

A *mixed account* is a margin account containing both long and short positions.

Example: The following is a mixed account.

Long Account		Short Account	
100 A @ 20	$2,000	100 X @ 10	$1,000
100 B @ 30	$3,000	100 Y @ 25	$2,500
100 C @ 40	$4,000	100 Z @ 15	$1,500
100 D @ 15	$1,500		

How are initial margin requirements determined for a mixed account?

In a mixed account, all the positions are netted out for the purpose of determining initial margin requirements.

Example: Is the following mixed account properly margined?

Long Account		Short Account	
100 A @ 20	$ 2,000	100 X @ 10	$1,000
100 B @ 30	$ 3,000	100 Y @ 25	$2,500
100 C @ 40	$ 4,000	100 Z @ 15	$1,500
100 D @ 15	$ 1,500		
Long market value	$10,500	Short market value	$5,000
Debit balance	$ 2,000	Credit balance	$5,000
Equity	$ 8,500		

Reg T requirements are applied to the total long and short market values.

Requirements:

Long market value: $10,500 × Reg T: .50	=	$5,250
Short market value: $ 5,000 × Reg T: .50	=	$2,500
Total requirement		$7,750

Equity:

Equity in margin account	$8,500
Equity in short account	-0-
Total equity	$8,500
SMA balance = $750	

Since the equity in the account ($8,500) is greater than the Regulation T requirement ($7,750), the account is properly margined. The difference of $750 ($8,500 less $7,750), in the form of Reg T excess equity, is put into the SMA.

Does the SMA notation apply to a mixed margin account as it does to a margin account with only long positions?

Yes. Equity noted in the SMA may be applied as in a margin account without short positions.

Example: The investor with the mixed account sells $4,000 worth of securities short. The Reg T call is for $1,250, calculated as follows:

Initial Reg T requirement	=	$2,000 (.50 × $4,000)
Less SMA balance	=	$ 750
Reg T call	=	$1,250

The broker has applied the $750 from the SMA to the initial Reg T requirement of $2,000 on the short sale. The result is a Reg T call for $1,250. After the short sale and deposit of $1,250, the account looks like this:

Long Account		*Short Account*	
100 A @ 20	$ 2,000	100 X @ 10	$1,000
100 B @ 30	$ 3,000	100 Y @ 25	$2,500
100 C @ 40	$ 4,000	100 Z @ 15	$1,500
100 D @ 15	$ 1,500	400 W @ 10	$4,000
Long market value	$10,500	Short market value	$9,000
Debit balance	$ 750	Credit balance	$9,000
Equity	$ 9,750		
SMA balance = zero			

Note: The amount deposited ($1,250) reduced the debit balance in the long account from $2,000 to $750.

What are the maintenance margin requirements for mixed accounts?

A mixed account involves far greater risk for an investor than a long margin account. When an investor buys securities, the risk is limited to the loss of the purchase price—the securities could theoretically become valueless. In a short position, however, there is no limit to how high a price can go. The short seller is obliged to cover the position sooner or later at whatever price is current. In recognition of this danger, the exchanges place stricter maintenance requirements on short positions, particularly for low-priced securities (with the potential for great gains).

- For stocks selling below $5.00 per share, the requirement is the greater of $2.50 per share or 100% of the market value.
- For stocks selling at $5.00 or more per share, the greater of $5.00 a share or 30% of market value is required.
- If all the short securities in a mixed account are $17.00 per share or more, a straight 30% is applied.

Example: What are the minimum maintenance requirements of the following mixed account?

Long Account		Short Account	
		100 A @ 10	$1,000
		200 B @ 10	$2,000
		100 C @ 20	$2,000
		100 D @ 2	$ 200
		100 E @ 5	$ 500
Long market value	$20,000	Short market value	$5,700
Debit balance	$12,000	Credit balance	$5,700
Equity	$ 8,000		

Long position:

$$\text{Minimum maintenance requirement} = \text{Long market value} \times .25$$
$$= \$20,000 \times .25 = \$5,000$$

Short positions: Each security has to be examined separately:

100 A @ 10	$ 500	The greater of $5.00 per share or 30%.
200 B @ 10	$1,000	The greater of $5.00 per share or 30%.
100 C @ 20	$ 600	The greater of $5.00 per share or 30%.
100 D @ 2	$ 250	The greater of $2.50 per share or 30%.
100 E @ 5	$ 500	The greater of $5.00 per share or 30%.
Maintenance requirement	$2,850	

Total maintenance requirement:

Long position	$5,000
Short positions	$2,850
Total	$7,850

$$\text{Maintenance excess} = \text{Equity} - \text{Maintenance requirement}$$
$$= \$8,000 - \$7,850$$
$$= \$150$$

With $8,000 equity in the account, this account meets minimum maintenance requirements. The maintenance excess of $150 may not be noted in the SMA because it is not Regulation T excess equity. Maintenance excess is the amount by which the equity exceeds the maintenance requirement. The opposite is a maintenance call, in which the maintenance requirement exceeds the equity.

KEY TERMS

Cover short: Any transaction in which an investor acquires securities and then uses the securities to replace previously borrowed shares (for a short sale). The investor is said to be "covering" the short sale.

Credit balance: The money held in an investor's account.

Debit balance: Money owed to the broker by an investor as a result of transactions in an account.

Down tick: A trade at a price lower than that of the immediately preceding trade.

Equity: The net worth in a customer's cash or margin account. In a margin account with only long positions, equity is the current market value of the securities held, less any debit balance. In a margin account with only short positions, it is the credit balance less the short market value.

House maintenance requirements: A brokerage firm's maintenance margin requirement, which is usually higher than the exchanges'.

Initial margin requirement: The portion of the purchase price that an investor must deposit with the brokerage firm upon entering into a margin trade commitment.

Loan value: See *Maximum loan value.*

Long market value: The total value of all long positions in an account, computed on the basis of the current prices of the securities.

Long position: Securities (stocks or bonds) held in a brokerage firm account for a client.

Maintenance margin: The amount of margin needed in an account after the initial requirements are met. An NYSE/NASD minimum percentage is 25% of long market value for marginable stocks.

Maintenance margin call: A demand, or call, by the broker for the investor to deposit cash and/or securities in a margin account as the result of a decrease in equity due to fluctuations in the market value of the securities acting as collateral.

Margin: The amount of money and/or collateral that must be deposited with a brokerage firm to secure a loan for securities. Margin is the equity required. It may be in the form of initial margin required for trade commitments or maintenance margin required due to a decrease in equity caused by market price fluctuations.

Marginable security: A security that is listed on a national exchange, included on the Federal Reserve's list of marginable securities, or traded on the NASDAQ National Market System.

Margin transaction: A trade in which the broker extends credit to the customer.

Maximum loan value: The maximum amount of money that an investor may borrow on a long security position. The loan value percentage is always the complement of the initial margin requirement.

Mixed account: A margin account with both long and short positions.

Odd lot: In a securities transaction, a number of shares, or of dollars in face value, that is not a multiple of the accepted unit of trading, or round lot.

Regulation T (Reg T): The Federal Reserve Board regulation that governs the extension of credit on securities transactions by brokers, dealers, and members of national securities exchanges.

Regulation T (Reg T) call: A demand, or call, by the broker for an investor to deposit cash or securities in the account following a margin trade commitment. Reg T calls must be met ''promptly,'' that is, within 7 business days.

Restricted margin account: A margin account in which the equity is below the initial margin required by Regulation T.

Round lot: A unit of trading, such as 100 shares of stock or $1,000 in face value for bonds.

Short market value: The total value of all short positions in an account, computed on the basis of the current prices of the securities.

Short position: Securities (stocks or bonds) sold or delivered out of an account in which they were not held.

Short sale: The sale of a security not owned by the seller or, if owned, not delivered.

Special Memorandum Account (SMA): An account set up alongside a margin account in which Regulation T excess equity is available and made note of; the purpose of the account is keep a "memorandum" of Regulation T excess equity so as to preserve it for future use.

Substitution: The purchase of one security and the sale of another on the same day so that the trade dates of the two transactions coincide.

Uptick (plus tick): A trade at a price that is higher than that of the immediately prior trade.

Zero plus tick: A trade at a price equal to that of the immediately prior trade, which in turn was higher than the last different price.

III

REAL ESTATE
AND RETIREMENT

8

Real Estate Investments

YOU WILL LEARN TO...

- Determine the monthly payment for a mortgage, given the rate, principal, and term.
- Calculate the principal and interest components of the monthly mortgage payment.
- Determine the "right" down payment.
- Compute the effects of points, loan origination fees, and prepayment penalties on the effective yield of a mortgage.
- Weigh the benefits of refinancing.
- Calculate payments on home equity loans.
- Compute property tax rates.
- Figure real estate broker's commissions.

INTRODUCTION

Many people buy real estate without realizing that it is an investment. We buy a place to live, to raise the kids, to retire. Many of us do not think of a home as a source of assets, of possible appreciation in value, and perhaps of income. This chapter provides you with many useful calculations related to the real estate that you own or that you intend to own.

Note: You can perform many of these computations without a calculator, but for some two things will be helpful:

- A calculator capable of raising a value to a given power.
- A couple of books, one containing monthly mortgage payment tables and annual amortization schedules, and

the other of annuity tables (with factors for present and future values for various compounding periods). Such books are available at larger bookstores.

If you cannot obtain these tables—or if you need to use them only once—call the lending institution (the bank or savings and loan association) with which you are doing business. Ask someone there to supply you with the information needed to make the calculations.

THE INTEREST EQUATION

What is interest?

Interest is the "cost" of borrowing money, and it is usually expressed as an *interest rate*, that is, as an annual percentage of the amount loaned, called the *principal*. The equivalent dollar value of the interest rate is a function of the rate applied to the principal over the period of time the money is out on loan, the *term*. At the end of the term, the loan *matures*, and the principal must be repaid.

$$\textbf{Interest} = \textbf{Principal} \times \textbf{Rate} \times \textbf{Time}$$

Example: A bank extends a one-year, $1,000 loan to a patron at an annual rate of 12%. The principal is $1,000, the term (or time) is 1 year, and the rate is 12%.

$$\text{Interest} = \text{Principal} \times \text{Rate} \times \text{Time}$$
$$= \$1,000 \times .12 \times 1 = \$120$$

Interest on the loan is $120. If the loan were for two years:

$$\text{Interest} = \text{Principal} \times \text{Rate} \times \text{Time}$$
$$= \$1,000 \times .12 \times 2 = \$240$$

What if a loan is for part of a year?

If the loan is extended for part of a year, then the time may be expressed in days, weeks, or months.

Example: The $1,000, 12% loan of the previous example is extended for nine months.

$$\text{Interest} = \text{Principal} \times \text{Rate} \times \text{Time}$$
$$= \$1,000 \times .12 \times \frac{9 \text{ months}}{12 \text{ months}}$$
$$= \$120 \times \frac{9}{12} = \$90$$

The interest for a nine-month loan is $90.

Note: Time in the formula can also be expressed as x weeks/52 weeks or x days/365 days.

What is the difference between "simple" interest and "compound" interest?

Simple interest is interest only on the original principal, or amount loaned. The calculation assumes that interest is paid to the lender and not included with the principal.

Example: Bill Malroni puts $1,000 into a 5-year, 12% simple interest time deposit. The bank pays Malroni $120 every year for the use of his money. Malroni is, in effect, lending the bank money. The principal of the loan is $1,000, the time 5 years, and the interest rate 12%. The interest payment on this account for each of the 5 years is the same:

$$\text{Interest} = \text{Principal} \times \text{Rate} \times \text{Time}$$
$$= \$1,000 \times .12 \times 1 = \$120$$

Note: This arrangement is an example of simple interest (and is not typical of a time deposit).

Compound interest results when interest is left to accumulate and becomes part of the principal, so that the borrower is paying interest on interest.

Example: Malroni deposits his $1,000 in another bank time deposit. The terms are the same—5-year maturity and 12% interest rate—but interest is "compounded annually." In year 1 the interest is the same as in a simple interest arrangement:

$$\text{Year 1 interest} = \text{Principal} \times \text{Rate} \times \text{Time}$$
$$= \$1,000 \times .12 \times 1 = \$120$$

The $120, however, is not withdrawn; it is left in the time deposit account, which now contains $1,120 ($1,000 principal plus $120 first year's interest). In the second year, the interest rate for the account is applied to the $1,120.

Year 2 interest = Principal × Rate × Time
= $1,120 × .12 × 1 = $134.40

The $134.40 in interest is added to the account for a total of $1,254.40. Each year the interest accumulates in the account and interest is paid on the interest (in addition to the principal):

Year 3 interest = Principal × Rate × Time
= $1,254.40 × .12 × 1 = $150.53
Year 4 interest = Principal × Rate × Time
= $1,404.93 × .12 × 1 = $168.59
Year 5 interest = Principal × Rate × Time
= $1,573.52 × .12 × 1 = $188.82

When the time deposit matures, the total compounded interest is $762.34.

How does simple interest compare to compound interest?

Compound interest accumulates more rapidly than simple interest and is therefore always more beneficial to lenders.

Example: Refer to the preceding example. Compare Malroni's return in the simple interest and compound interest accounts:

Year	Simple Interest	Compound Interest
1	$120.00	$120.00
2	$120.00	$134.40
3	$120.00	$150.53
4	$120.00	$168.59
5	$120.00	$188.82
	$600.00	$762.34

The longer interest is permitted to compound, the greater
the benefits to the lender (in this case, Malroni).

Can compounding occur more often than annually?

Yes. It can occur as often as daily. The more often interest
is compounded, the greater the benefit to the lender. The
interest calculation is simply adjusted for the compounding
period.

$$\text{Interest} = \text{Principal} \times \text{Rate} \times \frac{\text{Compound}}{\text{period (time)}}$$

Example: Malroni goes to a third bank and places $1,000
in a 5-year, 12% time deposit. In this account, however,
interest is compounding quarterly. The interest equation
applies, but the time component is adjusted to reflect the
portion of the year during which simple interest is being
paid.

$$\begin{aligned}
\text{Quarter 1 interest} &= \text{Principal} \times \text{Rate} \times \frac{\text{Compounding}}{\text{period (time)}} \\
&= \$1,000 \times .12 \times \frac{3 \text{ months}}{12 \text{ months}} \\
&= \$120 \times \frac{3}{12} = \$30
\end{aligned}$$

The interest for a 3-month term is $30. The $30 interest is
now included with principal, and the account's interest rate
is applied to the total, $1,030 ($1,000 principal plus $30
interest).

$$\begin{aligned}
\text{Quarter 2 interest} &= \text{Principal} \times \text{Rate} \times \frac{\text{Compounding}}{\text{period (time)}} \\
&= \$1,030 \times .12 \times \frac{3 \text{ months}}{12 \text{ months}} \\
&= \$123.60 \times \frac{3}{12} = \$30.90
\end{aligned}$$

Interest is again added to principal and the computation
repeated for the remaining two quarters of the year.

$$\text{Quarter 3 interest} = \text{Principal} \times \text{Rate} \times \text{Compounding period (time)}$$

$$= \$1,060.90 \times .12 \times \frac{3 \text{ months}}{12 \text{ months}}$$

$$= \$127.31 \times \frac{3}{12} = \$31.83$$

$$\text{Quarter 4 interest} = \text{Principal} \times \text{Rate} \times \text{Compounding period (time)}$$

$$= \$1,092.73 \times .12 \times \frac{3 \text{ months}}{12 \text{ months}}$$

$$= \$131.13 \times \frac{3}{12} = \$32.78$$

With interest compounding quarterly, Malroni earns $125.51 in the first year. Compare the following first-year returns:

Simple	Annually Compounding	Quarterly Compounding
$120.00	$120.00	$125.51

If interest were compounded "faster"—that is, more frequently per year—the total interest would be even higher. For example, $1,000 earning 12% compounded *daily* yields $129.40 in the first year. So an account that offers a slightly lower rate but faster compounding might offer a greater return than one with a higher rate but slower compounding. Computations must be done to determine which offers the greater dollar return.

Is there a simpler way to calculate compound interest?

Yes. There is a formula for calculating compound interest for any interest rate and for any number of periods. For short periods and relatively infrequent compounding, it might be useful. However, for most "real-world" situations, the compound interest tables should be consulted. These tables contain the total amount of principal and interest an investor would have at the end of a given period, at a given rate, for each dollar of principal invested. The values in the table are factors, which represent the *future value* of each dollar, that is, the value of a dollar earning a given interest rate, over a specified period of time, and at a certain frequency of compounding. Finding the total of principal and interest at the end of a given period involves a couple of simple steps:

● Go to the table with the applicable compounding period—quarterly, monthly, etc.
● Find the column headed by the relevant interest rate.
● Run down the column to the row at the end of the period.
● Multiply the future value factor there by the principal.

Future value = Principal × Factor

Example: Malroni invests $1,000 in a time deposit at 12%, compounded quarterly for 5 years. He wants to know how much the account will hold at maturity.

● *Go to the table with the applicable compounding period.* He consults the table for Quarterly Compounding:

Quarterly Compounding

Future Value of $1 Quarter	Annual Interest Rates			
	11%	11.5%	12%	12.5%
1	1.0275000	1.0287500	1.0300000	1.0312500
2	1.0557562	1.0583266	1.0609000	1.0634766
3	1.0847895	1.0887535	1.0927270	1.0967102
4	1.1146213	1.1200551	1.1255088	1.1309824
	. . .			
19	1.6743829	1.7135119	1.7535061	1.7943835
20	1.7204284	1.7627753	**1.8061112**	1.8504580
	. . .			
Year				
10	2.9598740	3.1073769	3.2620378	3.4241948
11	3.2991385	3.4804334	3.6714523	3.8727040
12	3.6772899	3.8982772	4.1322519	4.3799601
	. . .			

● *Find the column for the relevant interest rate:* He goes to the 12% column (heading in boldface).

● *Run down the column to the end of the compounding period:* In this case, the compounding period ends in 5 years, or 20 quarters (5 years times 4 quarters per year). (See the boldface entry in the row for "20.")

● *Multiply the future value factor by the principal:*

Future value = Principal × Factor
            = $1,000 × 1.8061112 = $1,806.11

Malroni will have $1,806.11 in his account at the end of five years.

Note: Refer to the previous example, in which the first year's interest ($125.51) was calculated for this account. If you use the factor from the table above for 12% over 4 quarters (1.255088), you will come up with the same amount.

Future value = Principal × Factor
            = $1,000 × 1.1255088 = $1,125.51

MORTGAGES

How do mortgages differ from most loans?

Mortgages are typically much longer arrangements than most loans, stretching out over 20, 25, 30, or more years. So in a mortgage agreement the lender is at risk for a much longer time than a lender in a time deposit arrangement of, say, less than a year. Also, each monthly payment is made up of some principal and some interest, whose proportions vary from month to month.

Monthly Payments

Is there a formula for calculating the monthly payment of a fixed-rate mortgage loan?

Yes. The formula, a modification of the interest equation that takes compounding into effect, requires the information on the principal, term, and rate. It assumes that the rate of interest is fixed to maturity of the loan.

$$\begin{matrix} \text{Monthly} \\ \text{payment} \end{matrix} = \text{Principal} \times \frac{\text{Rate}}{1 - [1/(1 + \text{Rate})^n]}$$

where:

$$\begin{matrix} \text{Rate} &=& \text{monthly rate (that is,} \\ && \text{the annual rate divided} \\ && \text{by 12 months).} \\ 1 - [1/(1 + \text{Rate})^n] &=& \text{the } \textit{mortgage constant.} \\ n &=& \text{number of monthly payment} \\ && \text{periods.} \end{matrix}$$

Example: Mary Kearney is buying a $100,000 home. She has $50,000 to put down and is seeking a 20-year mortgage of $50,000. Prevailing rates are such that she can obtain a fixed-rate mortgage of 12%.

- The amount borrowed (the principal) is $50,000.
- The rate is 1% (the annual rate of 12% divided by 12 months).
- The term (expressed in terms of months) is 240 (20 years times 12 months per year).

What is her monthly payment?

$$\begin{aligned} \begin{matrix} \text{Monthly} \\ \text{payment} \end{matrix} &= \text{Principal} \times \frac{\text{Rate}}{1 - [1/(1 + \text{Rate})^n]} \\[2mm] &= \$50,000 \times \frac{.01}{1 - [1/(1 + .01)^{240}]} \\[2mm] &= \$50,000 \times \frac{.01}{1 - [1/(1.01)^{240}]} \\[2mm] &= \$50,000 \times \frac{.01}{.009901^{240}} \\[2mm] &= \$50,000 \times \frac{.01}{.9081992} \\[2mm] &= \$50,000 \times .0110108 = \$550.54 \end{aligned}$$

Mary will make a payment of $550.54 a month. This payment will include both interest and principal components.

Notes: The formula does not enable you to determine their proportions.

Also, as you can see, this formula is a simple one, except for the one step in which a value must be raised to the power of 240! For this reason, the formula can be executed only on a calculator capable of computing exponents. Performing it on a nonautomated calculation device is unwieldy—in fact, all but impossible—and the results are prone to error.

Is there a way to determine monthly mortgage payments without an automated calculator?

Yes. You can determine monthly mortgage payments by means of *mortgage payment* tables. These tables are published in book form, and they are organized according to the interest rate. For each rate, the vertical columns represent the term (in years) and the rows reflect the principal.

Example: Part of a typical page in a mortgage payment table book might look like this:

Interest Rate: 12%

		Years		
Principal	18	19	20	21
100	1.13	1.12	1.10	1.09
200	2.26	2.23	2.20	2.18
500	5.66	5.58	5.51	5.44
1,000	11.32	11.15	11.01	10.89
		. . .		
10,000	113.20	111.54	110.11	108.87
20,000	226.39	223.08	220.22	217.74
30,000	339.59	334.62	330.33	326.61
40,000	452.78	446.15	440.43	435.48
50,000	565.98	557.69	**550.54**	544.35
		. . .		
100,000	1,131.95	1,115.39	1,101.09	1,088.70
105,000	1,188.55	1,171.15	1,156.14	1,143.13
110,000	1,245.15	1,226.92	1,211.19	1,197.57
		. . .		

Note: Actually, a page of mortgage payment figures will include many more entries for principal amounts, sometimes in only $1,000 increments. Typically, a book of payment tables will contain pages of terms and principal amounts, all under the heading of 12%. Terms may range from 1 to 40 years, and loan amounts from $100 to $250,000.

How are mortgage payment tables used?

Finding a monthly mortgage payment requires three steps. Given the same information as for the formula—principal, rate, and term—the steps are:

- Find the section containing payments for the interest rate.
- Find the column for the term.
- Run down the column to the row next to the principal amount. The figure in that cell is the monthly mortage payment.

Example: Eric Sigurd is applying for a $105,000 mortgage at 12% for 18 years. He has a book of mortgage payment tables. What is his monthly payment going to be be?

● *Find the section containing payments for the interest rate.* Eric flips to the section in the section in the book dealing with 12% interest.

Interest Rate: 12%

	Years			
Principal	18	19	20	21
100	1.13	1.12	1.10	1.09
200	2.26	2.23	2.20	2.18
500	5.66	5.58	5.51	5.44
1,000	11.32	11.15	11.01	10.89
	. . .			
10,000	113.20	111.54	110.11	108.87
20,000	226.39	223.08	220.22	217.74
30,000	339.59	334.62	330.33	326.61
40,000	452.78	446.15	440.43	435.48
50,000	565.98	557.69	550.54	544.35
	. . .			
100,000	1,131.95	1,115.39	1,101.09	1,088.70
105,000	**1,188.55**	1,171.15	1,156.14	1,143.13
110,000	1,245.15	1,226.92	1,211.19	1,197.57
	. . .			

● *Find the column for the term.* He reads from left to right until he finds the column headed by the number of years for his mortgage—18 years. (See the boldface heading in the preceding table.)

● *Run down the column to the row next to the principal amount.* He runs down the 18-year column until he comes to the row for the principal amount of the mortgage— $105,000. (See the boldface entry at the left of the table.) The entry at the juncture of the 18-year column and the $105,000 row is the amount of the monthly payment— $1,188.55. (See the boldface entry.)

Note: Refer to the example in the preceding section. Mary's monthly payment could just as easily have been determined from this table. Look down the 20-year column until you reach the $50,000 row, and you will find the payment amount of $550.54—exactly what was calculated.

What if the exact amount of the principal amount is not included in the payment table?

For amounts that are not included in the tables, you may "interpolate" or "extrapolate."

How do you interpolate using the mortgage payment tables?

This is a three-step process:

● Find the amount that is immediately greater than the loan amount.

● Find the monthly payment corresponding to the greater loan amount.

● Then apply the following formula:

$$\text{Monthly payment} = \text{Greater monthly payment} \times \frac{\text{Principal}}{\text{Greater principal}}$$

Example: Harvey Bender is seeking a 12%, 19-year loan for $47,000. The yield table does not have a row for this

amount. He must interpolate to determine his monthly
payment.

● *Find the amount that is greater than the loan amount.*
The amount in the following table is $50,000. (See the
boldface entry.)

Interest Rate: 12%

Principal	18	19	20	21
		Years		
100	1.13	1.12	1.10	1.09
200	2.26	2.23	2.20	2.18
500	5.66	5.58	5.51	5.44
1,000	11.32	11.15	11.01	10.89
		. . .		
10,000	113.20	111.54	110.11	108.87
20,000	226.39	223.08	220.22	217.74
30,000	339.59	334.62	330.33	326.61
40,000	452.78	446.15	440.43	435.48
50,000	565.98	**557.69**	550.54	544.35
		. . .		
100,000	1,131.95	1,115.39	1,101.09	1,088.70
105,000	1,188.55	1,171.15	1,156.14	1,143.13
110,000	1,245.15	1,226.92	1,211.19	1,197.57
		. . .		

● *Find the monthly payment corresponding to the greater loan amount.* The monthly payment for the larger
amount is $557.69. (See the boldface entry in the 19-year
column.)

● *Then apply the following formula:*

$$\text{Monthly payment} = \text{Greater monthly payment} \times \frac{\text{Principal}}{\text{Greater principal}}$$

$$= \$557.69 \times \frac{\$47,000}{\$50,000}$$

$$= \$557.69 \times .94 = \$524.23$$

Bender's monthly payment will be $524.23.

How do I extrapolate using the monthly mortgage tables?

This is a three-step process:

● Find a principal amount that is a "multiple" of the amount of the loan in question. A *multiple* may be less than or greater than the principal amount. If greater, the multiple must be the result of multiplying the loan amount by a whole number. If less, it must be the result of dividing the loan amount by a whole number.

Example: An investor is seeking a mortgage of $500,000, but the mortgage payment table only goes up to $250,000. The investor can use the maximum amount in the table ($250,000) as a "lesser" multiple of the loan amount ($500,000) because $250,000 can be multiplied by a whole number (2) to arrive at the principal amount of $500,000.

Another investor is seeking a mortgage of $45,000 but the tables do not contain such an amount. They do contain, however, $90,000. The investor can use $90,000 as a "greater" multiple of $45,000 because the result of dividing one into the other is a whole number (2).

● Find the corresponding monthly payment for the multiple amount.
● Apply one of the following formulas:

$$\text{Monthly payment} = \text{Monthly payment for multiple} \times \frac{\text{Greater multiple}}{\text{Principal}}$$

Or:

$$\text{Monthly payment} = \text{Monthly payment for multiple} \times \frac{\text{Principal}}{\text{Lesser multiple}}$$

Example: Alfredo Hernandez is applying for a $220,000 mortgage at 12% and for 21 years. The monthly mortgage table does not have an entry for that amount.

Interest Rate: 12%

	Years			
Principal	18	19	20	*21*
100	1.13	1.12	1.10	1.09
200	2.26	2.23	2.20	2.18
500	5.66	5.58	5.51	5.44
1,000	11.32	11.15	11.01	10.89
	. . .			
10,000	113.20	111.54	110.11	108.87
20,000	226.39	223.08	220.22	217.74
30,000	339.59	334.62	330.33	326.61
40,000	452.78	446.15	440.43	435.48
50,000	565.98	557.69	550.54	544.35
	. . .			
100,000	1,131.95	1,115.39	1,101.09	1,088.70
105,000	1,188.55	1,171.15	1,156.14	1,143.13
110,000	1,245.15	1,226.92	1,211.19	**1,197.57**
	. . .			

● *Find a principal amount that is a "multiple" of the amount of the loan in question.* He uses $110,000, which is a lesser multiple of $220,000 ($220,000 divided by $110,000 equals 2.)

● *Find the corresponding monthly payment for the multiple amount.* This is $1,197.57. (See the boldface entry under the 21-year heading.)

Apply the formula: In this case, Hernandez uses the one for the lesser multiple.

$$\text{Monthly payment} = \text{Monthly payment for multiple} \times \frac{\text{Principal}}{\text{Lesser multiple}}$$

$$= \$1,197.57 \times \frac{\$220,000}{\$110,000}$$

$$= \$1,197.57 \times 2 = \$2,395.14$$

Hernandez will pay $2,395.14 a month.

Example: Sylvia Kravitz is applying for a $15,000 mortgage at 12% for 20 years. The tables do not contain an entry for this amount.

Interest Rate: 12%

	Years			
Principal	18	19	20	21
100	1.13	1.12	1.10	1.09
200	2.26	2.23	2.20	2.18
500	5.66	5.58	5.51	5.44
1,000	11.32	11.15	11.01	10.89
	. . .			
10,000	113.20	111.54	110.11	108.87
20,000	226.39	223.08	220.22	217.74
30,000	339.59	334.62	**330.33**	326.61
40,000	452.78	446.15	440.43	435.48
50,000	565.98	557.69	550.54	544.35
	. . .			
100,000	1,131.95	1,115.39	1,101.09	1,088.70
105,000	1,188.55	1,171.15	1,156.14	1,143.13
110,000	1,245.15	1,226.92	1,211.19	1,197.57
	. . .			

● *Find a principal amount that is a "multiple" of the amount of the loan in question.* She uses $30,000, which is a "greater" multiple of $15,000 ($30,000 divided by $15,000 equals 2.)

● *Find the corresponding monthly payment for the multiple amount.* This is $330.33. (See the boldface entry under the 20-year heading.)

● *Apply the formula:* In this case, Kravitz uses the one for the greater multiple.

$$\text{Monthly payment} = \text{Monthly payment for multiple} \times \frac{\text{Principal}}{\text{Greater multiple}}$$

$$= \$330.33 \times \frac{\$15,000}{\$30,000}$$

$$= \$330.33 \times .5 = \$165.17$$

Kravitz will pay $165.17 a month.

Note: Both examples involve a multiple of 2. A multiple may be any whole number of 2 or more.

Determining Interest and Principal per Monthly Payment

Why do the monthly payments in the first few years of a mortgage consist of so much interest and so little principal?

Over the life of a fixed-rate mortgage, the borrower pays the same monthly amount, which contains some interest and some principal. Every month, however, the proportion of interest and principal changes. In the early years of a mortgage, the borrower is paying much more in interest in each payment than in principal.

The reason is that the interest rate per month is applied to the outstanding principal for that month. The outstanding principal will range from the full amount of the loan in the first month to zero by the time the loan matures. With each payment, the outstanding principal is reduced, and the interest amount decreases. Principal is paid off at an accelerating rate.

Example: For an 8%, 10-year mortgage for $50,000, the monthly payment is $606.64. (This figure is taken from the monthly payment tables, but could be calculated.) The monthly interest rate is .006667% (8% divided by 12 months). The first month's interest amount is:

$$\text{Interest} = \text{Principal} \times \text{Rate} \times \text{Time}$$
$$= \$50,000 \times .006667 \times 1 \text{ month} = \$333.35$$

When the homeowner makes the first monthly payment of $606.64, $333.35 of that payment is considered interest and the balance ($273.29) repayment of principal. In the second month, the principal is $49,726.71 ($50,000 less $273.29), and the proportions of interest and principal change.

$$\text{Interest} = \text{Principal} \times \text{Rate} \times \text{Time}$$
$$= \$49,726.71 \times .006667 \times 1 \text{ month} = \$331.53$$

Of the second month's payment of $606.64, $331.53 is interest and $275.11 repayment of principal. Going into the third month, the outstanding principal is $49,451.60 (the second month's balance of $49,726.11 less the second repayment of principal of $275.11).

This process continues for each of the 120 months of the mortgage (10 years times 12 months per year). Thus, for each monthly payment made, the outstanding principal and interest decreases. Given the fixed amount of the monthly payment, the proportion of interest goes down, while that of principal rises.

Can a real estate investor determine the amount of interest and principal for any given monthly payment?

No. Some lending institutions will routinely give mortgagees a printout of the loan's amortization, payment by payment, listing the amounts of principal and interest for each month. Most will prepare one for borrowers upon request and undoubtedly for a fee. But there is no practical formula for the individual real estate investor to use.

Instead, there are books of *amortization schedules*. These schedules itemize the interest and principal paid at the end of each year, in addition to the outstanding principal. The schedules enable real estate investors to determine how much interest and principal are paid each year. Organized by interest rate, they state the fixed monthly and annual payments. For each multiple of $10,000, they specify the amount of interest and principal paid for the year.

For most purposes, such as declaring interest expenses on a tax return, this information suffices. Given the information on your loan, you can determine how much interest was paid during the tax year. (IRS requires the lending institution to furnish the lender with this information once a year.)

Example: The following is a sample amortization schedule:

Amortization—30 Years at 9%
for Each $10,000 of Principal

Monthly payment: $80.46
Annual payment: $965.52

Year	Annual Interest	Annual Principal	Year-End Mortgage Balance
1	$897.20	$ 68.32	$9,931.68
2	$890.79	$ 74.73	$9,856.95

Year	Annual Interest	Annual Principal	Year-End Mortgage Balance
3	$883.78	$ 81.74	$9,775.21
4	$876.11	$ 89.41	$9,685.81
5	$867.73	$ 97.79	$9,588.01
		. . .	
26	$322.74	$642.78	$3,233.36
27	$262.44	$703.08	$2,530.28
28	$196.49	$769.03	$1,761.25
29	$124.35	$841.17	$ 920.08
30	$ 45.44	$920.08	$ 0.00

Note: As the loan nears the 30-year maturity, the interest component of each payment decreases as the principal component becomes greater.

How is the monthly payment found for a mortgage larger than the amount stated in the amortization tables?

The figures in the amortization tables generally are based on a principal amount of $10,000. To calculate the monthly payment for a given mortgage amount, use the following formula:

$$\frac{\text{Monthly payment}}{\text{for mortgage}} = \frac{\text{Monthly payment}}{\text{in table}} \times \frac{\text{Mortgage principal}}{\$10,000}$$

Example: In the amortization tables, the per-$10,000 monthly payment for 9%, 30-year mortgage is $80.46. What is the monthly payment for a $85,000 mortgage?

$$\frac{\text{Monthly payment}}{\text{for mortgage}} = \frac{\text{Monthly payment}}{\text{in table}} \times \frac{\text{Mortgage principal}}{\$10,000}$$

$$= \$80.46 \times \frac{\$85,000}{\$10,000}$$

$$= \$80.46 \times 8.5 = \$683.91$$

The monthly payment for an $85,000 mortgage is $683.91.

Note: Some mortgage amortization schedules use multiples of $10,000. If you are using a table with a different multiple, such as $1,000, simply substitute the $1,000 for $10,000 in the formulas.

Can the amortization tables be used to determine the amounts of interest and principal paid per year?

Yes. This is a three-step process:

- Find the table for the interest rate and term of the individual mortgage.
- Run down the left-hand column to the row for the year in question.
- For either the interest or the principal, use one of the following formulas to determine the amounts for the given mortgage amount.

$$\begin{matrix}\text{Interest} \\ \text{on mortgage}\end{matrix} = \begin{matrix}\text{Interest} \\ \text{in table}\end{matrix} \times \dfrac{\text{Mortgage amount}}{\$10,000}$$

Or:

$$\begin{matrix}\text{Principal} \\ \text{on mortgage}\end{matrix} = \begin{matrix}\text{Principal} \\ \text{in table}\end{matrix} \times \dfrac{\text{Mortgage amount}}{\$10,000}$$

Note: Some mortgage amortization schedules use multiples of $10,000. If you are using a table with a different multiple, such as $1,000, simply substitute the $1,000 for $10,000 in the formulas above.

Example: Sam Russell has a $114,000 mortgage at 9% for 30 years. Preparing his tax returns for the 26th year of the term, he needs to know how much he paid in interest for the year.

- *Find the table for the interest rate and term of the individual mortgage.* (See the next page.)

- *Run down the left-hand column to the row for the year in question.* The amount shown in boldface in the table ($322.74) is the interest paid per $10,000 of mortgage amount.

Amortization over 30 Years at 9%
for Each $10,000 of Principal

Monthly payment: $80.46
Annual payment: $965.52

Year	Annual Interest	Annual Principal	Year-End Mortgage Balance
		. . .	
26	**$322.74**	$642.78	$3,233.36
27	$262.44	$703.08	$2,530.28
28	$196.49	$769.03	$1,761.25
29	$124.35	$841.17	$ 920.08
30	$ 45.44	$920.08	$ 0.00

● *For the annual interest, use the following formula to determine the amount for the mortgage amount.*

$$\frac{\text{Interest}}{\text{on mortgage}} = \frac{\text{Interest}}{\text{in table}} \times \frac{\text{Mortgage amount}}{\$10,000}$$

$$= \$322.74 \times \frac{\$114,000}{\$10,000}$$

$$= \$322.74 \times 11.4 = \$3,679.24$$

Russell has paid $3,679.24 in interest on his mortgage over the course of the 26th year.

What is present value?

From the investor's point of view, *present value* is the amount of money that is invested now in order to receive a specified sum in the future, given the interest rate, term, and frequency of compounding. Present value factors are found in compounding, or annuity, tables, which are available at larger bookstores.

The procedure to find the present value consists of four steps:

● Find the page in the tables containing the interest rate and the frequency of compounding, such as 11% compounded monthly.

● Go down the left-hand column to the term in question, such as 18 months or 20 years.

● Read across that row to the column head by the interest rate in question.

● Multiply the present value factor (often referred to as "PVF") found there by the amount invested.

Example: What would someone have to invest today at a rate of 11.5%, compounded monthly, in order to have $1 in 20 years?

● *Find the page in the tables containing the interest and the frequency of compounding.* Go to the page with the present value of 11% compounded monthly.

Present Value of $1
Compounded Monthly

| | Annual interest rate: | | | |
Months	11%	11.5%	12%	12.5%
1	.9909166	.9905076	.9900990	.9896907
2	.9819157	.9811054	.9802960	.9794877
3	.9729966	.9717924	.9705901	.9693899
4	.9641584	.9625678	.9609803	.9593962
	. . .			
Years				
20	**.1119192**	.1013628	.0918058	.0831533
21	.1003113	.0904009	.0814730	.0734300
	. . .			

● *Go down the left-hand column to the term in question.* In this find the row for 20 years.

● *Read across that row to the column head by the interest rate in question.* The present value factor (PVF) is .1119192.

● *Multiply the present value factor by the amount invested.* $1 times .1119192 is $.11—eleven cents. This means that, in order to have $1 at the end of 20 years, someone would have to invest 11 cents today.

Note: The factor works with any sum of money. If the desired sum at the end of 20 years were $15,000, the factor is applied to the $15,000 instead of to $1.

$$\$15,000 \times .1119192 = \$1,678.79$$

Investing $1,678.79 at 11%, compounded monthly for 20 years, would result in a sum of $15,000.

How does "present value of $1" differ from "present value"?

"Present value" answers the question, How much must I invest today to have a desired lump sum at some specified point in the future, given the interest rate and frequency of compounding? *Present value of $1* answers the question, How much must I invest now in order to make periodic withdrawals starting at a specific point in the future and extending for a certain period (again, given the interest rate and frequency of compounding)? The periodic withdrawals are referred to as an *annuity*.

To find the amount to be invested, the steps are the same as for present value:

● *Find the page in the tables containing the interest rate and frequency of compounding.*

● *Go down the left-hand column to the term in question.*

● *Read across that row to the column headed by the interest rate in question.*

● *Multiply the present value of $1 factor, or present value of an annuity factor (PVAF), by the amount invested.*

Example: How much would someone have to invest now at 11.5% compounded monthly in order to be able to withdraw $1 per month for 20 years?

● *Find the page in the tables containing the interest and the frequency of compounding.* Go to the page with the present value of $1 per month 11.5% compounded monthly.

Present Value of $1 Per Month
Compounded Monthly

Months	11%	11.5%	12%	12.5%
		Annual interest rate:		
1	.9909166	.9905076	.9900990	.9896907
2	1.9728323	1.9716130	1.9703951	1.9691784
3	2.9458289	2.9434054	2.9409852	2.9385684
4	3.9099873	3.9059731	3.9019656	3.8979646
		...		
Years				
20	96.8815390	**93.7708378**	90.8194163	88.0172792
21	96.1478563	94.9146932	91.8526982	88.9507174

...

● *Go down the left-hand column to the term in question.*
In this find the row for 20 years.

● *Read across that row to the column head by the*
interest rate in question. The factor is 93.7708378.

● *Multiply the factor by the amount invested.* $1 times
93.7708378 is $93.77. This means that, in order to with-
draw $1 per month for 20 years, someone would have to
invest $93.77 cents today.

Note: The factor works with any sum of money. If the
desired monthly withdrawal were $200, the factor is ap-
plied to the $200 instead of to $1.

$$\$200 \times 93.7708378 = \$18,754.17$$

Investing $18,754.17 at 12%, compounded monthly,
would enable an investor to have an annuity of $200 per
month for 20 years.

Effective Yield

Is the contract rate of a mortgage really the rate
investors pay?

In most cases, yes. The rate stated in a mortgage agreement, the *contract rate*, is the rate the investor pays.
Certain conditions—such as discounts (points), penalties
for early repayment, or loan origination fees—can cause
the investor to pay more. Given one or more of such
conditions, the rate that the investor really pays is called
(from the lender's point of view) the *effective yield*, or the
effective cost from the borrower's point of view.

Discounts, Points, Loan Origination Fees

What are discounts?

Discounts are deductions from the loan proceeds. Although
the mortgage document states the bank will extend x
amount of money (the contract amount) to the borrower,
the amount disbursed is actually less than x. The difference
between the contract amount and the (lower) amount
actually disbursed is called the *loan discount*. The discount
is usually expressed as a percentage, or in terms of

"points," a *point* being a percentage point of the mortgage principal.

$$\textbf{Points (\$) = Principal} \times \textbf{Points (\%)}$$

Example: A mortgage agreement is drawn up in which the local S&L agrees to lend $150,000 to buyer-borrower Wysocki. The contract rate is 10%. A clause in the agreement, however, states that the Wysocki will pay 2 "points" on the loan. The 2 points translate into $3,000.

$$\text{Points (\$)} = \text{Principal} \times \text{Points (\%)}$$
$$= \$150,000 \times .02 = \$3,000$$

The S&L cuts a check for only $147,000. Since the mortgage is amortized as if it were for $150,000, Wysocki pays interest on money that he never received.

Note: Why don't lending institutions simply raise the contract rate, instead of playing games with points? The answer is that, psychologically, the lower contract rate sounds better to the borrower and is easier for the lender to "sell." Also, state usury laws may place ceilings on contract rates.

Loan origination fees also raise the effective yield. The same formula may be used.

Is it worth paying points?

The answer depends on the alternatives available to the buyer-borrower. Discounts, or points, raise the effective yield on a mortgage. Because the contract rate is fixed but the actual amount of loan money reduced, the yield to the lending institution increases—and the borrower pays more for less. But the real question is whether the discount raises the effective rate so much that another financing alternative becomes more cost-effective. So step one in determining whether paying points is "worth it" is ascertaining the effective yield of the mortgage with the points deducted. Then the effective yield can be compared to other mortgage arrangements. Calculating effective yield is possible but complicated. It is generally easier to ask the loan officer of the lending institution for the effective yield of the mortgage with points.

Prepayment

Does prepaying a mortgage raise the effective yield?

Prepaying a mortgage, or paying back principal before maturity, raises the effective yield only if there is a discount, loan origination fee, or prepayment penalty.

REFINANCING

If interest rates on mortgages have declined, is it worthwhile to refinance?

In many cases, the decision to refinance a mortgage is an easy one. When a mortgage has been held for a number of years and prevailing interest rates have declined by several percentage points, there is little doubt that refinancing— even with closing and other costs—will save the investor money. When the refinancing rate is close to the current rate, however, the investor should calculate the effective yield upon repayment and compare it to the new rate.

When the spread between the current and refinancing rates is wide (2 or more points), the procedure to determine savings is:

- From the annual amortization tables, find the remaining principal of the current mortgage as of the date of prepayment.
- From the annual amortization tables, find the total interest on the remaining principal for the current and refinancing rates.
- Calculate the savings:

$$\begin{matrix} \text{Savings} \\ \text{in} \\ \text{interest} \end{matrix} = \begin{matrix} \text{Total interest} \\ \text{on remaining} \\ \text{principal at} \\ \text{current rate} \end{matrix} - \begin{matrix} \text{Total interest} \\ \text{on remaining} \\ \text{principal at} \\ \text{refinancing rate} \end{matrix}$$

- Compare the savings with any out-of-pocket expenses incurred as a part of the refinancing, such as prepayment penalties on the existing loan or closing costs, points, or origination fees on the new loan.

Example: Samantha Stone has been paying off a $50,000, 30-year, 12% mortgage for 5 years. There was no discount or loan origination fee. In that time, mortgage rates have declined to the extent that the local S&L is willing to give her a 25-year, 8.5% mortgage on the remaining principal, if she were to repay her existing mortgage. She is considering refinancing, but she will have to pay a prepayment penalty of 2 points on the remaining principal but no closing fees. There is no doubt that she will save a great deal in interest by refinancing. The only question is whether the prepayment penalties will offset those savings.

● *From the annual amortization tables, find the remaining principal of the current mortgage as of the date of prepayment.* The remaining principal per $10,000 is $9,766.32; that's $48,831.60 for a $50,000 mortgage ($9,766.32 times 5).

● *From the annual amortization tables, find the total interest on the remaining principal for the current and refinancing rates.* To find this, you must add the interest portions of each year's payments to maturity. From year 6 through year 30, interest on the existing mortgage is $21,091.70. For the new (25-year) mortgage, it would be $17,680.35.

● *Calculate the savings:*

$$\begin{matrix} \text{Savings} \\ \text{in} \\ \text{interest} \end{matrix} = \begin{matrix} \text{Total interest} \\ \text{on remaining} \\ \text{principal at} \\ \text{current rate} \end{matrix} - \begin{matrix} \text{Total interest} \\ \text{on remaining} \\ \text{principal at} \\ \text{refinancing rate} \end{matrix}$$

$$= \$21,091.70 - \$17,680.35 = \$3,411.35$$

● *Compare the savings with any out-of-pocket expenses incurred as a part of the refinancing.* There are no closing costs, but Samantha will have to pay a 2% prepayment penalty.

$$\begin{matrix} \text{Prepayment} \\ \text{penalty (\$)} \end{matrix} = \begin{matrix} \text{Remaining} \\ \text{principal} \end{matrix} \times \begin{matrix} \text{Prepayment} \\ \text{penalty (\%)} \end{matrix}$$

$$= \$46,831.60 \times .02 = \$936.63$$

Her total saving on the refinancing would be $2,474.72 ($3,411.35 in interest savings less the prepayment penalty of $936.63).

MORTGAGES FOR OWNER-OCCUPIED HOMES

Note: The guidelines in this section may be adjusted depending on the circumstances of the borrower and the property. Considerations include: the investor's credit history and ability to budget, the borrower's potential for income growth, the size of the down payment, the nature or the source of income, the borrower's net worth, the quality and energy efficiency of the property, and so on.

How does an individual determine how much of a mortgage he or she is eligible for?

Many factors go into the lender's decision to extend credit—interest rate risk, the borrower's creditworthiness, the value of the property, and so on. There are, however, a few rules of thumb that enable individuals to determine the amount of mortgage they are financially eligible for. The lender's evaluation of the prospective mortgager is called *borrower analysis*, part of which entails certain ratios:

- Mortgage expense to gross income.
- Household expense to gross income.
- The borrower's fixed expenses to gross income.
- Monthly income less monthly expenses to monthly mortgage payment.
- Total income to mortgage amount.
- Total income to price of house.

The lender also considers the market value of the house in connection with the amount of mortgage being sought; this is called the *loan-to-value (LTV) ratio*. Essentially, the question is, if the borrower defaults on the loan, will the bank be able to sell the property for enough to recoup the amount of the loan and delinquent costs, including delinquent interest, taxes, insurance, and so on?

What does a lender consider "income"?

In addition to the borrower's gross salary from full-time employment or self-employment, income includes:

- Overtime or part-time wages, if they are historically "regular."
- Spouse's income, as long as it is for an extended period.
- Commissions and bonuses only if they have a regular track record.
- Disability payments, child support or alimony, and investment earnings only if they are assured to continue in the future.

Given total income, what amount of mortgage may an investor expect to be granted?

A typical guideline is that the mortgage amount should not exceed twice the investor's total annual income. Depending on the financial circumstances of the borrower, as well as a number of other circumstances, this factor may be adjusted slightly upward or downward.

Mortgage amount = 2 × Total annual income

Example: Bill and Nancy Perrine both work full time, with a combined annual income of $75,000. Disregarding extenuating circumstances, they may expect to be granted a mortgage of about $150,000.

$$\text{Mortgage amount} = 2 \times \text{Total annual income}$$
$$= 2 \times \$75,000 = \$150,000$$

How much of a monthly payment should an investor take on?

The guideline is that the total mortgage expense should not be more than 26% of total income, with "total mortgage expense" defined as the sum of principal, interest, taxes, and insurance. This percentage may be as high as 33% to include other fixed expenses. What this means is that the borrower may want to adjust either the principal (by putting down more or less up front) or the term (by extending or shortening the maturity of the loan).

Total mortgage expense = .26 × Total annual income

Example: Refer to the preceding example. The Perrines have $20,000 to put down and want to buy a $160,000 home. They ask the local S&L for a 10-year, $140,000 mortgage at 12.5%. The monthly payment for this loan would be $2,049.27, or $24,591.24 for the year. (This figure is taken from the Monthly Payment tables.) The monthly payment (that is, only principal and interest) is higher than the guideline permits for the Perrines.

$$\text{Total mortgage expense} = .26 \times \text{Total annual income}$$
$$= .26 \times \$75,000 = \$19,500$$

The local S&L refuses to extend the loan, but they offer one for 15 years, for which the monthly payment is $1,725.53 ($20,706.36 for the year). This amount leaves "room" for taxes and insurance.

Is the total value of the house considered in relation to the size of the mortgage?

Yes. Generally—and again depending on many circumstances—the house price should be about 2.5 times the investor's total annual income. The figure may be adjusted upward to about 2.75 or downward to 2.25.

Price of house = 2.5 × Total annual income

Example: Refer to the preceding example. The Perrines should be looking for a house in the range of $187,500.

$$\text{Price of house} = 2.5 \times \text{Total annual income}$$
$$= 2.5 \times \$75,000 = \$187,500$$

If an investor can make a very large down payment, why wouldn't the lender permit the person to buy a more expensive home than is permitted by the guidelines?

The rationale is that, as the price of a home increases, so does the cost of its upkeep. Investors may be able to handle the mortgage payments, but can they meet the expenses of maintaining a larger home?

Example: Refer to the preceding example. If the Perrines had $75,000 to put down, theoretically they could be eligible to own a house with a market value in excess of $250,000.

$$\begin{aligned}
\text{Price of house} &= 2.5 \,(\text{Total annual income}) + \text{Down payment} \\
&= 2.5\,(\$75{,}000) + \$75{,}000 \\
&= \$187{,}500 + \$75{,}000 = \$262{,}500
\end{aligned}$$

But, on $75,000 a year, would they be able to pay for the upkeep expenses of the larger home (taxes, insurance, utilities, landscaping, maintenance, etc.)? The lender assumes not and may not extend a loan.

Is there a guideline on how much of a housing expense an investor should assume?

The investor should get as much information as possible on every aspect of house-related expenses: heating and air conditioning, mortgage and homeowner's insurance, an estimate of typical repairs over the course of the year, the cost of a paint job, new rugs, and so on. When these expenses are all added up, they should not exceed about a third of the investor's total annual income.

$$\textbf{House expense} = \frac{\textbf{Total annual income}}{3}$$

Example: The Perrines estimate that running the home of their choice will cost about $1,300 a month, or $15,600 a year. This is well within the house expense guideline of $25,000.

$$\begin{aligned}
\text{House expense} &= \frac{\text{Total annual income}}{3} \\
&= \frac{\$75{,}000}{3} = \$25{,}000
\end{aligned}$$

Do an investor's other expenses figure into a lender's decision to extend a loan?

Yes. A would-be borrower may be deeply in debt—high credit card balances, heavy car payments, child support or alimony obligations, and so on. All such expenses detract from the borrower's ability to make monthly mortgage payments and to meet household expenses. The rule of thumb is that all fixed expenses, including mortgage payments, should not exceed one-half the investor's total annual income.

$$\text{Fixed expenses} = \frac{\text{Total annual income}}{2}$$

Example: The Perrines have the following annual fixed expenses:

Car payment #1	$ 2,100
Car payment #2	$ 2,760
Average credit card payments	$ 850
10-year, $70,000 college loan	$11,568
Total fixed expenses	$17,278

This is within the guideline of one-half their total income.

$$\text{Fixed expenses} = \frac{\text{Total annual income}}{2}$$

$$= \frac{\$75,000}{2} = \$37,500$$

The Perrines could afford a mortgage payment of up to a little over $20,000 a year ($37,500 less $17,278 is $20,222).

ADJUSTABLE RATE MORTGAGES (ARMs)

What are adjustable rate mortgages?

When a lending institution commits capital to a loan, it becomes exposed to *interest rate risk*. If prevailing interest rates rise, the lender could command higher rates of interest for the money it loans out. If the money is committed—locked into a long-term mortgage commitment of 20–40 years—it is being "underutilized"; that is, it is not earning as much interest as it could

Many banks, S&Ls, and other lenders now offer home buyers a type of mortgage whose contract rate is pegged to the rate of some negotiable debt security, such as the 1-year

Treasury bill. As the yield on the security rises or falls, so does the contract rate of the mortgage. The rate is "adjustable." These are *adjustable rate mortgages* (ARMs).

The terms vary widely, but many ARMs guarantee:

- Fixed rates for one year (usually for no less than six months), at which time the rate is adjusted according to the terms of the contract.

- First-year rates that are generally lower than fixed-rate (conventional) mortgages, so as to compensate borrowers for the increased risk of higher rates in the future.

- A cap and a floor on rates, that is, maximum and minimum rates for the life of the mortgage.

- An ARM rate pegged to an index that the borrower can verify, such as the rate of a Treasury security.

- Monthly payments adjusted so as to fully amortize the remaining principal over the remaining time to maturity.

- For the borrower, 30–45 days' notice before an adjusted rate goes into effect.

- The right of the borrower to prepay the mortgage without penalty after being notified of the first scheduled rate adjustment.

- The offer of a fixed-rate mortgage at the same time as the ARM.

Example: A local S&L is offering an 8% adjustable rate mortgage, when fixed-rate mortgages are going at about 10%. There is a cap of 12.25% and a floor of 7%. The rate is pegged to the 1-year Treasury bill; the contract rate is 2 percentage points above the T bill rate on the anniversary of the mortgage. If a $100,000, 30-year, 8% adjustable-rate mortgage agreement is closed on May 1 of this year and the T bill rates move upward 2 points (from 6% to 8%) by May 1 of next year, the contract rate will be 10% (the T bill rate of 8% plus 2%).

Does the adjusted rate in an ARM apply to the original principal amount or to remaining principal?

The adjusted rate applies to the principal remaining at the time of adjustment. Early in the life of the mortgage, this distinction does not make much difference because principal is not reduced greatly in the early years. Only later in the life of the mortgage will the difference in principal have a significant effect on the monthly payment.

Example: Refer to the preceding example. Assume that the T bill rate remained so constant for 4 years that the contract rate did not change. (Assume this unlikely occurrence for the sake of illustration.) For 4 years, the borrower has been making monthly payments of $733.80 (the payment for an 8%, 30-year, $100,000 mortgage, according to the Monthly Payment tables). By the 5th anniversary of the mortgage, however, the T bill rate has risen to 9.5% and the mortgage contract rate to 11.5%. The 11.5% now applies to the remaining principal, which is $95,069.90 (according to the amortization tables) over the next 25 years. In effect, the remaining principal ($95,069.90) becomes a new mortgage with an adjusted rate and a term equal to the time remaining to the original maturity.

Looking at the adjusted rate in this manner, you can approximate the new monthly payment. According to the Mortgage Payment tables, the monthly payment for a mortgage at 8% over 25 years is $965.68. The precise amount is $966.36, which is arrived at by means of the formula on page 317.

$$\begin{aligned} \text{Monthly payment} &= \text{Principal} \times \frac{\text{Rate}}{1 - [1/(1 + \text{Rate})^n]} \\ &= \$95,069.90 \times \frac{.115}{1 - [1/(1 + .115)^{25}]} \\ &= \$966.36 \end{aligned}$$

Note: The mortgage payment tables do not always provide the listings for the quarter or eighth points of ARM rates, or for the odd-year maturities of, say, 27 years or 19 years. In such cases, a calculator is needed.

When are ARMs better than fixed-rate mortgages?

The answer to that question requires a crystal ball. If the home buyer anticipates prevailing interest rates to decline or at least to remain constant, then an ARM is probably the way to go. If interest rates are expected to climb, the question becomes whether rates will climb and remain elevated to the extent that the borrower will be paying the cap rate (which is generally higher than the fixed rate offered at the same time as the ARM). So deciding on adjustable versus fixed-rate mortgage calls for some forecasting of interest rates, an ability that few possess. While knowing where interest rate levels will be a week or month from now is difficult, predicting their levels a year, five years, or twenty years in the future is impossible. Who in 1960, if offered a 30-year ARM, would have foreseen the double-digit rates of the early eighties?

Perhaps a more reasonable task is to take the short-term view.

Example: Jack and Susan Powers are buying a new home at the same time their son is starting college. The local S&L is offering a 9% adjustable rate mortgage, along with a fixed-rate mortgage at 11%. There is a cap of 12.5% and a floor of 8%. The rate is pegged to the 1-year Treasury bill, with the contract rate 1 percentage point above the T bill rate on the anniversary of the mortgage. The Powers anticipate interest rates will remain steady for at least a year or two. To save on the monthly payments for as long as possible, so as to make payments on a college tuition loan to be paid off in two years, the Powers take the $100,000, 30-year, 9% adjustable-rate mortgage agreement, closing on June 1.

By June 1 of the next year, the T bill rate has remained at 8%. The Powers continue to pay a 9% contract rate. At this point, they enjoy a savings of 2% interest for two years (paying off the mortgage at 9% rather than at 11%, which was the rate of the fixed-rate mortgage).

By the anniversary of the third year, however, the T bill has climbed to 13%, which pushes the contract rate of the Powers' mortgage to the cap of 12.5%. If the T bill stays high (reflecting elevated prevailing interest rates), the Powers will be paying considerably more for their mortgage than they would had they taken out a fixed rate.

It is also possible that, in a couple of years more, if the T bill rate stays high, the Powers might consider refinancing.

On the other hand, if rates remain steady, or even decline, over the life of the mortgage, Powers may wind up paying far less for the mortgage.

HOME EQUITY LOANS

How does a homeowner calculate the equity in a home?

Equity is the difference between market value and any indebtedness on the property.

$$\text{Equity} = \begin{matrix}\text{Appraised} \\ \text{value}\end{matrix} - \begin{matrix}\text{Indebtedness} \\ \text{on property}\end{matrix}$$

Example: The Carruthers bought a home for $97,000 10 years ago, putting down $10,000. Since the purchase, they have reduced the principal on their mortgage to $91,000, and the home has appreciated in value to $175,000.

$$\begin{aligned}\text{Equity} &= \begin{matrix}\text{Appraised} \\ \text{value}\end{matrix} - \begin{matrix}\text{Indebtedness} \\ \text{on property}\end{matrix} \\ &= \$175,000 - \$91,000 = \$84,000\end{aligned}$$

The Carruthers have $84,000 of equity in their home.

What are home equity loans?

Home equity loans are loans taken out by homeowners who pledge a part of the "equity" in their home. Generally, lenders accept only a percentage of the total amount of equity, so as to protect themselves against a decline in the value of the home during "soft" real estate markets. Lenders will extend credit of up to 75% of the market value of the home.

$$\begin{matrix}\text{Equity loan} \\ \text{amount}\end{matrix} = \begin{matrix}\text{Market} \\ \text{value}\end{matrix} \times \begin{matrix}\text{Lender's} \\ \text{percentage}\end{matrix} - \begin{matrix}\text{Indebtedness} \\ \text{on property}\end{matrix}$$

Example: Refer to the preceding example. Homeowner's Equity Credit Corp. will lend homeowners up to 65% of the equity in their home. The Carruthers could apply for a home equity loan of $22,750.

$$\begin{aligned}\begin{matrix}\text{Equity loan} \\ \text{amount}\end{matrix} &= \begin{matrix}\text{Market} \\ \text{value}\end{matrix} \times \begin{matrix}\text{Lender's} \\ \text{percentage}\end{matrix} - \begin{matrix}\text{Indebtedness} \\ \text{on property}\end{matrix} \\ &= \$175,000 \times .65 - \$91,000 \\ &= \$22,750\end{aligned}$$

How are equity loans structured?

There is no "typical" home equity loan. It can be a credit line with a maximum amount, a collateralized personal loan from an S&L of five to ten years maturity, or a long-term second mortgage with closing costs.

How do homeowners determine whether they are able to carry the payments on a home equity loan?

One way is to use the same ratios that a lender uses in its borrower analysis when processing a loan application. In other words, consider the home equity loan payment and monthly mortgage payment as one, and apply the ratios.

Given total income, what combined amount of home equity and mortgage payment may a homeowner carry?

A typical guideline is that the combined mortgage and loan principal should not exceed twice the investor's total annual income. Depending on the financial circumstances of the homeowner, this ratio may be adjusted slightly upward or downward.

$$\text{Mortgage} + \frac{\text{Home equity}}{\text{principal}} \leq 2 \times \frac{\text{Total annual}}{\text{income}}$$

Example: Bill and Nancy Perrine both work full time, with a combined annual income of $75,000. They are carrying a $140,000 mortgage and are eligible for a home equity loan of up to $30,000.

$$\text{Mortgage} + \frac{\text{Home equity}}{\text{principal}} \leq 2 \times \frac{\text{Total annual}}{\text{income}}$$

$$\$140,000 + \$30,000 \leq 2 \times \$75,000$$

$$\$170,000 \leq \$150,000$$

The Perrines would probably be straining their financial resources by taking out a home loan of $30,000.

How much of a combined loan and monthly mortgage payment should an investor take on?

The guideline is that the total mortgage expense should not be more than 26% of total income, with "total mortgage expense" defined as the sum of principal, interest, taxes, and insurance. This percentage may be as high as 33% to include other fixed expenses. If the homeowner's mortgage expense is much lower than this guideline, then a home loan may not be out of picture.

$$\text{Total mortgage and loan payment} = .26 \times \text{Total annual income}$$

Example: The Mensching family has an 8%, 30-year, $50,000 mortgage, which has five years left to maturity. The total family income is $40,000 a year. Their monthly mortgage payment is $366.90 ($4,402.80 per year). Their home has appreciated greatly in value, and they are eligible for up to $100,000 in home equity loans at 12%. What size home equity loan might the family carry?

$$\text{Total mortgage and loan payment} = .26 \times \text{Total annual income}$$
$$= .26 \times \$40,000 = \$10,400$$

With $4,402.80 in mortgage payments a year, the Menschings might consider a loan whose term and rate enables them to make payments of $5,997.20 or less a year ($10,400 maximum according to the guideline less $4,402.80 already being paid on the mortgage).

Do an investor's other expenses figure into a lender's decision to extend a loan?

Yes. As in a mortgage loan application, the borrowers in an equity loan arrangement must consider their other fixed expenses. Adapting the rule of thumb for borrower analysis in a mortgage application, other fixed expenses should not exceed one-half the investor's total annual income.

$$\text{Fixed expenses} = \frac{\text{Total annual income}}{2}$$

Example: Refer to the preceding example. The Menschings have the following annual fixed expenses:

Car payment #1	$ 2,400
Personal loan payments	$ 1,230
Average credit card payments	$ 725
Child support	$ 6,000
Total fixed expenses	$10,355

This is well within the guideline of one-half their total income.

$$\text{Fixed expenses} = \frac{\text{Total annual income}}{2}$$

$$= \frac{\$40,000}{2} = \$20,000$$

PROPERTY-RELATED CALCULATIONS

How do homeowners calculate the tax rate for their community?

The tax rate is the result of dividing the community's total tax revenues by the total assessed value of the property in the community.

$$\textbf{Tax rate} = \frac{\textbf{Total tax revenues}}{\textbf{Total assessed value of property in community}}$$

Example: The Town of Belsinger's total tax revenues are $752,300, and all the property in the town is assessed at a total of $13,560,000.

$$\text{Tax rate} = \frac{\text{Total tax revenues}}{\text{Total assessed value of property in community}}$$

$$= \frac{\$752,300}{\$13,560,000} = .0555 \text{ or } 5.6\%$$

The Town of Belsinger taxes property at an average rate of 5.6%.

Note: Not all real property in a community is taxed at the same rate. For example, residential property is often taxed at a different rate than commercial property.

How is a real estate broker's commission calculated?

The seller of a house pays the real estate broker a fee that is negotiable but that is usually set by the real estate company's policy. The fee is expressed as a percentage of the sale proceeds. A typical rate is 6%.

$$\text{Broker's fee (\$)} = \text{Sale price of house} \times \text{Broker's fee (\%)}$$

Example: The Carruthers sell their home for $172,900. Their broker charges a 6% commission.

$$\begin{aligned} \text{Broker's fee (\$)} &= \text{Sale price of house} \times \text{Broker's fee (\%)} \\ &= \$172,900 \times .06 = \$10,374 \end{aligned}$$

At the closing, the Carruthers will have to pay the broker $10,374 out of the sales proceeds.

When lawyers handle the sale or purchase of a home, how are they compensated?

Lawyers' fees may be a fixed dollar amount or a percentage of the sale or purchase price of the home. If the fee is a percentage:

$$\text{Lawyer's fee (\$)} = \text{Sale price of home} \times \text{Lawyer's fee (\%)}$$

Example: Refer to the preceding example. The Carruthers' lawyer charges 1% to handle a closing. At the closing, they will have to pay her $3,458.

$$\begin{aligned} \text{Lawyer's fee (\$)} &= \text{Sale price of home} \times \text{Lawyer's fee (\%)} \\ &= \$172,900 \times .01 = \$1,729 \end{aligned}$$

How does a homeowner know how much he or she will "walk away with" from the sale of a home?

To know *roughly* how much the sale of a home will actually yield, all expenses must be deducted from the sales proceeds. The remaining principal on the home must be paid, as well as all fees and closing costs.

Net proceeds	=	Sale price	−	Remaining principal	+	Broker's fees	+	Lawyer's fees	−	Closing costs

Example: Refer to the preceding examples. The Carruthers sell their home for $172,900. The principal remaining on the mortgage is $91,000. The broker charges them $10,374, and the lawyer is paid $1,729. Closing costs amount to $7,500.

Net proceeds	=	Sale price	−	Remaining principal	+	Broker's fees	+	Lawyer's fees	−	Closing costs

= $172,900 − ($91,000 + $10,374 + $1,729 + $7,500)

= $172,900 − $110,603 = $62,297

The Carruthers "clear" $62,297 from the sale.

KEY TERMS

Adjustable rate mortgage (ARM): A mortgage whose rate is adjusted periodically to reflect current prevailing rates.

Amortization tables: Mortgage tables that list the monthly payment, the amount of interest and principal paid within each period (usually monthly), as well as the remaining principal at the end of each period.

Annuity: Series of payments over a given period.

Borrower analysis: The lender's analysis of a loan applicant as a creditworthy borrower.

Broker's commission: The fee, usually expressed as a percentage of the sale price, paid to the real estate broker by the seller of a house.

Compound interest: Interest resulting when interest is left to accumulate with principal, so that the borrower is paying interest on interest.

Contract rate: The rate of interest on the loan stated in the mortgage agreement.

Discounts: Deductions from the loan proceeds, usually expressed as a percentage of the principal.

Down payment: The amount of cash a home buyer must put down on the house.

Effective yield (effective borrowing cost): The true rate of interest a borrower pays on a mortgage when added costs are figured, such as points, loan origination fees, and prepayment penalties.

Equity: The value of the home represented by the down payment plus an appreciation in appraised value.

Future value: The value of a sum earning a given interest rate, over a specified period of time, and at a certain frequency of compounding.

Home equity loan: A loan taken out by homeowners who pledge a part of the equity in their home.

Interest: The cost of borrowing money.

Interest rate: The annual percentage of the amount loaned.

Lawyer's fee: The fee charged by a lawyer who handles the sale or purchase of a home.

Loan discount: See *Discounts.*

Loan origination fees: Fees paid by the borrower, incurred in the process of securing a loan. These are usually expressed as a percentage of principal.

Loan-to-value ratio: The ratio between the mortgage amount (the loan) and the value of the house. If the borrower defaults on the loan, will the bank be able to sell the property for enough to recoup the amount of the loan and other costs?

Maturity: The date on which borrowed money is due to be repaid.

Monthly payment: The fixed amount that the borrower pays the lender in a mortgage arrangement each month. Each payment has a different ratio of interest to principal.

Mortgage: A long-term loan, usually for 20, 25, 30, or more years, that is secured by real property.

Mortgage expense: The amount the borrower will have to pay each month to pay off a mortgage—the monthly payment.

Points: Discounts from the principal, expressed as a percentage of the amount loaned.

Prepayment penalty: A penalty sometimes assessed by the lender when a borrower repays a mortgage before maturity. It is expressed as a percentage of the remaining principal.

Present value per period: Tables that list the sum that must be invested now, at a given rate of interest and compounding, in order to withdraw a desired sum on a periodic basis for a specified term.

Present value tables: Tables that list the sum that must be invested now, at a given rate of interest and frequency of compounding, in order to have a desired amount at the end of the term.

Principal: The amount loaned.

Refinancing: Paying off the remaining principal on an existing mortgage with the proceeds of a new mortgage loan, usually at a lower rate of interest.

Renegotiable rate (rollover) mortgage (RRM): A long-term, fixed-rate mortgage with repayment due in 3 to 5 years. The principal for the repayment is "rolled over" into a new mortgage, that is, it is refinanced as a new long-term, fixed-rate mortgage at the then current rates. This process may be repeated indefinitely.

Simple interest: Interest only on the original principal, or amount loaned.

Tax rate: The rate resulting from dividing the community's total tax revenues by the total assessed value of the property in the community.

Term: The time during which money is out on loan.

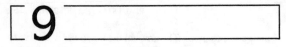

9

Retirement Planning

YOU WILL LEARN TO:

- Calculate your net worth.
- Compute the effects of compounding on net worth.
- Project your monthly retirement budget.
- Estimate how much of a "nest egg" you need for retirement.
- Determine how much you must put aside each month in order to achieve your retirement goals.
- Gauge the effect of inflation and prevailing interest rates on retirement planning.

INTRODUCTION

Retirement planning is actually much simpler than many people think. It is like planning a trip—knowing where you are and determining where you want to go. Many fine books deal with the many questions people must ask themselves about retirement: where they want to live, how they wish to spend their time, whether children will still be dependent, and in general how they want their lives in retirement to be structured and spent.

The purpose of this chapter is limited to assisting individual investors in their retirement planning by enabling them to use several very useful tools—the tables of present value, future value, and sinking fund factors. Knowing how to use these tables gives you the capability of projecting your expenses, net worth, and other financial data. With these tools, you become able to define your retirement hopes in terms of hard dollars and cents.

Under no circumstances should the information in this chapter be considered an adequate substitute for the individualized guidance and counsel of a competent financial advisor. Before taking any steps with your assets, seek the assistance of such a professional.

Note: All computations in this chapter assume that all tax obligations have been met either before or after retirement. When before-tax dollars are invested in a retirement-oriented plan, those dollars (the principal) and interest earned are taxable upon withdrawal. When after-tax dollars are placed in deferred compensation (retirement) plans or in other retirement-oriented investments, the return of those dollars (the principal) is not a taxable event. Interest earned by the principal generally is taxable, and, depending on circumstances, penalties may also be assessed if principal and/or interest is withdrawn prior to retirement. A competent tax advisor should be consulted in all cases.

NET WORTH

What is "net worth"?

Net worth is the value of a person's financial assets after all obligations are met at any given point in time. It is something like the equity in a corporation's balance sheet—the value of a business's assets after all liabilities are met. Thus an individual's net worth is calculated by means of a variation of the accounting equation.

$$\text{Assets} = \text{Liabilities} + \text{Stockholders' equity}$$

Or:

$$\text{Stockholders' equity} = \text{Assets} - \text{Liabilities}$$

A person's net worth is like stockholders' equity in a corporation. Hence it is computed by essentially the same equation:

Net worth = Assets − Liabilities

To arrive at your net worth, total up all your *assets* (anything you own or anything that is owed to you), and add up all your *liabilities* (anything you owe, short or long term). Then you apply the net worth equation.

Example: Gary Trudell has assets totaling $320,270 and liabilities of $172,250. His net worth is $148,020.

$$\text{Net worth} = \text{Assets} - \text{Liabilities}$$
$$= \$320,270 - \$172,250 = \$148,020$$

What are included in a person's "assets"?

Assets are anything of value that you own, from the loose change in your pockets to a securities portfolio. Most people have more assets than they realize. To arrive at the value of your assets, use the following inventory of personal assets:

Inventory of Assets

Cash

Checking accounts

Savings

Short-term accounts (certificates of deposit and the like)

Long-term accounts (loans to be paid back to you)

Stocks

Bonds

Precious metals, commodities

Life insurance cash value

Market value of home

Market value and cash flow from income-producing property

Mutual funds (government securities, stocks, money market, REITs, etc.)

Ownership in a business (proprietorship, partnership)

Personal property (silverware, paintings, collectibles, etc.)

Automobiles

Furnishings

Equipment

Retirement plans (pensions, profit sharing, etc.)

Annuities

Trusts
Inheritances
Other
    Total assets

Example: Refer to the preceding example. Gary Trudell arrives at a total value of his assets by taking the following inventory:

Inventory of Assets

Cash	$ 150
Checking accounts	$ 1,120
Savings	$ 4,300
Short-term accounts (certificates of deposit)	$ 19,500
Long-term accounts (loans to be paid back to him)	-0-
Stocks	-0-
Bonds (Series EE)	$ 6,200
Precious metals, commodities	-0-
Life insurance cash value	$ 12,000
Market value of home	$175,000
Market value and cash flow from income-producing property	-0-
Mutual funds (government securities, stocks, money market, REITs, etc.)	$ 5,100
Ownership in a business (proprietorship, partnership)	-0-
Personal property (silverware, paintings, collectibles, etc.)	$ 1,500
Automobiles	$ 6,400
Furnishings	$ 4,000
Equipment	-0-
Retirement plans (pensions, profit sharing, etc.)	$ 85,000
Annuities	-0-
Trusts	-0-
Inheritances	-0-
Other	-0-
Total assets	**$320,270**

What are "liabilities"?

Liabilities are any money amounts that an individual owes, in either the long or the short term. Like assets, total liabilities can be inventoried.

Inventory of Liabilities

Monthly living expenses (phone, utilities, insurance premiums, but *not* installment payments on mortgages, credit cards, loans, etc.)

Charge and/or credit balances (the amount you owe, not the monthly payment due)

Loan balances (on the car, a personal loan, home equity, life insurance, credit union, IOUs, etc.)

Mortgage(s) balance

College tuition or loan balances

Child support or alimony

Any other debt or financial obligation

    Total liabilities

Example: Refer to the preceding two examples. Gary Trudell inventories his liabilities as follows:

Inventory of Liabilities

Monthly expenses:	$ 3,400
Charge and/or credit balances	$ 1,200
Loan balances	$ 13,350
Mortgage balance	$111,300
College tuition or loan balances	$ 43,000
Child support or alimony	-0-
Any other debt or financial obligation	-0-
Total liabilities	**$172,250**

Using his total assets and total liabilities, Trudell can then calculate his net worth.

How is net worth increased?

Net worth can be increased in two ways:

- Decreasing liabilities.
- Increasing assets.

Net worth = Assets − Liabilities
= \$320,270 − \$172,250 = \$148,020

How does decreasing liabilities affect net worth?

Net worth and expenses (or liabilities) have an *inverse* relationship. That is, when one goes down (liabilities), the other goes up (net worth).

Example: Refer to the preceding example. If Gary Trudell's son were to work his way through college, the tuition loan would be unnecessary. Trudell's liabilities would be lower and his net worth greater.

Inventory of Assets		
Cash	\$	150
Checking accounts (etc.)	\$	1,120
. . .		
Other		-0-
Total assets		**\$320,270**

Inventory of Liabilities	
Monthly expenses:	\$ 3,400
Charge and/or credit balances	\$ 1,200
Loan balances	\$ 13,350
Mortgage balance	\$111,300
College tuition or loan balances	**-0-**
Child support or alimony	-0-
Any other debt or financial obligation	-0-
Total liabilities	**\$129,250**

Net worth = Assets − Liabilities
= \$320,270 − \$129,250 = \$191,020

Thus Trudell's net worth is greater by \$43,000 (\$191,020 versus \$148,020), which is the amount of the tuition loan. By bringing expenses down, Trudell has brought his net worth up.

What is the relationship between assets and net worth?

Net worth and assets have a *direct* relationship; that is, net worth increases as assets do.

Example: Refer to the preceding example. Gary Trudell's uncle dies, leaving him his home and savings account balances. After estate taxes are paid, the sale of the home and the savings accounts come to a net total of $253,000. Trudell's assets increase to $573,270 ($320,270 plus $253,000). His net worth correspondingly jumps to $444,020.

$$\text{Net worth} = \text{Assets} - \text{Liabilities}$$
$$= \$573,270 - \$129,250 = \$444,020$$

How does ongoing debt affect net worth?

One of the most common eroders of net worth is debt. Granted, a mortgage is the only way most individuals can hope to own a home, and very few people can pay cash for a new car these days. But the overuse of credit cards, personal loans, credit lines, and other forms of debt almost always leads to an erosion of wealth by reason of the interest payments. These payments, or *debt service*, erode net worth in two ways:

- The monthly loan payments represent increased expenses.

- The money being paid out as an expense could be invested, thereby increasing assets.

Example: Ann Sanders's assets and liabilities are as follows:

Inventory of Assets

Cash	$ 250
Checking accounts	$ 900
Savings	-0-
Short-term accounts (certificates of deposit)	-0-
Long-term accounts (loans to be paid back to her)	-0-
Stocks	-0-
Bonds	-0-
Precious metals, commodities	-0-
Life insurance cash value	-0-
Market value of home	$230,000
Market value and cash flow from income-producing property	-0-

Mutual funds (government securities, stocks, money market, REITs, etc.)	-0-
Ownership in a business (proprietorship, partnership)	-0-
Personal property (silverware, paintings, collectibles, etc.)	$ 45,000
Automobiles	$ 22,400
Furnishings	$ 62,300
Equipment	-0-
Retirement plans (pensions, profit sharing, etc.)	$121,000
Annuities	-0-
Trusts	-0-
Inheritances	-0-
Other	-0-
Total assets	$481,850

Inventory of Liabilities

Bills that are due (phone, utilities, insurance premiums, but *not* installment payments on mortgages, credit cards, loans, etc.)	$ 2,500
Charge and/or credit balances (the amount you owe, not the monthly minimum due)	$ 21,200
Loan balances (on the car, a personal loan, home equity, life insurance, credit union, IOUs, etc.)	$ 44,450
Mortgage(s) balance	$165,100
College tuition or loan balances	-0-
Child support or alimony	-0-
Other	-0-
Total liabilities	$233,250

$$\text{Net worth} = \text{Assets} - \text{Liabilities}$$
$$= \$481,850 - \$233,250 = \$248,600$$

Looking only at the net worth figure, one might say that Sanders is doing pretty well. But the quality of her net worth is not high. The equity in her home and retirement plan assets are of good quality. The home is likely to appreciate in value, perhaps even at a rate greater than the interest rate she pays on the mortgage. The retirement plan is compounding to her benefit.

But the value of such things as furniture and automobiles depreciates, often very quickly. If, as seems to be
the case, she has financed much of her assets (through car
loans, personal loans, etc.), then she is incurring high
interest expenses for assets that do not appreciate in value
and that in fact do not endure in their current value.

What are some ways to increase net worth?

Barring inheriting a million dollars or hitting the lottery, it
is up to the individual to minimize expenses and to increase
assets over time. This can be done by placing disposable
income into investments that appreciate in value (such as
mutual funds, stocks, real estate, etc.), rather than in assets
that lose value (like cars, appliances, and so on). In this
way, the investor makes maximum effective use of compounding.

How do appreciating assets affect net worth?

A common scenario is the *inordinate* use of credit cards,
credit lines, home equity loans, retail financing, and other
forms of debt arrangements to purchase things that decline
in value: cars, appliances, furniture, clothing, and so on.
The payments on these loans drain income that could be put
into assets that appreciate in value: a second home, a
mutual fund, government bonds, and the like. A person's
immediate net worth might even be reduced because the
market value of depreciating assets is for the moment high,
whereas the current value of an investment is low. But even
the lower net worth is of a much higher quality because it
has the potential to grow, not decline, in value.

Example: Suppose Ann Sanders had not purchased such a
costly car, furnished her home so extravagantly, or otherwise used her income to pay off depreciating assets. Suppose instead that she had taken the money that went toward
credit card and other debt service payments, and put it into a
mutual fund earning 10% annually. Compare her assets and
liabilities under her current status and her ''supposed''
status:

Inventory of Assets

	Current	Proposed
Cash	$ 250	$ 250
Checking accounts	$ 900	$ 900
Savings	-0-	-0-
Short-term accounts (certificates of deposit)	-0-	-0-
Long-term accounts (loans to be paid back to her)	-0-	-0-
Stocks	-0-	-0-
Bonds	-0-	-0-
Precious metals, commodities	-0-	-0-
Life insurance cash value	-0-	-0-
Market value of home	$230,000	$230,000
Market value and cash flow from income-producing property	-0-	-0-
Mutual funds (government securities, stocks, money market, REITs, etc.)	-0-	$ 12,450
Ownership in a business (proprietorship, partnership)	-0-	-0-
Personal property (silverware, paintings, collectibles, etc.)	$ 45,000	$ 5,000
Automobiles	$ 22,400	$ 15,600
Furnishings	$ 62,300	$ 25,000
Equipment	-0-	-0-
Retirement plans (pensions, profit sharing, etc.)	$121,000	$121,000
Annuities	-0-	-0-
Trusts	-0-	-0-
Inheritances	-0-	-0-
Other	-0-	-0-
Total assets	$481,850	$410,200

Inventory of Liabilities

	Current	Proposed
Bills that are due	$ 2,500	$ 2,500
Charge and/or credit balances	$ 21,200	$ 4,240
Loan balances	$ 44,450	$ 19,800
Mortgage(s) balance	$165,100	$165,100
College tuition or loan balances	-0-	-0-
Child support or alimony	-0-	-0-
Other	-0-	-0-
Total liabilities	$233,250	$191,640

Current net worth:

Net worth = Assets − Liabilities
= $481,850 − $233,250 = $248,600

"Proposed" net worth:

Net worth = Assets − Liabilities
= $410,200 − $191,640 = $218,560

Sanders's net worth is actually less than it was before, but the quality of the net worth is much greater. She has taken roughly $12,000 in debt payments on depreciating assets and swung them over into an asset (the mutual fund) that appreciates in value. In the years to come, her loans and credit card balances are going to be paid off (because they are more manageable). And the mutual fund is a much higher-quality investment than furnishings and fancy cars. The mutual fund account will grow as she puts more money into it and as the earnings are left in the account to produce more earnings. Her net worth now has much greater potential for growth.

How does compounding affect net worth?

Compounding occurs when earned interest is left to accumulate with principal, thereby allowing it to earn interest. If you are the lender, compounding benefits you; if you are a borrower, it works against you. If you are a heavy user of credit—a borrower—and make only the minimum payments each month, you are probably increasing the total principal of all outstanding loans—getting deeper into debt, not paying it off. By paying interest on an increasing amount of principal, you are, in a sense, allowing compounding to work against you and to decrease your net worth.

The interest paid on credit card or other types of loan balances is money that could be invested so that compounding can work to your benefit. In effect, you turn yourself from a borrower into a lender, thereby enabling compounding to work for you.

Example: Refer to the preceding example. Ann Sanders continues to use debt prudently, paying off her loans over the course of five years. At the same time, she invests $12,000 per year (which would have been used up in debt service) in the mutual fund, which yields an average return of 10%. In five years, her net worth is greatly increased and of very high quality.

Inventory of Assets

	Year 1	Year 5
Cash	$ 250	$ 250
Checking accounts	$ 900	$ 900
Savings	-0-	-0-
Short-term accounts (certificates of deposit)	-0-	-0-
Long-term accounts (loans to be paid back to her)	-0-	-0-
Stocks	-0-	-0-
Bonds	-0-	-0-
Precious metals, commodities	-0-	-0-
Life insurance cash value	-0-	-0-
Market value of home	$230,000	$ 273,500
Market value and cash flow from income-producing property	-0-	-0-
Mutual funds (government securities, stocks, money market, REITs, etc.)	$ 12,450	$ 366,306
Ownership in a business (proprietorship, partnership)	-0-	-0-

Inventory of Assets

	Year 1	Year 5
Personal property (silverware, paintings, collectibles, etc.)	$ 5,000	$ 8,000
Automobiles	$ 15,600	-0-
Furnishings	$ 25,000	$ 5,000
Equipment	-0-	-0-
Retirement plans (pensions, profit sharing, etc.)	$121,000	$ 350,000
Annuities	-0-	-0-
Trusts	-0-	-0-
Inheritances	-0-	-0-
Other	-0-	-0-
Total assets	$410,200	$1,003,956

Notes: Three things have been done to keep the illustration simple:

● The investor has the same amount of cash and checking account balance.

● Sanders writes a $12,000 check to the mutual fund once at the beginning of each year. More likely, she would make monthly payments of $1,000. This amount is therefore the future value of $12,000 per year, compounded annually at 10%. More frequent compounding and more frequent periodic payments (such as monthly) would increase the amount.

● She is driving the same car five years later.

Inventory of Liabilities

	Year 1	Year 5
Bills that are due	$ 2,500	$ 4,000
Charge and/or credit balances	$ 4,240	-0-
Loan balances	$ 19,800	-0-
Mortgage(s) balance	$165,100	$150,000
College tuition or loan balances	-0-	-0-
Child support or alimony	-0-	-0-
Other	-0-	-0-
Total liabilities	$191,640	$154,000

Year 1 net worth:

Net worth = Assets − Liabilities
             = \$410,200 − \$191,640 = \$218,560

Year 5 net worth:

Net worth = Assets − Liabilities
             = \$1,003,956 − \$154,000 = \$849,956

This is obviously a simplified illustration of how someone can turn disposable income from servicing debt to generating high net worth through compounding. She has reduced the effects of compounding her liabilities by entering into sensible debt agreements that she can pay off, at the same time maximizing her assets through compounding.

RETIREMENT-RELATED CALCULATIONS

How much does a person need to retire?

Estimating how much of a "nest egg" you need to retire is a three-step process:

- Estimate your monthly budget upon retirement.
- Assuming you want to leave the "nest egg" (the principal) intact and live on interest payments, calculate the amount of principal needed to yield enough for you to live on each month. (Many financial planners these days *do* consider the withdrawal of principal upon or after retirement; ruling out this possibility, however, simplifies the illustrations.)
- Calculate how much you have to put away periodically between now and retirement to have that principal upon retirement.

Projecting a Monthly Budget at Retirement

How does a person know what something will cost upon retirement?

Most costs are subject to inflation. How does one account for the effect of inflation over the period remaining to retirement? To do this, you need a set of tables containing future values, which are available in book form and which can be used in many ways. For the purpose of calculating the future cost of things, they give you the value of $1 after the effects of an assumed rate of inflation over the years left to retirement.

To determine the approximate increased cost of something due to inflation:

● Go to the annual compounding section of the tables showing the future value of $1.

● Find the percentage that you estimate will be the *average* inflation rate over the years remaining to retirement.

● Go down that column to the row for the years remaining to retirement, where you will find a factor.

● Multiply this future value, or "inflation," factor by the present cost to arrive at the future cost of the item in your budget.

Future cost = Present cost × Inflation factor

Example: Burt Gallant retires in 15 years, and he is trying to work out a monthly budget at retirement. He wants to know the factor by which he must multiply each item in order to arrive at a realistic budget.

● *Go to the annual compounding section of the future value tables.*

Annual Compounding
Future Value of $1

	Interest Rate [Rate of Inflation]			
Year	5%	5.5%	6%	6.5%
		• • •		
13	1.8856491	2.0057739	2.1329283	2.2674875
14	1.9799316	2.1160915	2.2609040	2.4148742
15	**2.0789282**	2.2324765	2.3965582	2.5718410
16	2.1828746	2.3552627	2.5403517	2.7390107
		• • •		

● *Find the percentage that you estimate will be the average inflation rate over the years remaining to retire-*

ment. Based on the last 25 years' history of inflation, Burt feels that 5% is a safe estimate. (See the boldface column head for 5%.)

● *Go down that column to the row for the years remaining to retirement, where you will find a factor.* The factor for 15 years at 5% inflation is 2.0789282. (See the boldface entry.)

● *Multiply the factor by the present cost to arrive at the future cost of the item in your budget.* For any item in his budget that is subject to inflation, Burt simply multiplies by this factor. For example, his monthly food budget is $650 now, but that includes food for two growing children, who will be independent by the time he retires. The cost of food for him and his wife, he figures, is about $350.

$$\text{Future cost} = \text{Present cost} \times \text{Inflation factor}$$
$$= \$350 \times 2.0789282 = \$727.62$$

All other things being equal, Burt can expect to pay over $700 per month for food in 15 years.

What constitutes a budget?

A family budget includes:

● All expenses that you may expect to pay on a monthly basis, such as mortgage payments or phone bills.

● Per-month allocations of expenses that are paid on a nonmonthly basis, such as property taxes or insurance premiums.

How are annual expenses prorated for inclusion in a monthly budget?

Annual expenses are simply divided by 12 months.

$$\textbf{Prorated expense} = \frac{\textbf{Annual expense}}{\textbf{12 months}}$$

Example: Life insurance premiums might be paid quarterly, but their annual cost can be prorated per month. Assume the annual premium is $2,000.

$$\text{Prorated expenses} = \frac{\text{Annual expense}}{12 \text{ months}}$$

$$= \frac{\$2,000}{12 \text{ months}} = \$166.67 \text{ per month}$$

For an annual $2,000 premium, $166.67 should be budgeted each month.

What should be included in a budget?

All you need to do is total up the expenses you may expect to be paying when you retire. This step takes a lot of thought because it entails visualizing your situation some years in the future. Will the mortgage be paid off? Will you be renting? What kind of insurance do you need, given Medicare? How much of a monthly Social Security payment will you be eligible for? Will the children, if any, be out of the house by the time you retire? And so on.

The following checklist helps that thought process:

Projected Monthly Retirement Budget

	Now	At Retirement
Housing (mortgage or rental)		
Property taxes		
Household maintenance		
Food		
Utilities		
Water		
Telephone		
Waste disposal		
Insurance:		
Auto		
Medical		
Life		
Homeowner		
Transportation (car?)		
Income taxes		
Dependent care		
Recreation		
Travel		
Education		
Loan payments		
Total monthly budget		

In the "Now" column are your current expenses (pro-rated per month, if need be). In the "At Retirement" column are the projected expense, prorated per month and factored for inflation, as necessary.

Example: Burt Gallant will be retiring in 15 years. The kids will be off on their own by then, and he and his wife intend to do more traveling than they have had a chance to do while raising the family. The house will be paid off, and they intend to remain in it. From the future value tables, he has determined that his "inflation factor" is 2.0789282. He has prepared the following budget, prorating annual expenses and applying the inflation factor as necessary.

Projected Monthly Retirement Budget

	Now	At Retirement
Housing (mortgage or rental)	$ 468	-0-
Property taxes	$ 125	$ 260
Household maintenance	$ 100	$ 208
Food	$ 350	$ 728
Utilities	$ 65	$ 135
Water	$ 5	$ 10
Telephone	$ 35	$ 73
Waste disposal	$ 35	$ 73
Insurance:		
Auto	$ 50	$ 104
Medical	$ 150	$ 312
Life	Paid up	-0-
Homeowner	$ 10	$ 21
Transportation (car?)	$ 350	$ 728
Income taxes	$ 625	$1,299
Dependent care	$ 650	$1,351
Recreation	$ 50	$ 104
Travel	$ 200	$ 831
Education	NA	-0-
Loan payments	NA	-0-
Total monthly budget	$3,268	$6,237

Gallant knows that he needs at least $6,237 of income per month at retirement. The figures in the retirement column (rounded to the nearest dollar) were arrived at by applying the inflation factor. For instance, if the telephone is costing the Gallants $35 per month now, 15 years from now it may cost $73.

$$\text{Future cost} = \text{Present cost} \times \text{Inflation factor}$$
$$= \$35 \times 2.0789282 = \$72.76 \text{ or } \$73$$

In the case of "Travel," Gallant doubled the present figure of $200 (since he and his wife want to do more traveling) before applying the inflation factor.

$$\text{Future cost} = \text{Present cost} \times \text{Inflation factor}$$
$$= \$400 \times 2.0789282 = \$831.57 \text{ or } \$831$$

Calculating the Size of the "Nest Egg"

Once a projected budget is established, how much of a "nest egg" (or principal sum) does a person need to provide the necessary income?

Assuming you want to leave your principal intact, calculating the amount of principal that will yield enough interest to meet your needs is fairly simple.

$$\text{Principal} = \frac{\text{Monthly income} - (\text{Social Security, other payments})}{\text{Earning rate} / 12}$$

Monthly income is the projected monthly retirement budget less monthly payments of Social Security, pension, or other benefits. The earning rate is the annual percentage that you may reasonably expect the principal to earn at retirement. And the annual earning rate is divided by 12 (months) to convert it into a monthly rate.

Example: Burt Gallant estimates that he will need roughly $6,500 per month at retirement. After making a call to the local Social Security office, he knows that, given his anticipated contributions, he can expect approximately $900 per month upon retirement. Someone at the Benefits Department where Gallant works advises him that his pension will

provide him with $2,500 per month, if he chooses install-
ment payments as opposed to a lump sum withdrawal. He
expects to be able to earn at least 8% on some kind of
fixed-income investment.

$$\text{Principal} = \frac{\text{Monthly income} - (\text{Social Security, other payments})}{\text{Earning rate} / 12}$$

$$= \frac{\$6,500 - (\$900 + \$2,500)}{.08 / 12}$$

$$= \frac{\$3,100}{.00667} = \$464,767.61$$

Gallant knows he needs about $465,000 in principal to live
as he wishes to at retirement (without having to withdraw
principal).

Calculating the Annuity

*How does someone know what to save each month in
order to have enough to retire?*

This is a three-step process:

● *Step 1:* Determine how much your current savings can
earn over the years remaining to retirement. The answer
to this question involves the use of the "*Future Value of
$1*" tables, which in this case give you the future value
of an investment, given a rate of earning and time.

● *Step 2:* Deduct the results of Step 1 from the amount
needed at retirement.

● *Step 3:* Calculate how much you have to put away each
month, or quarter, or year to make up the balance, if any.
This step involves the use of "*Sinking Fund*" tables,
which tell you how much you have to put away each
compounding period in order to have the money desired.
Sinking Fund tables are usually available in the same
publication as the Future Value and Present Value
tables.

How do you find out what an investment will be worth at a given number of years in the future (Step 1)?

Using the future value of $1 tables:

- Estimate an average annual rate of earning for the years remaining to retirement.
- Establish the rate of compounding (monthly, quarterly, etc.).
- Go to the Future Value tables section for the rate of earning and compounding.
- Read down the right-hand column to the number of years to retirement.
- Read across the columns to the one for the appropriate rate of interest.
- Multiply the factor at the intersection of that column and row by the original investment amount to arrive at the value of the investment at retirement.

$$\begin{array}{c}\text{Future value}\\\text{of investment}\end{array} = \begin{array}{c}\text{Current value}\\\text{of investment}\end{array} \times \begin{array}{c}\text{Future value}\\\text{factor}\end{array}$$

Example: Burt Gallant has $45,000 in a savings account and in matured savings bonds. He can put that into a variable annuity contract that historically has averaged a 9% per year (before taxes), with earnings compounded quarterly. How much will the $45,000 be worth in 15 years when he retires.

Note: Gallant chooses a variable annuity contract because the return is taxable only upon withdrawal. The return on many other investments, such as a mutual fund, is taxable each year.

- *Estimate an average annual rate of earning for the years remaining to retirement.* Gallant decides to go with the 9% variable annuity contract.
- *Establish the rate of compounding (monthly, quarterly, etc.).* The annuity compounds principal and earnings quarterly.
- *Go to the future values tables section for the rate of earning and compounding.*

*Quarterly Compounding
Future Value of $1*

Years	8%	8.5%	9%	9.5%
		. . .		
13	2.8003282	2.9844727	3.1804785	3.3890936
14	3.0311653	3.2463541	3.4765280	3.7227102
15	3.2810308	3.5312151	**3.8001348**	4.0891674
16	3.5514932	3.8410720	4.1538639	4.4916980
		. . .		

Annual Rate of Earning spans the 8%–9.5% columns.

• *Read down the right-hand column to the number of years to retirement.* The number of years remaining to retirement is 15.
• *Read across the columns to the one for the appropriate rate of interest.* Gallant goes to the 9% column.
• *Multiply the factor at the intersection of that column and row by the original investment amount to arrive at the value of the investment at retirement.*

$$\begin{array}{ccc}
\text{Future} & & \text{Current} & & \text{Future} \\
\text{value of} & = & \text{value of} & \times & \text{value} \\
\text{investment} & & \text{investment} & & \text{factor}
\end{array}$$

= \$45,000 \times 3.8001348 = \$171,006.06

Gallant will have at least $171,000 upon retirement.

Notes: The Gallants wish to stay in their home, which will be paid off by retirement. So the equity in their home will not be considered as part of the principal needed for retirement. If they wished, they could sell the home, rent a place to live, and include the sales proceeds as principal. This would raise their monthly needs slightly, but would greatly reduce the need to put away money before retirement. (They could also arrange to use the equity in their homes without having to sell it.)

Gallant chooses a variable annuity contract because the return is taxable only upon withdrawal. The return on many other investments, such as a mutual fund, is taxable every year.

How much does a person have to put away each month in order to have enough principal to provide the needed income (Steps 2 and 3)?

First, deduct the results of Step 1 from the principal needed.
  The procedure is:

- Determine the number of years remaining to retirement.
- Estimate the average rate of interest that your investments can earn over the years to retirement.
- Determine the rate of compounding (monthly, quarterly, etc.).
- Go to the section of sinking fund tables for the compounding and interest rates.
- Read down the right-hand column to the number of years remaining to retirement.
- Read across to the column headed by the appropriate interest rate.
- Multiply that factor by the desired amount of principal to arrive at how much has to be put away per compounding period, in order to have the principal.

$$\begin{array}{c}\textbf{Investment per}\\\textbf{compounding}\\\textbf{period}\end{array} = \begin{array}{c}\textbf{Desired}\\\textbf{principal}\end{array} \times \begin{array}{c}\textbf{Sinking}\\\textbf{fund}\\\textbf{factor}\end{array}$$

Example: Refer to the preceding example. Gallant expects to have $171,000 in principal upon retirement. That means he needs an additional $292,000 ($463,000 less $171,000). He figures on putting additional funds, every quarter, into the same 9% variable annuity, which compounds quarterly.

  • *Determine the number of years remaining to retirement.* Gallant retires in 15 years.

  • *Estimate the average rate of interest that your investments can earn over the years to retirement.* The annuity averages 9% per year (pretax).

  • *Determine the rate of compounding (monthly, quarterly, etc.).* The fund compounds quarterly.

  • *Go to the section of sinking fund tables for the compounding and interest rates.*

*Quarterly Compounding
Sinking Fund Factors*

	Annual Rate of Earning			
Year	8%	8.5%	9%	9.5%
	. . .			
13	.0111091	.0107081	.0103188	.0099410
14	.0098466	.0094598	.0090853	.0087229
15	.0087680	.0083952	**.0080353**	.0076882
16	.0078385	.0074796	.0071341	.0068018
	. . .			

● *Read down the right-hand column to the number of
years remaining to retirement.* In this case, the number is
15.

● *Read across to the column headed by the appropriate
interest rate.* The column is 9%.

● *Multiply that factor by the desired amount of principal
to arrive at how much has to be put away per compounding
period, in order to have the principal.*

$$\begin{matrix} \text{Investment per} \\ \text{compounding} \\ \text{period} \end{matrix} = \begin{matrix} \text{Desired} \\ \text{principal} \end{matrix} \times \begin{matrix} \text{Sinking} \\ \text{fund} \\ \text{factor} \end{matrix}$$

$$= \$292,000 \times .0080353 = \$2,346.31$$

Gallant will have to put away $2,346 every quarter.

*What effect does time remaining to retirement have on
the amount a person has to set aside?*

The cardinal rule in planning for retirement, and in financial planning in general, is to start putting money aside as
early in life as possible—even small amounts of it. Many
people don't do so because their incomes are limited early
in their careers, they have children to raise, or they just
don't think about retiring at a young age. Nevertheless,
people are well advised to start as soon as possible to invest
a little each month. *The sooner you start investing, the less
you have to invest to achieve the desired principal.*

Example: Suppose Gallant begin his planning 25 years
before retirement, with $45,000 in savings. His projected

budget would be higher after applying 25 years worth of inflation, but the value of his savings would be greater after 25 years of compounding, and the amount he has to put away would be less because he has 10 more years to accumulate the desired principal.

The projected retirement budget is simplified by applying a 5% inflation factor for 25 years to the overall budget (the future value of $1 after 25 years at 5%):

Projected budget = Current budget × Inflation factor

$$= \$3,268 \times 3.3863549 = \$11,066.61$$

The future value of the $45,000 (25 years compounded quarterly at 9%):

Future value of investment	=	Current value of investment	×	Future value factor

$$= \$45,000 \times 9.2540463 = \$416,432.08$$

The desired principal:

$$\text{Principal} = \frac{\text{Monthly income} - (\text{Social Security, other payments})}{\text{Earning rate} / 12}$$

$$= \frac{\$11,067 - (\$900 + \$2,500)}{.08 / 12}$$

$$= \frac{\$7,667}{.00667} = \$1,149,475.20$$

The Gallants need $773,043 ($1,149,475 less $416,432).

Amount to be put away quarterly (sinking fund factor for 25 years, compounded quarterly at 9%):

Investment per compounding period	=	Desired principal	×	Sinking fund factor

$$= \$733,043 \times .0027259 = \$1,998.20$$

The Gallants need to put away a little under $2,000 ($1,998) each quarter.

What if inflation averages more or less than expected?

Higher-than-projected inflation rates means your dollars will buy less at retirement, and your budget will be bigger. Lower means that your dollars will buy more at retirement, your budget will be smaller, and you will not need as much principal.

Example: At retirement Gallant realizes that inflation actually averaged 6% over the 25 years to retirement. If his budget 25 years before retirement is $3,268, the projected retirement budget at 5% is:

Projected budget = Current budget × Inflation factor
$$= \$3,268 \times 3.3863549 = \$11,066.61$$

The projected retirement budget at 6% is:

Projected budget = Current budget × Inflation factor
$$= \$3,268 \times 4.2918707 = \$14,025.83$$

Note: The inflation factor is obtained from the future value of $1 tables, 5% or 6% for 25 years. The factors are applied to the budget as a whole, although some items in a budget (such as a monthly mortgage payment) would not be altered by inflation.

What effect do higher yields on investments have on achieving the desired principal?

Higher yields, if they are left with principal to compound, help you build the nest egg faster. Lower yields will make it harder for you to accumulate the principal needed.

Example: Suppose the Gallants' mutual fund averages 11% over the 25 years remaining to retirement, instead of the anticipated 9%.

The future value of the $45,000 (25 years compounded quarterly at 11%):

Future value of investment	=	Current value of investment	×	Future value factor	
				$= \$45,000 \times 15.0724223 = \$678,258.99$	

If the desired principal is $1,144,328, then the Gallants need $466,069 ($1,144,328 less $678,259).

Amount to be put away quarterly (sinking fund factor for 25 years, compounded quarterly at 11%):

$$\begin{array}{c} \text{Investment per} \\ \text{compounding} \\ \text{period} \end{array} = \begin{array}{c} \text{Desired} \\ \text{principal} \end{array} \times \begin{array}{c} \text{Sinking} \\ \text{fund} \\ \text{factor} \end{array}$$

$$= \$466,069 \times .0019542 = \$910.79$$

This compares very favorably with the figure $1,998 that would be needed every quarter at 9%.

What protection does a person have against inflation?

Generally, inflation affects the cost of everything, including money. If interest is regarded as the cost of money, then interest rates will rise when inflation rates do. If you are lender (which you are when you put your money into a certificate of deposit or other interest-earning investment), then you are "charging" more for your money. Thus the amount you earn should compensate, more or less, for the erosion of buying power by inflation.

Example: Refer to the preceding two examples. If over 25 years, inflation rates average 6% (higher than planned by the Gallants), then it is likely that they could find investments yielding more than the 9% they budgeted for.

HOW TO USE HOME EQUITY WITHOUT SELLING THE HOME

What can a person do if he or she cannot put enough money away for the needed principal?

The equity in a person's home can be used by various means of *home equity conversion*, by which the equity in a home can be "converted" into cash without having to sell it and move out. Some of the more common arrangements are:

- Sale-and-leaseback arrangement.
- Reverse mortgage.
- Deferred payment loan.
- Property tax deferral.

Note: None of these income-generating or expense-saving methods should be confused with a home equity loan.

How does a sale-and-leaseback arrangement work?

In the *sale-and-leaseback*, the owners can sell the home (to another member of the family or to an investor who is not interested in taking occupancy), and they continue to reside in it on a long-term lease. They have the use of their equity for investment, in addition to the home they are accustomed to.

Example: Refer to the example on page 380. Burt Gallant needs $292,000 by retirement, which means that he will have to invest $2,346 every quarter for 15 years. The Gallants' home, however, will be paid off by then and, according to a projection by a local real estate appraiser, worth about $195,000. It is possible that the Gallants could sell the home to an investor or to someone who does not wish to occupy it. The proceeds of the sale, after broker's commissions, lawyer's fees, and closing costs are estimated at $177,500. The proceeds may then be added to the principal, thereby reducing the amount of money that the Gallants need to accumulate to $114,550 ($292,000 less $177,500). The amount to be put away each quarter is also greatly reduced:

$$\begin{array}{c}\text{Investment per}\\\text{compounding}\\\text{period}\end{array} = \begin{array}{c}\text{Desired}\\\text{principal}\end{array} \times \begin{array}{c}\text{Sinking}\\\text{fund}\\\text{factor}\end{array}$$

$$= \$114,500 \times .0080353 = \$920.04$$

The Gallants now have to put away only $920 each quarter.

How does a reverse mortgage work?

A *reverse mortgage* (*RM*) is exactly what it is called. The lending institution makes monthly payments to the homeowners, and the homeowners "repay" the loan when the house is sold or when the last joint owner dies. The amount of a reverse mortgage is usually not more than 60% to 80% of the value of the house, since the lender is exposed to the risk that the home might decline in value. If the RM's term is fixed—for, say, 30 years—then the loan must be repaid, which usually requires the sale of the home. If the home has appreciated enough in value, however, the loan might be renegotiated. An *open-ended RM* has a term that is indefinite, extending to the death of the last joint owner or to whenever the house is sold.

Example: Refer to the example on page 374. The Gallants figure that putting away more than $2,300 per quarter is too much of a strain on their income. Given a projected appraisal of their home's value in 15 years of $195,000, they find that they can obtain a 30-year reverse mortgage of 70% of their equity. In this case, since the home will be paid off, their equity is 100% of its appraised market value. If they can obtain a 10%, 30-year (that is, fixed-term) mortgage on $136,500 of the equity in their home, the lending institution will pay them $1,197.89 a month for 30 years (that is, until Burt Gallant is 95 and his wife 91). (The monthly payment was interpolated from the monthly mortgage tables for a 30-year, 10% mortgage.) This income reduces what the Gallants need to put away each quarter.

$$\text{Principal} = \frac{\text{Monthly income} - \text{(Social Security, other payments)}}{\text{Earning rate} / 12}$$

$$= \frac{\$6,500 - (\$900 + \$2,500 + \$1,198)}{.08 / 12}$$

$$= \frac{\$1,902}{.00667} = \$285,157.42$$

Deducting $171,000 that he will have in a variable annuity contract by retirement, he needs to accumulate only $114,157.42 ($285,157.42 less $171,000). Thus he needs to put away less each quarter.

$$\begin{array}{c}\text{Investment per}\\\text{compounding}\\\text{period}\end{array} = \begin{array}{c}\text{Desired}\\\text{principal}\end{array} \times \begin{array}{c}\text{Sinking}\\\text{fund}\\\text{factor}\end{array}$$

$$= \$114,158 \times .0080353 = \$917.29$$

Note: Reverse mortgage credit lines are also available. These make cash available to homeowners but do not oblige them to receive a payment every month.

How does a deferred property tax loan work?

A lending institution pays the homeowner's taxes, charging an interest rate that is usually lower than the prevailing loan rate. The loan—interest and principal—is repaid upon the last joint homeowner's death, when the house is sold.

Example: Local S&L will pay the Gallants' property taxes, estimated to be $260 monthly at retirement. Interest will be charged, but both interest and the principal (the amount advanced to pay taxes) do not have to be repaid until the house is sold, which will be no later than upon the death of the last joint owner. This reduces the Gallants' projected retirement budget, thereby reducing the amount they need to put away.

$$\text{Principal} = \frac{\text{Monthly income} - \begin{pmatrix} \text{Social} \\ \text{Security, other payments} \end{pmatrix}}{\text{Earning rate} / 12}$$

$$= \frac{\$6,500 - (\$900 + \$2,500 + \$260)}{.08 / 12}$$

$$= \frac{\$2,840}{.00667} = \$425,787.10$$

Deducting $171,000 that he will have in a variable annuity contract by retirement, he needs to accumulate only $254,787.10 ($425,787.10 less $171,000). Thus he needs to put away slightly less each quarter.

$$\begin{matrix} \text{Investment per} \\ \text{compounding} \\ \text{period} \end{matrix} = \begin{matrix} \text{Desired} \\ \text{principal} \end{matrix} \times \begin{matrix} \text{Sinking} \\ \text{fund} \\ \text{factor} \end{matrix}$$

$$= \$254,787.10 \times .0080353 = \$2,047.29$$

TYPES OF RETIREMENT ACCOUNTS

Note: The laws governing retirement plans can be complex, particularly with respect to taxation. The aim of this book is not a detailed account of such plans, but rather simplified explanations of their mathematics.

How does a 401(K) plan work?

Full-time employees of companies with 401(K) plans may put a fixed dollar amount of pretax earnings into a fund. The maximum amount is set by federal regulation and adjusted for inflation annually. Companies may permit employees to invest less than the government maximum because the employer usually matches all or part of the employee's contribution.

Example: In 19XX, the federal maximum for an employee's contribution to the company's 401(K) plan is $8,000. The company, however, limits employees' contributions to $4,000, but matches it dollar for dollar. An employee could therefore have as much at $76.92 deducted weekly from his or her paycheck ($4,000 divided by 52 weeks) and contributed to the fund, not pay any income taxes on that income, and have the company contribute the same amount.

What is a 403(B) plan?

Available to employees of nonprofit organizations, such as public schools or charitable groups, this plan allows employees to contribute a percentage of their pretax income (currently 16⅔%), but not more than $9,000, annually. Contributions for prior years in which employees did not work are also possible.

Example: Betty Largent works for a charitable organization that offers its employees a 403(B) plan. She earns $25,000 a year and opts to contribute the full percentage allowable to the plan, which is $4,167.50 ($25,000 annual salary times .1667). Each week $80.14 is deducted from her paycheck.

In addition, she has worked for the organization for two years without taking part in the program. If she desires, she could have additional amounts taken out for those years.

Can anyone open an individual retirement account (IRA)?

Whether covered by another retirement plan or not, any wage earner under age 70½ can open an individual retirement account. Contributions may be equal to your annual earnings up to a maximum of $2,000, with an additional

$250 for an unemployed spouse (in a separate account), if the spouse does not earn enough to contribute. The accounts of the spouses may be divided any way, as long as one does not receive less than $250. Withdrawals may begin without penalty any time between the ages of 59½ and 70½.

Example: Peter Largent is several years older than his wife. He elects to put "his" $2,000 into his spouse's account, and "her" $250 into his account. The effect is that "his" $2,000 will compound a few years longer in "her" account before it must be withdrawn.

Who is eligible for Keogh plans?

Sole proprietors, partners, and employees of proprietorships and partnerships may participate in Keogh plans. There are two types of this plan:

- Defined contribution.
- Defined benefit.

How does a defined contribution Keogh plan work?

In a *defined contribution plan*, a partner or proprietor may contribute up to 20% of pretax earnings, with a maximum of $15,000, a year. Employers make similar contributions for employees, who may make additional contributions of the lesser of 10% of annual earnings or $2,500.

Example: Joe Isso owns a chauffeur service, which is a proprietorship. He withdraws $75,000 a year in salary. He may contribute up to $15,000 a year, which is 20% of his salary ($75,000 times 20%). For one of his drivers, earning $22,000 a year, Isso contributes $4,400 (20% of $22,000), and the driver contributes another $220 (10% of his annual earnings, which is less than $2,500).

How does a defined benefit Keogh plan work?

This plan, which benefits the business owner over 50 years of age, is based on a future retirement goal. The Keogh participant sets a desired monthly payout figure and arrives at the contributions necessary to achieve that goal. The closer the business owner is to retirement, the higher the contributions will be.

Example: The process is similar to the series of Gallant examples in this chapter on pages 374–378.

LIFE INSURANCE

What is a term life insurance policy?

A *term* life insurance policy is issued to an individual by an insurance company for a specified number of years. The cost of the policy is pure premium; that is, it only covers the risk assumed by the insurer that the insured may die during the term of the policy. If the insured does not die, the company does not pay out, and the premium payments are not refunded.

Example: The Smiths buy a new home with a $125,000, 25-year mortgage. Since both spouses are wage earners, each takes out a 25-year, decreasing term life insurance policy for the outstanding principal on the house. In the first month, they are insured for the full amount, $125,000. As payments are made and principal is reduced, the amount payable upon either of their deaths also decreases. The amount they pay each month, however, remains level. When the mortgage is paid off, or when the house is sold, the insurance policy is terminated.

What is a whole life insurance policy?

A *whole life* policy is issued to an individual by an insurance company for the life of the insured. The cost of the policy is partly premium and partly savings. The savings component of the payments accumulate in the form of *cash value*, which may be withdrawn, borrowed, used as collateral, or applied to make premium payments.

• *Straight life* policies require the insured to pay for as long as the policy is in effect, that is, until the insured dies or the policy is terminated.

• *Limited payment life* policies, which entail a higher premium than straight life contracts, are structured so that some or all of the cash value is applied to paying up the policy in full. In a specified number of years (usually 20 or 30), the insured no longer has to make payments and remains insured, sometimes even retaining some cash value.

• *Endowment policies* are really insured savings plans.

These contracts permit the insured to put away a certain amount of money, which earns interest, as they protect themselves against the risk of premature death. The policy provides for the payout of a lump sum or annuity upon maturity of the contract, usually either in 20 years or at age 60 to 65.

What are the benefits of a straight life policy?
A straight life policy is the least expensive of all types of whole life contracts, and it provides the greatest protection. The cash value, however, is low compared to other types.

Example: Each of the Smiths elects to take out a $125,000 straight life policy. The premium is higher than what it would be for a term policy, but lower than for a limited payment or endowment. Each is insured for $125,000 for as long as they make payments, and they must make payments for the rest of their lives. Each payment, however, contributes to a cumulative cash value.

What are the benefits of a limited-payment life contract?
A limited-payment life insurance policy has greater cash value than a straight life contract, and it can be structured so as to be fully paid up at some specified time in the future. It offers less protection than a straight policy.

Example: The Smiths could opt to take out limited-payment life contracts on each other, each for $125,000, to be become fully paid up in 20 or 25 years (as the mortgage is paid off). With this contract, the Smiths not only have the house "free and clear," but some cash value in the policy.

Why take out an endowment policy?
The aim of an endowment policy is to have a specified amount of money at the end of the endowment period. The risk protection is therefore the lesser part of the premium. It is the most "expensive" type of contract because it enforces saving on the insured.

Example: If the Smiths, who are just married, intend to have children and hope for them to attend college, they might consider a 20-year endowment policy. The monthly payments might pinch their budget, but in 20 to 25 years they will have a mortgage-free home and a reserve of money for their children's education.

Note: There are many "brand name" policies available (insurance companies often package policies to make them more salable), and many offer significantly different features from the ones described here. Most, however, are best understood as variations of these four basic types.

KEY TERMS

Assets: Anything of value that a person owns.

Budget: An item-by-item account of (1) all expenses that you may expect to pay on a monthly basis, such as mortgage payments or phone bills, and (2) per-month allocations of expenses that are paid on a nonmonthly basis, such as property taxes or insurance premiums.

Compounding: The effect on earnings when earned interest is left to accumulate with principal, thereby allowing it to earn interest.

Defined benefit plan: A retirement plan, such as a Keogh, in which a business owner sets a retirement goal (that is, a desired monthly payout figure upon retirement) and calculates the contributions necessary to achieve that goal.

Defined contribution plan: A retirement plan, such as a Keogh, in which a partner or proprietor may contribute up to 20% of pretax earnings, with a maximum of $15,000, a year. Employers make similar contributions for employees, who may make additional contributions of the lesser of 10% of annual earnings or $2,500.

401(K) plan: A retirement plan in which full-time employees of companies with such plans may put a fixed dollar amount of pretax earnings into a fund. The maximum amount is set by federal regulation and adjusted for inflation annually. Companies may permit employees to invest less than the government maximum because the employer usually matches all or part of the employee's contribution.

403(B) plan: A retirement plan in which employees of nonprofit organizations may contribute a percentage of their pretax income (currently 16⅔%), but not more than

$9,000, annually. Contributions for prior years in which employees did not work are also possible.

Future value of $1: A series of tables that contain the future values of an investment, given a rate of earnings and time.

Individual retirement acccount (IRA): Any savings or investment account designated as a retirement account; that is, the funds are deposited for purposes of retirement, not for withdrawal sooner than age 59½ (without penalty).

Keogh plan: A retirement plan for sole proprietors, partners, and employees of proprietorships and partnerships may participate in Keogh plans.

Liabilities: Any money amounts that an individual owes, in either the long or the short term.

Net worth: The value of a person's financial assets after all obligations are met at any given point in time.

Open-ended reverse mortgage: A reverse mortgage in which the term is indefinite, extending to the death of the last joint owner or to whenever the house is sold.

Reverse mortgage (RM): An arrangement in which the lending institution makes monthly payments to the homeowners, and the homeowners ''repay'' the loan when the house is sold or when the last joint owner dies.

Sale-and-leaseback: An arrangement in which the owners can sell their home (to another member of the family or to an investor who is not interested in taking occupancy), but they continue to reside in it on a long-term lease.

Sinking fund tables: A series of tables containing factors that enable you to calculate, given the rate of earning and compounding frequency, how much you have to put away each compounding period in order to have a desired amount at the end of a number of compounding periods.

Index